PRENTICE-HALL INTERNATIONAL SERIES IN MANAGEMENT

Baumol	*Economic Theory and Operations Analysis*
Boot	*Mathematical Reasoning in Economics and Management Science*
Brown	*Smoothing, Forecasting and Prediction of Discrete Time Series*
Chambers	*Accounting, Evaluation and Economic Behavior*
Churchman	*Prediction and Optimal Decision: Philosophical Issues of a Science of Values*
Clarkson	*The Theory of Consumer Demand: A Critical Appraisal*
Cohen and Cyert	*Theory of the Firm: Resource Allocation in a Market Economy*
Cyert and March	*A Behavioral Theory of the Firm*
Fabrycky and Torgersen	*Operations Economy: Industrial Applications of Operations Research*
Greenlaw, Herron, and Rawdon	*Business Simulation in Industrial and University Education*
Hadley and Whitin	*Analysis of Inventory Systems*
Holt, Modigliani, Muth, and Simon	*Planning Production, Inventories, and Work Force*
Hymans	*Probability Theory with Applications to Econometrics and Decision Making*
Ijiri	*The Foundations of Accounting Measurement: A Mathematical, Economic, and Behavioral Inquiry*
Kaufmann	*Methods and Models of Operations Research*
Lesourne	*Economic Analysis and Industrial Management*
Mantel	*Cases in Managerial Decision*
Massé	*Optimal Investment Decisions: Rules for Action and Criteria for Choice*
McGuire	*Theories of Business Behavior*
Miller and Starr	*Executive Decisions and Operations Research*
Muth and Thompson	*Industrial Scheduling*
Nelson (editor)	*Marginal Cost Pricing in Practice*
Nicosia	*Consumer Decision Process: Marketing and Advertising Implications*
Peters and Summers	*Statistical Analysis for Business Decisions*
Pfiffner and Sherwood	*Administrative Organization*
Simonnard	*Linear Programming*
Singer	*Antitrust Economics: Selected Legal Cases and Economic Models*

PRENTICE-HALL, INC.
PRENTICE-HALL INTERNATIONAL, INC., UNITED KINGDOM AND EIRE
PRENTICE-HALL OF CANADA, LTD., CANADA
J. H. DE BUSSY, LTD., HOLLAND AND FLEMISH-SPEAKING BELGIUM
DUNOD PRESS, FRANCE
MARUZEN COMPANY, LTD., FAR EAST
HERRERO HERMANOS, SUCS., SPAIN AND LATIN AMERICA
R. OLDENBOURG VERLAG, GERMANY
ULRICO HOEPLI EDITORE, ITALY

ANTITRUST ECONOMICS

Selected Legal Cases and Economic Models

EUGENE M. SINGER

Prentice-Hall, Inc.
Englewood Cliffs, New Jersey

Library of Congress Catalog Card No.: 68-13646

Printed in the United States of America

Current Printing (last digit)

10   9   8   7   6   5   4   3   2

PRENTICE-HALL INTERNATIONAL, INC., *London*
PRENTICE-HALL OF AUSTRALIA, PTY. LTD., *Sydney*
PRENTICE-HALL OF CANADA, LTD., *Toronto*
PRENTICE-HALL OF INDIA PRIVATE LTD., *New Delhi*
PRENTICE-HALL OF JAPAN, INC., *Tokoyo*

Foreword

Teachers and practitioners of antitrust would readily agree that one ventures only a short distance into this arena before encountering the concepts of monopoly and competition. These are the concepts on which public policy toward the private economic sector of the United States — and to a lesser extent of other nations giving considerable scope to private enterprise — has been erected.

Similarly, all would agree with Dr. Singer's opening statement in his preface to this book that "antitrust by its very essence is a mixture of law and economics." In fact, as Professor Edward S. Mason pointed out so eloquently three decades ago in his much-cited article "Monopoly in Law and Economics" (*Yale Law Journal*, November 1937), this identifies an important historical difficulty in formulating and administering an effective and entirely rational antitrust policy. While both the law and economics of antitrust use the concepts of monopoly and competition, they have often used them in different ways and attached to them different meanings.

In the law the term monopoly has been identified with "unreasonable," and hence illegal, restraints of trade. Accordingly, as Professor Mason explained, the term monopoly as used in the law came to be a standard of evaluation — it existed when the courts found the restraint at bar "unreasonable." By extension, competition prevailed when the courts found no such restraint. In the law, then, monopoly and competition were ultimately what the judicial mind asserted they reasonably might be, and preoccupation was with tests that distinguished monopoly from competition, not with the formulation of the concepts.

In economics, on the other hand, monopoly and competition are defined as market structural conditions determining the business firm's conduct — they are subsumed in the underlying assumptions of the economist's "model" that permit his analysis to yield particular and determinate solutions. Accordingly, economics has been preoccupied with the concepts of competition and monopoly and not with the design of operable tests for distinguishing one from the other. Since the design of rational tests cannot be separated from the formulation of the relevant concepts, the disciplines of law and economics have needed to be joined.

The economics and the law of antitrust have no doubt travelled along converging paths in the three decades that have transpired since Mason noted their sharply distinguishable differences. But in no single treatment of antitrust have they been so explicitly and so effectively coalesced as they have in this book by Dr. Singer. He is unusually well qualified to bring about the long overdue union of the two disciplines for a more penetrating analysis of this vital public policy. Dr. Singer is a legal scholar, having graduated from the University of Michigan Law School where he studied under, and worked with, Professor S. Chesterfield Oppenheim. He is a member of the New York Bar. He is on the Board of Editors of *The Antitrust Bulletin*. He holds a Ph.D. degree in economics from Princeton University, where he also majored in economics as an undergraduate. For the past five years he has been an independent economic consultant on antitrust matters to numerous law firms and corporations, a frequent contributor to legal and economic journals, and an active participant in various antitrust conferences and symposia.

This book reflects Dr. Singer's thorough training and rich experience. In his hands classic legal passages take on added significance and meaning when translated into the theoretical models of micro-economic analysis. His application of the concept of leverage to vertical and conglomerate mergers, tying contracts and full line forcing add clarity and new understanding to these business practices. Throughout, Singer combines rigorous analysis and the requisite appreciation of the politics — the "art of the possible" — of public policy. Lawyers, economists, those who administer the day-to-day affairs of the antitrust agencies, congressional committees, the judiciary and all those concerned with antitrust policy generally, will enthusiastically welcome Dr. Singer's new and stimulating text. It fills a gap that has long needed filling.

JESSE W. MARKHAM

Princeton University

Preface

Antitrust by its very essence is a mixture of law and economics. Legal judgments as to competition must be made within economic settings. This book is concerned with the legal and economic methods of analyzing market structures and business practices encompassed by the antitrust statutes of the United States.

Antitrust cases are examined with a legal analysis, documented by passages from court opinions, and an economic analysis, which includes excerpts from economic treatises and articles. This technique reflects a compromise between a law casebook designed for economists and a commentary on the economic implications of a number of landmark antitrust decisions. Furthermore, the classic legal passages by such distinguished justices as White, Peckham, and Learned Hand present a more stimulating introduction to the subject of antitrust than a paraphrased summary.

Seven major topics in antitrust have been chosen: monopoly, oligopoly, concentration, tying arrangements, vertical integration, price discrimination, and mergers. The book is oriented principally to the student who seeks to pursue the implications of basic issues in antitrust, rather than to the policy maker called upon to decide a specific course of action. The policy maker faces the more burdensome task of resolving conflicts in the numerous views, counterpoints, and empirical studies.

I have not followed the course of others in attempting to reconcile antitrust law and economics. The legal and economic analyses have been arranged, for several reasons, in separate chapters. Primarily, the separation offers readers less sophisticated in economic theory, or perhaps less interested in some of the more abstract antitrust problems, an easier access to the legal analysis. The approach also permits a digression into purely theoretical economic areas which have no immediate relationship to law cases, but which offer a valuable methodology of their own.

Economic theory cannot be expected to solve the judicial question as to whether the business practices or conduct of defendants in an antitrust proceeding may tend to lessen competition. The assumptions of economic theory limit the application of models to specific settings. However, economic models, in providing a framework for examining the relevant variables, offer insights into the problems which face both lawyers and economists.

Economic and legal analysis in the field of antitrust has proceeded from a single product context, inherent in the concept of monopoly and reflected in the name *antitrust*, to a multiple product context in which firms compete with each other in terms of a diversity of product lines and geographic areas. Vertical integration and merger cases raise problems which require an analysis of interrelated markets. An understanding of the operations of economic forces at work in these areas provides an incentive to look further at the surrounding markets associated with the different stages of production, at the potential injury to buyers and sellers, and on the effect the exercise of economic power in one market will have on other geographic and product markets.

Since the economics of antitrust are taught in a course covering the subject of industrial organization and public policy, this book is designed basically as a supplemental text. The student is expected to have completed an introductory economic theory course and to be familiar with demand and supply curves, marginal cost and revenue curves, and indifference curve analysis. Although this book has been written primarily for advanced undergraduate and graduate students in a university department of economics, I have also endeavored to make it useful for law and business administration schools, as well as for lawyers specializing in the field of antitrust.

For helpful suggestions, criticisms, and encouragement, the author gratefully acknowledges, without implicating, S. Chesterfield Oppenheim, Jesse W. Markham, Betty Bock, William L. Baldwin, Almarin Phillips, James M. Ferguson, Peter Asch, Maurice Singer and Raymond A. Ochacher.

EUGENE M. SINGER

Harrison, New York

Table of Contents

The Sherman Antitrust Act. The Federal Trade Commission Act. The
Clayton Act. *The Robinson-Patman Price Discrimination Act Amendment to
Section 2. Section 3: Tying Arrangements and Exclusive Dealings. Section 4:
Private Suits for Treble Damages. The Celler-Kefauver Antimerger Act
Amendment to Section 7.* Federal Antitrust Statutes Applying to State Fair
Trade Laws. *The Miller-Tydings Act. The McGuire Act.*

Definition of Pure Competition. *Definition of Pure Monopoly.* Comparison
of the Theoretical Results of the Models. Welfare Implications of the Model
of Perfect Competition. The Inadequacies of the Model of Pure Competition
for Antitrust Policy.

Part II.
ANTITRUST IN A SINGLE PRODUCT CONTEXT

SECTION B *MONOPOLY*

PART I

Foundations of Antitrust

SECTION A

Antitrust Policy

CHAPTER ONE

Selected Political and Economic Aims

Antitrust policy has a heritage which includes a distaste for concentrated economic power groups, a respect for equality of opportunity, and a hope for a strong productive economy that can furnish an increasingly higher standard of living for the nation. Broad political goals to protect democratic institutions, set in juxtaposition to economic objectives for higher efficiency and technical progress, mark the outer boundaries for the course of antitrust policy in the United States.

The technological accomplishments of larger-sized and smaller firms, and their continued introduction of new products, have contributed to the high rate of economic growth of the United States. The encouragement of new entry and protection of small business reflects a traditional American belief in economic liberties: the right of a producer to have an equal opportunity to enter a trade, the right of a consumer to have a multitude of alternative sources of supply, and the right of the people to have a government free from the pressures of special economic interest groups.

Political and economic goals in antitrust policy do not always coincide. There is often a price for economic growth and a cost for economic freedom. Government procurement policies and the awarding of research and development contracts for national security and aerospace projects, which may favor only a few large firms, exemplify the ambivalence of economic and political policies. The future structure of a defense industry composed of numerous small producers may be deemed in some situations to be less important than the objective of most effectively insuring success of a project for a military exigency. Consequently, the preservation of democratic standards through the fostering of industries composed of numerous small units cannot be the solitary objective of the antitrust statutes.[1] The existence of a powerful, productive economy is a matter of necessity both for satisfying the internal demands of society for an increasingly higher standard of living, and for facing the external international challenges which threaten its very existence.

A fundamental question in antitrust is whether a strong policy against concentrated economic power groups impedes or is conducive to our goals for efficiency and technical progress. Do leading firms in highly concentrated industries account for greater shares of the industry output than is necessary for achieving the lowest possible per unit costs? To answer this question an examination of accounting records, which generally involves different cost systems, and engineering studies are necessary in order to ascertain the average costs and economies of scale of the different-sized firms in an industry. Since most small, medium-sized, and larger plants in an industry generally produce a heterogeneous output that crosses over a number of industrial classifications, the problem of ascertaining whether smaller or medium-sized firms are as efficient as the larger-sized firms is exceedingly complex.[2]

---

[1]See M. Massel, *Competition and Monopoly* (Washington, D.C.: Brookings Institution, 1962), especially pp. 15–41. For a sympathetic attitude toward the important role of the larger firms in a free enterprise system, see J. Schumpeter, *Capitalism, Socialism, and Democracy* (New York: Harper & Row, Publishers, 1942); J. K. Galbraith, *American Capitalism* (Boston: Houghton Mifflin Company, 1952); D. Lilienthal, *Big Business: A New Era* (New York: Harper & Row, Publishers, 1953); A. D. H. Kaplan, *Big Enterprise in a Competitive System*, rev. ed. (Washington, D.C.: Brookings Institution, 1964); and S. H. Slichter, "In Defense of Bigness in Business," *New York Times Magazine* (August 4, 1957) reprinted in E. Mansfield, *Monopoly Power and Economic Performance* (New York: W. W. Norton & Company, Inc., 1964), pp. 13–18. Compare to G. J. Stigler, "The Case Against Big Business," *Fortune*, Vol. XLV (May, 1952), 123; T. K. Quinn, *Giant Business: Threat to Democracy* (New York: Exposition Press, 1953); and H. C. Simons, *Economic Policy for a Free Society* (Chicago: University of Chicago Press, 1948).

[2]See J. S. Bain, *Barriers to New Competition* (Cambridge, Mass.: Harvard University Press, 1956) and "Relation of Profit Rate to Industry Concentration: American Manufacturing, 1936–1940," *Quarterly Journal of Economics*, Vol. LXV (August, 1951), 293–324; C. A. Smith, "Survey of the Empirical Evidence on Economies of Scale," and Comment by M. Friedman, in *Business Concentration and Price Policy*, Universities-National Bureau Committee for Economic Research (Princeton, N.J.: Princeton University Press, 1955), pp. 213–38; J. Johnston, *Statistical Cost Analysis* (New York: McGraw-Hill Book Company, 1960); J. M. Blair, "Technology and Size," *American Economic Review*, Vol. XXXVIII (1948), 121–53 and "The Relation Between Size and Efficiency of Business," *Review of Economics and Statistics*, Vol. XXIV (1942), 125–36; R. B. Heflebower. "The Economics of Size," *Journal of Business of the University of Chicago*, Vol. XXIV (1951), 253–68; United States, Federal Trade Commission, *Relative Efficiency of Large, Medium-Sized, and Small Business*, Temporary National Economic Committee Monograph No. 13 (Washington, D.C.: Government Printing Office, 1941); A. Phillips, "Concentration, Scale and Technological Change in Selected Manufacturing

The comparison of the size characteristics of the larger-sized companies in industries with respect to the remaining member firms has been the focal point of empirical studies of economic concentration. Do large firms have economic advantages which permit them to enjoy a larger differential growth rate than medium- or smaller-sized firms? Are the leading firms in industries increasing their market positions and raising levels of concentration throughout various sectors in the economy? These questions raise problems of industry classification, reliability of underlying data especially for the smaller- and medium-sized firms, selection of measurement units, such as value of shipments or employment, types of concentration indexes, and appropriate time periods for measuring changes in economic concentration. There has not been unanimity among economists as to whether overall concentration in the manufacturing sector of the United States economy has been increasing, has been declining, or has remained relatively stable since the early 1930's.[3]

Large firms, as well as smaller-sized firms, have made vital contributions to the economic progress of our nation. The larger firms have an advantage in being able more easily to finance costly research and development projects in which the risk of success is limited. But after a medium-size level is attained, the inventive output of a firm may not continue to increase

Industries, 1899–1939," *Journal of Industrial Economics*, IV (1955–1956), 179–93; W. L. Crum, *Corporate Size and Earning Power* (Cambridge, Mass.: Harvard University Press, 1939); J. Steindt, *Small and Big Business* (Oxford: Basil Blackwell, 1945); and S. Alexander, "The Effect of Size of Manufacturing Corporations on the Distribution of the Rate of Return," *Review of Economics and Statistics*, Vol. XXXI (August, 1949), 229–35; R. C. Osborn, "Efficiency and Profitability in Relation to Size," *Harvard Business Review*, Vol. XXIX (February, 1951), 82; J. Schmookler, "The Changing Efficiency of the American Economy, 1869–1938," *Review of Economics and Statistics*, Vol. XXXIV (May, 1952), 214–31; A. C. Harberger, "Monopoly and Resource Allocation," *American Economic Review*, Vol. XLIV (May, 1954), 77–87; and D. Schwartzman, "The Burden of Monopoly," *Journal of Political Economy*, Vol. LXVIII (December, 1960), 627–30.

[3]For the views of a number of economists, see United States, Senate Hearings before the Subcommittee on Antitrust and Monopoly of the Committee of the Judiciary, *Economic Concentration, Part I*, "Overall and Conglomerate Aspects," 88th Cong., 2nd Sess. (Washington, D.C.: Government Printing Office, 1964); M. A. Adelman, "The Measurement of Industrial Concentration, 1940–1947," *Review of Economics and Statistics*, Vol. XXXIII (November, 1951), 269–96, reprinted in American Economic Association, *Readings in Industrial Organization and Public Policy*, R. B. Heflebower and G. W. Stocking, eds. (Homewood, Ill.: Richard D. Irwin, Inc., 1958), p. 8; I. Rottenberg, "New Statistics on Companies and on Concentration in Manufacturing from the 1954 Census," *American Statistical Association Proceedings of the Business and Economic Section, 1957*, p. 225; R. L. Nelson, *Concentration in the Manufacturing Industries of the United States* (New Haven: Yale University Press, 1963); and B. Bock and J. Farkas, *Concentration in Manufacturing* (New York: National Industrial Conference Board, 1966).

proportionately with its growth of sales.[4] However, economic progress is difficult to measure: the number of patents issued to a company, for example, does not reflect the substantially different kinds of technical progress contributed by larger-, medium- and smaller-sized firms.[5]

The introduction of new products, innovations in production processes, and improvements in merchandising methods provide the economy with a constant competitive stimulus, or, in the words of Professor Schumpeter, "a perennial gale of creative destruction,"[6] in which new products and processes supplant the old. This continual substitution places the economy and society in a state of flux, serving to challenge petrified market structures, and encourage the flexibility associated with change and economic growth. But it can be argued with equal cogency that in concentrated industries in which the leading companies have substantial market power, the environment breeds stagnation; it lacks the pressure to develop new products and innovate.

Paradoxically, the small, weak firms in the model of pure competition also stagnate, since by definition they earn only normal profits, which preclude an allotment for research and development. Thus, at the extremes of

[4]J. S. Worley, "Industrial Research and the New Competition," *Journal of Political Economy*, Vol. LXIX (April, 1961), 183–86. Also see United States, Senate Hearings Before the Subcommittee on Antitrust and Monopoly of the Committee on the Judiciary, *Economic Concentration, Part III*, "Concentration, Invention and Innovation," 89th Cong., 1st Sess. (1965); H. Villard, "Competition, Oligopoly, and Research, *"Journal of Political Economy*, Vol. LXVI (December, 1958), 483–97; Reply by J. Schmookler, "Bigness, Fewness, and Research," *ibid.*, Vol. LXVII (December, 1959), 628–32; Reply by Villard, *ibid.*, 633–35; J. Jewkes, D. Sawers, and R. Stillerman, *The Sources of Invention* (London: Macmillan & Co. Ltd., 1958); G. W. Nutter, "Monopoly, Bigness, and Progress," *Journal of Political Economy*, Vol. LXIV (1956), 520–27; W. Maclaurin, "Technical Progress in Some American Industries," *American Economic Review*, Vol. XLIV (1954), 178–90; E. Mansfield, "Size of Firm, Market Structure, and Innovation," *Journal of Political Economy*, Vol. LXXI (December, 1963), 565–68 and "Industrial Research and Development Expenditures," *ibid.*, Vol. LXXII (August, 1964), 333–34; I. Horowitz, "Firm Size and Research Activity," *Southern Economic Journal*, Vol. XXVII (January, 1962), 298–301; W. L. Baldwin, "Contracted Research and the Case for Big Business," *Journal of Political Economy*, Vol. LXX (June, 1962), 294–98; D. Hamberg, "Size of Firm, Oligopoly, and Research: The Evidence," *Canadian Journal of Economics and Political Science*, Vol. XXX (February, 1964), 62–75; Reply by F. M. Scherer, *ibid.*, Vol. XXXI (May, 1965), 256–66, and "Firm Size and Patented Inventions, *American Economic Review*, Vol. LV (December, 1965), 1097–1125; and J. W. Markham, "Market Structure, Business Conduct and Innovation," *ibid.*, Vol. LV (May, 1965), 323–42.

[5]D. Dewey, "Competitive Policy and National Goals: the Doubtful Relevance of Antitrust," *Perspectives on Antitrust Policy*, A. Phillips, ed. (Princeton, N.J.: Princeton University Press, 1965), p. 74; and M. J. Peck, *Competition in the Aluminum Industry, 1945–1958* (Cambridge, Mass.: Harvard University Press, 1961).

[6]J. A. Schumpeter, *Capitalism, Socialism and Democracy*, Chap. VII.

theoretical market structures, monopoly and pure competition, there exists no incentive for technical development. A number of firms and some inequality of firm sizes in an industry is, therefore, an essential prerequisite for an industrial climate conducive to innovation and inventive activity. Unanswered is the question of what degree of imbalance between large-, medium-, and smaller-sized firms will encourage economic growth and industrial vitality in a particular industry and will also confer a net benefit on the aggregate economy.

CHAPTER TWO

Antitrust Laws of the United States

There are three principal antitrust statutes in the United States: the Sherman Antitrust Act,[1] the Federal Trade Commission Act,[2] and the Clayton Act.[3] The Sherman Act, enacted in 1890, was subsequently amended by the Miller-Tydings Act[4] in 1937. The Federal Trade Commission Act was enacted in 1914, and amended by the Wheeler-Lea Act[5] in 1938 and by the McGuire Act[6] in 1952. The Clayton Act was enacted in 1914 and was amended in 1936 by the Robinson-Patman Act[7] and in 1950 by the Celler-Kefauver Antimerger Act.[8] A brief explanation of these statutes and the text of the basic substantive provisions are given below.[9]

The Sherman Antitrust Act

Section 1 of this Act provides in part that:

Every contract, combination in the form of trust or otherwise, or conspiracy, in restraint of trade or commerce among the several States, or with foreign nations, is hereby declared to be illegal.

[1]26 Stat. 209 (1890); 15 U. S. C., Sec. 1–7.

[2]38 Stat. 717 (1914); 15 U. S. C. Sec. 41–58.

[3]38 Stat. 730 (1914); 15 U. S. C. Sec. 12–27.

[4]50 Stat. 693 (1937); 15 U. S. C. Sec. 1.

[5]52 Stat. 111 (1938); 15 U. S. C. Sec. 41.

[6]66 Stat. 632 (1952); 15 U. S. C. Sec. 45.

[7]49 Stat. 1526 (1936); 15 U. S. C. Sec. 13.

[8]64 Stat. 1125 (1950); 15 U. S. C. Sec. 18.

[9]For further discussion, see J. G. Van Cise, *Understanding the Antitrust Laws* rev. ed. (New York: Practicing Law Institute, 1966).

This section requires generally the existence of two or more persons, since a contract, combination, or conspiracy must be formed as a prerequisite to a finding of illegality. Agreements between competitors to fix prices, allocate geographic markets, or boycott third parties are practices condemned by this section of the Sherman Act.

Section 2 of the Sherman Act is directed toward actual or attempted monopolization and provides in part that: ·

Every person who shall monopolize, or attempt to monopolize, or combine or conspire with any other person or persons, to monopolize any part of the trade or commerce among the several States, or with foreign nations, shall be guilty of a misdemeanor, . . .

The Federal Trade Commission Act

Section 5 of the Federal Trade Commission Act, as amended, provides in part that:

Unfair methods of competition in commerce, and unfair or deceptive acts or practices in commerce, are hereby declared illegal.

In 1938 the Federal Trade Commission Act was amended by the Wheeler-Lea Act to read as shown above. The amendment added the phrase "and unfair or deceptive acts or practices in commerce." The Wheeler-Lea Act broadened the Commission's powers to include jurisdiction over not only unfair methods of business conduct which injured competing companies, but also deceptive or unfair acts in which no business competitors were harmed but the public was injured. Typical proceedings brought by the Federal Trade Commission under Sec. 5 include false or misleading advertising claims concerning the quality, physical ingredients, or performance of a product, or the "regular price" of a product from which a discount is offered. There is considerable overlap of Sec. 5 of the Federal Trade Commission Act with the major provisions of the Sherman and Clayton Acts.

The Clayton Act

THE ROBINSON-PATMAN PRICE DISCRIMINATION ACT AMENDMENT TO SECTION 2. Section 2 of the Clayton Act was amended in 1936 by the Robinson-Patman Act. The Act was passed in response to the complaints of independent wholesalers, that chain stores were obtaining from their suppliers unwarranted advantage in the form of lower prices, greater advertising allowance, and discounts. Those concessions that could not be justified by lower costs as a result of the large volume purchases by chain stores and, in turn, adversely affected competitors were to be curbed by the passage of the Robinson-Patman Act.

Section 2(a) of the Robinson-Patman Act condemns illegal price discrimination by providing in part that:

> It shall be unlawful for any person engaged in commerce, in the course of such commerce, either directly or indirectly, to discriminate in price between different purchasers of commodities of like grade and quality, where either or any of the purchasers involved in such discriminations are in commerce, where such commodities are sold for use, consumption, or resale within the United States . . . (or any place under its jurisdiction) and where the effect of such discrimination may be substantially to lessen competition or tend to create a monopoly in any line of commerce, or to injure, destroy, or prevent competition with any person who either grants or knowingly receives the benefit of such discrimination, or with customers of either of them . . . .

Section 2(a) also includes the following "cost justification" defense to a charge of price discrimination:

> . . . That nothing herein contained shall prevent differentials which make only due allowance for differences in the cost of manufacture, sale or delivery resulting from the differing methods or quantities in which such commodities are to such purchasers sold or delivered . . . .

Section 2(b) of the Robinson-Patman Act covers the "meeting competition" defense to a charge of price discrimination covered in Sec. 2(a). This section permits price discrimination if it is justified by the necessity of a seller to meet in good faith the equally low price of a competitor.

Section 2(b) of the Robinson-Patman Act provides in part:

> That nothing herein contained shall prevent a seller rebutting the prima facie case thus made by showing that his lower price or the furnishing of services or facilities to any purchaser or purchasers was made in good faith to meet an equally low price of a competitor, or the services or facilities furnished by a competitor.

Section 2(c) of the Robinson-Patman Act is directed against arrangements whereby buyers exact price discriminations disguised as brokerage commissions. It provides in part:

> That it shall be unlawful for any person engaged in commerce, in the course of such commerce, to pay or grant, or to receive or accept, anything of value as a commission, brokerage, or other compensation, or any allowance or discount in lieu thereof, except for services rendered in connection with the sale or purchase of goods, wares, or merchandise, either to the other party to such transaction or to an agent, representative, or other intermediary therein where such intermediary is acting in

fact for or in behalf, or is subject to the direct or indirect control, of any party to such transaction other than the person by whom such compensation is so granted or paid.

Sections 2(d) and 2(e) cover discriminations in promotional allowances and services made available to purchasers who buy for resale. Promotional allowances and services include cooperative payments by manufacturers to retailers for advertising, special featuring of a product in a store sale, or having a representative of a supplier give a demonstration in a store of the advantages of a particular product. Section 2(d) applies where the supplier gives a payment to the buyer for the buyer to perform the services. Section 2(e) applies where the supplier furnishes the service itself to the buyer. Both sections require the supplier to treat his competing customers on proportionally equal terms.

Section 2(d) of the Robinson-Patman Act provides:

> That it shall be unlawful for any person engaged in commerce to pay or contract for the payment of anything of value to or for the benefit of a customer of such person in the course of such commerce as compensation or in consideration for any services or facilities furnished by or through such customer in connection with the processing, handling, sale or offering for sale of any products or commodities manufactured, sold, or offered for sale by such person, unless such payment or consideration is available on proportionally equal terms to all other customers competing in the distribution of such products or commodities.

Section 2(e) of the Robinson-Patman Act provides:

> That it shall be unlawful for any person to discriminate in favor of one purchaser against another purchaser or purchasers of a commodity bought for resale, with or without processing, by contracting to furnish or furnishing, or by contributing to the furnishing of, any services or facilities connected with the processing, handling, sale, or offering for sale of such commodity so purchased upon terms not accorded to all purchasers on proportionally equal terms.

Section 2(f) was directed against large buyers who use their buying power to exact more favorable treatment from their suppliers. Section 2(f) of the Robinson-Patman Act provides:

> That it shall be unlawful for any person engaged in commerce, in the course of such commerce, knowingly to induce or receive a discrimination in price which is prohibited by this section.

SECTION 3: TYING ARRANGEMENTS AND EXCLUSIVE DEALING. Section 3 covers tying sales where the purchase of one good is conditioned upon the purchase of another good; exclusive dealing, where the purchaser cannot handle competing lines; and requirements contracts, where the purchaser fulfills all or most of his needs from a single supplier. These restraints are condemned where their effect may substantially lessen competition or tend to create a monopoly.

Section 3 of the Clayton Act provides in part:

> It shall be unlawful for any person engaged in commerce, in the course of such commerce, to lease or make a sale or contract for sale of goods, wares, merchandise, machinery, supplies, or other commodities . . . on the condition, agreement, or understanding that the lessee or purchaser thereof shall not use or deal in the goods, wares, merchandise, machinery, supplies, or other commodities of a competitor or competitors of the lessor or seller, where the effect of such lease, sale, or contract for sale or such condition, agreement, or understanding may be to substantially lessen competition or tend to create a monopoly in any line of commerce.

SECTION 4: PRIVATE SUITS FOR TREBLE DAMAGES. Section 4 of the Clayton Act gives a private party the right to sue for treble damages for an injury to his property or business received as a result of violations of the antitrust laws by an individual or corporation. The section has been resorted to in price-fixing cases, where customers purchased goods at prices higher than would have prevailed in the absence of a conspiracy to fix prices by suppliers, in boycott cases, where a buyer was unable to find suppliers or a seller was unable to find customers, and in price discrimination cases, where a customer paid more than his competitors or a competitor was intentionally destroyed by price cutting.

Section 4 of the Clayton Act provides:

> That any person who shall be injured in his business or property by reason of anything forbidden in the antitrust laws may sue therefor in any district court of the United States in the district in which the defendant resides or is found or has an agent, without respect to the amount in controversy, and shall recover threefold the damages by him sustained, and the cost of suit, including a reasonable attorney's fee.

THE CELLER-KEFAUVER ANTIMERGER ACT AMENDMENT TO SECTION 7. Section 7 of the Clayton Act covers corporate acquisitions and mergers. It condemns those mergers or acquisitions, between corporations engaged in interstate commerce, where the effect of the transaction may be substantially to lessen competition or to tend to create a monopoly. The 1950 Celler-Kefauver Act amendment broadened this section to cover mergers accomplished both through asset and stock purchases.

Section 7 of the Clayton Act, as amended by the Celler-Kefauver Antimerger Act, provides in part that:

> No corporation engaged in commerce shall acquire, directly or indirectly, the whole or any part of the stock or other share capital and no corporation subject to the jurisdiction of the Federal Trade Commission shall acquire the whole or any

part of the assets of another corporation engaged also in commerce, where in any line of commerce in any section of the country, the effect of such acquisition may be substantially to lessen competition, or to tend to create a monopoly.

Federal Antitrust Statutes Applying to State Fair Trade Laws

THE MILLER-TYDINGS ACT. The Miller-Tydings Act was passed in 1937 as an amendment to Sec. 1 of the Sherman Antitrust Act. The amendment exempted from the federal antitrust laws certain interstate contracts that are made between manufacturers, wholesalers, or other suppliers, and retailers, and covered products identified by a brand name or trademark, which are to be resold at a fixed or minimum price. The product had to be in open competition with goods of the same general class produced by other manufacturers. The Miller-Tydings Act did not imply federal approval of the resale price maintenance system. It simply sanctioned interstate resale price contracts where the resale is to take place in states which have their own fair trade laws. In 1965 there were only seven states without fair trade laws: Alaska, Kansas, Missouri, Nebraska, Nevada, Texas, and Vermont. The District of Columbia does not have fair trade legislation. The amendment does not permit horizontal resale price maintenance agreements between manufacturers, between wholesalers, or between retailers.

The Miller-Tydings Act amendment to Sec. 1 of the Sherman Act provides in part:

> That nothing herein contained shall render illegal, contracts or agreements prescribing minimum prices for the resale of a commodity which bears, or the label or container of which bears, the trademark, brand, or name of the producer or distributor of such commodity and which is in free and open competition with commodities of the same general class produced or distributed by others, when contracts or agreements of that description are lawful as applied to intrastate transactions, under any statute, law, or public policy now or hereafter in effect in any State, Territory, or the District of Columbia in which such resale is to be made, or to which the commodity is to be transported for such resale . . .

THE McGUIRE ACT. The McGuire Act, enacted in 1952 as an amendment to Sec. 5 of the Federal Trade Commission Act, specifically allows enforcement of a "nonsigners" clause in a resale price maintenance contract made between parties in different states. A "nonsigners" clause requires all retailers in a state, even those who do not sign a contract, to follow the manufacturer's resale price maintenance program once one retailer signs a contract and the other retailers are served notice. However, the fair trade laws in the state of resale must permit the enforcement of nonsigner clauses in resale price contracts. Thus, a manufacturer of a product with a brand name or trademark can, by virtue of a single contract, compel acceptance of the same price for its product by all retailers in the state, including non-signers.

The McGuire Act amendment to Sec. 5(a) of the Federal Trade Commission Act provides in part that:

Nothing contained in this Act or in any of the Antitrust Acts shall render unlawful the exercise or the enforcement of any right or right of action created by any statute, law, or public policy now or hereafter in effect in any State, Territory, or the District of Columbia, which in substance provides that willfully and knowingly advertising, offering for sale, or selling any commodity at less than the price or prices prescribed in such contracts or agreements whether the person so advertising, offering for sale, or selling is or is not a party to such a contract or agreement, is unfair competition and is actionable at the suit of any person damaged thereby.

CHAPTER THREE

Pure Competition and Economic Welfare

Definition of Pure Competition

The economic model of pure competition is a market structure with the following features: (1) a large number of buyers and sellers, (2) a standardized product, (3) freedom of entry and exit, (4) inability of any individual buyer or seller to influence price, and (5) absence of any collusion. The adjective "pure" indicates an absence of all monopoly elements. In contrast, the term "perfect competition" implies an absence of monopoly elements, and in addition, instantaneous mobility of factors of production, and complete knowledge as to prevailing prices and future events.

In pure competition a firm can sell at the going market price as many units as it produces. Its demand curve is a horizontal line at a height corresponding to the going market price. In Fig. 3-1 the equilibrium output for the competitive firm is at OM, where the marginal cost curve MC is rising and intersects the horizontal demand curve D' at the going market price P. The demand curve (or average revenue curve) coincides with the marginal revenue curve and, in equilibrium, the following conditions exist: $P = MC = MR$. The competitive firm will continue to increase its output and sell it at the going market price until the total cost of producing an additional unit (MC) is equal to the revenue $(MR = P)$ derived from its sale. In the long run, as a result of freedom of entry into and exit out of an industry, the average cost curve will be tangent at its minimum point to the demand curve and the competitive firm will achieve a normal return, which is the minimum remuneration necessary to keep the firm in business.

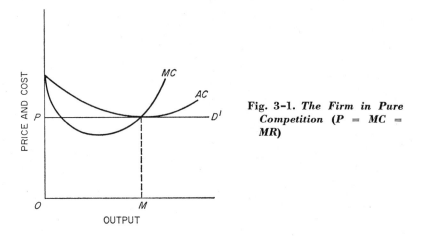

Fig. 3-1. *The Firm in Pure Competition (P = MC = MR)*

DEFINITION OF PURE MONOPOLY. The economic model of pure monopoly is a market structure of one firm which faces neither the threat of entry of other firms into its industry nor the competition of close substitute products. The pure monopolist controls a complete industry. It competes only in the restricted sense of vying with all other firms in the economy for the limited incomes of consumers.

The monopolist, unlike the purely competitive firm, cannot sell all its output at a going market price. As a monopolist increases output the market price for its product can be expected to decline. Thus, the monopolist faces a downward sloping demand curve. In Fig. 3-2 the monopolist will

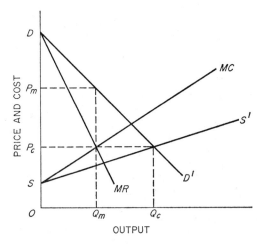

Fig. 3-2. *Pure Monopoly (P > MR = MC)*

maximize its profits by increasing its output to Q_m, where its marginal revenue curve MR intersects its marginal cost curve MC. Note that as a consequence of the downward sloping demand curve DD', the price charged by the monopolist OP_m will be greater than marginal revenue OP_c at the profit maximizing output Q_m.

Comparison of the Theoretical Results of the Models

The output of a monopolist, which represents the total industry output, can be compared with the output of the same industry under pure competition. Assume that DD' in Fig. 3-2 represents the demand curve for the monopolist as well as the demand curve for the competitive industry. SS' represents the long run competitive supply curve and is equal to the average cost curve.[1] The competitive industry will be in equilibrium at output Q_c, where the industry demand curve DD' intersects the industry supply curve SS'.

If the monopolist takes over this competitive industry, and no changes in cost or demand occur, the industry output will be contracted to Q_m. At Q_m the monopolist's marginal cost MC, which is marginal to the average cost curve SS', intersects the marginal revenue curve MR, and the profits of the monopolist are maximized. Thus, the monopolist by restricting output to maximize profits would appear to produce a lower level of output than that achieved by a purely competitive industry.[2]

A number of objections have been raised to the comparison between monopoly and purely competitive outputs. First, the larger output of the competitive industry versus the monopolist may be, during periods of full employment, at the expense of other more important industries, and can result in a misallocation of resources. Second, the cost curves and demand curves can be expected to change after an industry has been altered from pure competition to a pure monopoly. For example, the monopolist may be able to achieve *real economies* through lower costs per unit of output by economies of large-scale production.[3]

---

[1]See J. Robinson, *Economics of Imperfect Competition* (London: Macmillan & Co. Ltd., 1961; 1st ed., 1933), Chap. 9.

[2]It can be proved that in Fig. 3-2, as drawn with linear demand and supply curves, the monopoly output Q_m is exactly one-half Q_c, the competitive output.

[3]In contrast, *pecuniary economies* result from the ability of the monopolist to buy its raw materials at lower prices by virtue of its superior bargaining power. These lower costs may not offer any net benefit to society.

Welfare Implications of the Model of Perfect Competition

If the productive resources and technology of an economy were fully utilized under perfect competition, the welfare of society would be optimized and an ideal allocation of resources would be achieved according to the economist Pareto, provided no person could be made more satisfied without at the same time making another person less satisfied. This state of economic efficiency is often referred to as the Pareto optimum.[4]

A number of economic conditions must be fulfilled before the consumer sector and producer sector of an economy can reach a Pareto optimum.[5] In the consumer sector an optimum allocation of goods will be realized when there exist no further situations in which a mutual advantage can be obtained by any two consumers in further exchanging goods. In the producer sector an optimum allocation of resources will be realized when inputs cannot be further reallocated among firms in order to increase the output of one firm without at the same time decreasing the output of another firm, and when inputs cannot be further reallocated in one firm to increase the output of one good without at the same time decreasing the output of some other good produced by the firm.

An optimum allocation of goods in the consumer sector requires that the ratio of marginal utilities for any two goods should be the same for any pair of individuals consuming both of them. Any two consumers, denoted by superscripts i and j, must face the same prices under conditions of perfect competition. A consumer maximizes his satisfaction when the ratio of his marginal utilities for any two goods, denoted by subscripts x and y, equals the ratio of their respective prices. Only in this position will the consumer be unable to increase his total utility by reallocating his limited funds in order to obtain more of a good X and less of good Y, or *vice versa*. Since both

---

[4]See J. M. Henderson and R. E. Quandt, *Microeconomic Theory* (New York: McGraw-Hill Book Company, 1958), pp. 202–8. Also see T. Scitovsky, *Welfare and Competition: The Economics of a Fully Employed Economy* (Homewood, Ill.: Richard D. Irwin, Inc., 1951); R. H. Leftwich, *The Price System and Resource Allocation* (New York: Holt, Rinehart & Winston, Inc., 1956); A. Lerner, *The Economics of Control: Principles of Welfare Economics* (New York: The Macmillan Company, 1944); and J. W. Markham, "Goals for Industrial Organization: A Theoretical Analysis," *The American Economy*, J. W. Markham, ed. (New York: George Braziller, Inc., 1963), pp. 28–42.

[5]Only the necessary marginal conditions will be discussed; these first-order conditions are necessary but not sufficient for an optimum. For a discussion of second-order conditions, which must be satisfied for a welfare optimum, see J. de V. Graaff, *Theoretical Welfare Economics* (London: Cambridge University Press, 1957), pp. 66–70; and W. J. Baumol, "External Economies and Second-Order Optimality Conditions," *American Economic Review*, Vol. LIV (June, 1964), 358–71.

consumers face the same fixed prices, the ratios of their marginal utilities for any two goods are equal. The consumers' rate of substitution (CRS) represents the rate at which consumers can substitute one good, such as X, for another good, such as Y, given a limited budget. The following chain equation summarizes these relationships:

$$(3\text{-}1) \qquad CRS = \frac{P_x}{P_y} = \frac{MU_x^i}{MU_y^i} = \frac{MU_x^j}{MU_y^j}$$

An optimum allocation of resources in the producer sector requires that the ratio of marginal products for any two inputs should be the same for any pair of products using both of these inputs. In other words, the marginal product of input A (or the extra output of good X resulting from an additional unit of input A) over the marginal product of input B in the production of good X should be equal to the ratio of the marginal products for input A and B which are used also in the production of another good Y. If the ratios are not equal, a more suitable allocation of resources can be obtained by shifting resources from the production of X into the production of Y, or *vice versa*, as the case may be. Furthermore, inputs A and B will be combined efficiently when the ratios of their marginal products equal the ratio of their respective prices. Denoting the inputs A and B as superscripts, and the final goods X and Y as subscripts, the condition for an optimum allocation of the inputs is as follows:

$$(3\text{-}2) \qquad \frac{P_a}{P_b} = \frac{MP_x^a}{MP_x^b} = \frac{MP_y^a}{MP_y^b}$$

The above marginal productivity analysis can be translated into the more familiar marginal cost analysis. By definition, the cost of an input such as A, which contributes to an increase in one unit of product X, is the same as the marginal cost of product X. Hence, for inputs A and B, which are used in the production of good X, the following relationships exist when the inputs are optimally allocated:

$$(3\text{-}3) \qquad \frac{P_a}{MP_x^a} = \frac{P_b}{MP_x^b} = MC_x$$

$$(3\text{-}4) \qquad \frac{P_a}{MP_y^a} = \frac{P_b}{MP_y^b} = MC_y$$

The above equations state the proper proportions in which a firm should combine optimally inputs A and B. The absolute amount of these resources which the firm should employ in terms of its optimum output level is determined by the profit maximizing condition equating marginal cost to marginal revenue. Under conditions of perfect competition, the firm expands its output until its marginal cost is equal to the product price. Hence,

$$(3-5) \qquad\qquad P_x = MC_x$$

$$(3-6) \qquad\qquad P_y = MC_y$$

The producers' rate of transformation (PRT) is the rate at which producers can substitute the output of product X for product Y given a fixed level of inputs. The producers' rate of transformation between goods X and Y is equal to the ratio of their marginal costs under conditions of perfect competition. Therefore, for an optimum allocation of resources the ratio of market prices for a pair of goods must be equal to their respective marginal costs:

$$(3-7) \qquad\qquad \frac{P_x}{P_y} = \frac{MC_x}{MC_y} = PRT$$

Alternatively stated, and generalized for Z products, the condition for efficient allocation of resources between the consumer and producer sectors becomes

$$(3-8) \qquad\qquad \frac{P_x}{MC_x} = \frac{P_y}{MC_y} = \ldots = \frac{P_z}{MC_z}$$

The final step in achieving the necessary conditions for a Pareto optimum allocation of resources requires the efficient product mix of the producer sector to conform to the preferences of the consumer sector. This is accomplished by having the producers' rate of transformation (PRT) between any two products equal the consumers' rate of substitution (CRS) for the same two products:

$$(3-9) \qquad\qquad PRT = CRS$$

The transition in the preceding analysis from the individual consumer or firm to the totality of all firms and consumers did not take into account the interdependence of the actions among both consumers and producers. Each consumer or producer simply maximized in an isolated fashion his private interests. However, the actions of one individual generally have repercussions on the conduct of other members of society. For example, fashions and luxury items reflect an interdependence of consumption functions among members of a community. The movement of a large firm to a relatively isolated sector of a country may attract other firms, develop roads and school systems for the area, and generally bring a multitude of benefits to neighboring consumers and producers. These benefits are referred to as external economies.

External *diseconomies* are present where a firm depletes a natural resource and deprives other firms and industries from the benefits of this resource. The introduction of external economies and diseconomies into the preceding theoretical framework demonstrates the importance of interdependence between the various producer equations and consumer equations. The presence of interdependence also raises serious doubts as to whether the pursuit of private interests by consumers and producers will be sufficient, by itself, to bring society to a welfare optimum.

The presence of interdependence among the various equations in the producer sector and the consumer sector has been the basis for a frontal attack on the marginal analysis used to derive the Paretian optimum. Critics of the "classical welfare economics" have contended that if there is introduced into a general equilibrium system a constraint which prevents the attainment of one of the Paretian conditions, the remaining Paretian conditions are in general no longer desirable. Thus, in a mixed economy with a number of regulated and unregulated industries not operating under conditions of pure competition, it may be *undesirable* in terms of economic welfare to attempt to restructure some but not all of these monopolistic industries.

The *theory of second best* states, ". . . there is no *a priori* way to judge as between various situations in which some of the Paretian optimum conditions are fulfilled while others are not."[6] Furthermore, the theory states," . . . it is *not* true that a situation in which more, but not all, of the optimum conditions are fulfilled is necessarily, or is even likely to be, superior to a situation in which fewer are fulfilled."[7] If the Paretian optimum condition that marginal cost equal marginal revenue is not established for one firm in the economy, the second best optimum requires that this equality be departed from in other firms. The second best position can therefore be one in which some firms have marginal revenues greatly in excess of their marginal costs and others have only a slight departure, with the remaining firms having their marginal revenues falling short of their marginal costs.

The theory of second best presents a profound lesson to the antitrust

[6]R. G. Lipsey and K. Lancaster, "The General Theory of Second Best," *Review of Economic Studies*, Vol. XXIV (1956–57), 11. Also see C. Morrison, "The Nature of Second Best," *Southern Journal of Economics*, Vol. XXXII (July, 1965), 49–52; E. J. Mishan, "Second Thoughts on Second Best," *Oxford Economic Papers*, Vol. XIV (October, 1962), 205–17; M. McManus, "Comments on the General Theory of Second Best," *Review of Economic Studies*, Vol. XXVI (June, 1959), 209–24; and L. W. McKenzie, "Ideal Output and the Interdependence of Firms," *Economic Journal*, Vol. LVI (December, 1951), 785–803.

[7]Lipsey and Lancaster, "The General Theory of Second Best," p. 11.

policy maker: "To apply to only a small part of an economy welfare rules which would lead to a Paretian optimum if they were applied everywhere, may move the economy away from, not toward, a second best optimum position."[8] There may exist, of course, political or competitive advantages far outweighing economic welfare disadvantages. But the interdependence of the network of industries in an economy must be carefully considered in effecting any structural changes.[9] The marginal rules of the model of perfect competition and the Pareto optimum, taken alone, offer no *a priori* guide in a mixed economy for an antitrust policy which takes into account economic objectives reflecting increased welfare for a country.

The Inadequacies of the Model of Pure Competition for Antitrust Policy

Antitrust statutes have not been directed to the narrow task of eliminating all monopolistic elements in our economy. Variations in products, advertising, and brand names give product diversity to our economy in contrast to the standardized products found in countries not operating within a free enterprise system. These monopolistic elements would not exist in a world of pure competition where a large number of firms manufacture a homogeneous product, and no one firm can materially affect the market price. To eliminate these monopolistic elements would destroy the distinctive traits and individuality of firms with respect to their services, products, and price policies. The basic point is that a belief in the value of competition does not require each and every move in antitrust policy to be made in the direction of a pure competition model. The pure competition model is neither a description of reality nor a normative standard toward which antitrust policy makers should strive.

Professor Edward Chamberlin, in describing his term "monopolistic competition," reaches basically the same conclusion:

Now if pure competition is the ideal, the direction in which we should move is very clear. For it is easy enough to show that the actual economy is shot full of monopoly elements, and hence that any move to get rid of them or to diminish their importance is in the right direction. The main point I want to make is that the welfare ideal itself (as well as the description of reality) involves a blend of monopoly and competition and is therefore correctly described as one of monopolistic competition. If this is true, it is no longer self-evident which way we should move, for it is no longer self-evident on which side of the ideal lies the actuality for which a policy

[8]*Ibid.*, p. 17.

[9]W. J. Baumol, "Informed Judgment, Rigorous Theory, and Public Policy," *Southern Journal of Economics*, Vol. XXXII (October, 1965), 137–45.

is sought. It is possible that the economy should be made 'more competitive,' but it is also quite possible that it should be made 'more monopolistic' instead.[10]

An encouragement of some monopolistic elements does not require an advocacy of monopolies.[11] It is rather a recognition that the term competition encompasses a vitality of interacting market forces that are not always provided by moving in the direction of pure competition. The term "competitiveness" should not be shackled with the connotation that unless the market conditions simulate those of a theoretical model containing a large number of firms no one of which has any influence on price, and all of which produce a standardized product, the market structure lacks the vital rivalry and stimulus associated with a free enterprise system.

In a world of pure competition an optimum allocation of resources is determined only after the consumer preferences or the demand conditions of a community are known. The assortment of goods which maximizes the total utility of a community has presented economists with insuperable difficulties because of the incomparability and incommensurability of the utilities of different individuals. There is no economic or objective solution for finding a "bliss point" which maximizes the satisfaction of consumers.[12]

---

[10]E. H. Chamberlin, *Towards A More General Theory of Value* (New York: Oxford University Press, 1957), p. 93. The Chamberlin model of monopolistic competition is discussed in Chap. 8 in this book.

[11]Monopolists, in their attempt to maximize profits, restrict output. Therefore, in an economy mixed with monopolies and competitive industries resources will tend to be over-allocated to competitively produced commodities and under-allocated to monopolistically produced commodities. However, in a world of monopolies, where no industries are competitive, a misallocation of resources does not necessarily result. Professor William Baumol makes this point with an interesting metaphor: "Given the level of employment of resources, a misallocation can arise only if the demand for inputs of one set of industries (the monopolists) is low *in comparison with* that of the remaining industries. If each of a number of runners slows down, none of them need come in ahead of the others, and if each industry is weak in its bidding for resources, no lopsided allocation of these resources need result. We see, then, that some competition may conceivably be worse than none!" *Economic Theory and Operations Analysis* (Englewood Cliffs, N. J.: Prentice-Hall, Inc., 1961), p. 257. Cf. J. S. Bain, *Price Theory* (New York: John Wiley & Sons, Inc., 1966), pp. 240–47; and Lipsey and Lancaster, "The General Theory of Second Best," p. 12.

[12]Professor Paul Samuelson states, ". . . the new welfare economics is a body of doctrines which attempts to go as far as possible in preparing the way for the final a-scientific step involving value judgments...." See his "Evaluation of Real National Income," *Oxford Economic Papers*, New Series, Vol. II (1950), 1–29. Also see T. C. Koopsmans, "Allocation of Resources and the Price System, " the first of *Three Essays on the State of Economic Science* (New York: McGraw-Hill Book Company, 1957), pp. 41–66; M. W. Reder, *Studies in the Theory of Welfare Economics* (New York: Columbia University Press, 1947); I. M. D. Little, *A Critique of Welfare Economics*, 2nd ed. (London: Oxford University Press, 1957); A. Bergson, "A Reformulation of Certain Aspects of Welfare

Resort must be made to value judgments as to the favorability of income distribution, individuals' preferences and social preferences. Thus, models dealing with optimum allocation of resources have not met the problem of determining the ideal product mix of the economy.

If a number of different advertised brands of a product are preferred by our society over a single standardized product, our economy will have to maintain a greater number of plants, many of which may be operating at less than their minimum long-term average cost. But this state of the economy is not one of misallocation of resources — if society prefers a wide proliferation of sizes, shapes, and types of products.

The unique features of products and services are emphasized by advertising. To the extent that consumers accept these differences as important, a differential in value is created between related products. Individualism becomes the keynote. Individualism in product encourages each company to manufacture, not an identical product, but a better product than its competitor. Individualism in service encourages each company to try harder to please customers. Individualism in price means that a company has some limited degree of price flexibility. These features are not present in a model of pure competition. However, each of these forms of individualism has been recognized as fundamentally important to the free enterprise system of the United States.

Economics," *Quarterly Journal of Economics*, Vol. LII (February, 1938), 310–34; W. J. Baumol, *Welfare Economics and the Theory of the State* (London: Longmans, Green & Company, Ltd., 1952); and J. de V. Graaff, *Theoretical Welfare Economics*.

PART II

Antitrust in
A Single Product Context

SECTION B

Monopoly

CHAPTER FOUR

The Standard Oil Case (1911)

The Standard Oil Company of New Jersey, the largest manufacturing corporation in terms of assets in the United States in the mid-1960's, had its genesis only a century ago.[1] In 1862 John D. Rockefeller and his partner

[1]For background information on the petroleum industry, see J. McGee, "Price Discrimination and Competitive Effects: The Standard Oil of Indiana Case," *University of Chicago Law Review*, Vol. XXIII (Spring, 1956), pp. 398–473; J. S. Bain, *The Economics of the Pacific Coast Petroleum Industry*, 3 vols. (Berkeley, Calif.: University of California Press, 1944, 1945, and 1947); K. Beaton, *Enterprise in Oil: A History of Shell in the United States* (New York: Appleton-Century-Crofts, 1957); R. Cassady, Jr., *Price Making and Price Behavior in the Petroleum Industry* (New Haven: Yale University Press, 1954); R. Cassady, Jr. and W. L. Jones, *The Nature of Competition in Gasoline Distribution at the Retail Level* (Berkeley, Calif.: University of California Press, 1951); R. C. Cook, *Control of the Petroleum Industry by Major Oil Companies*, T. N. E. C. Monograph No. 39 (Washington, D.C.: Government Printing Office, 1941); L. Cookenboo, Jr., *Crude Oil Pipe Lines and Competition in the Oil Industry* (Cambridge, Mass.: Harvard University Press, 1955); J. B. Dirlam, "The Petroleum Industry," in *The Structure of American Industry*, Walter Adams, ed. (New York: The Macmillan Company, 1954), and "Leadership and Conflict in the Pricing of Gasoline," *Yale Law Journal*, Vol. LXI (1952), 818–55; G. S. Gibb and E. H. Knowlton, *The Resurgent Years, 1911–1927, History of the Standard Oil Company (New Jersey)*, (New York: Harper & Row, Publishers, 1956); R. W. Hidy and M. E. Hidy, *Pioneering in Big Business, 1882-1911, History of the Standard Oil Company (New Jersey)*, (New York: Harper & Row, Publishers, 1955); J. H. McLean and R. W. Haigh, *The Growth of Integrated Oil Companies* (Cambridge, Mass.: Harvard University Graduate School of Business Administration, 1954); G. H. Montague, *The Rise and Progress of the Standard Oil Company* (1904); E. V. Rostow, *A National Policy for the Oil Industry* (New Haven: Yale University Press, 1948); E. V. Rostow and A. S. Sachs, "Entry into the Oil Refining Business; Vertical Integration Re-examined," *Yale Law Journal*, Vol. LXI (1952), 856–914; G. W. Stocking, *The Oil Industry and the Competitive System, A*

advanced $4,000 to Samuel Andrews to enable the latter to improve an oil refinery. The oil refinery prospered and in 1870 John D. Rockefeller, William Rockefeller, Henry M. Flagler, and several other individuals formed the Standard Oil Company of Ohio. In two years Standard of Ohio had obtained almost all of the forty oil refineries in Cleveland. By 1880 Standard had acquired a large number of refineries in New York, Pennsylvania, and in other parts of Ohio. From 1882 to 1899 over forty corporations, including Standard of Ohio, were reorganized into the Standard Oil Trust. The stock of the trust was subsequently transferred to the Standard Oil Company of New Jersey, which acted as a holding company.

The United States government brought legal proceedings in 1906 against Standard of New Jersey, John D. and William Rockefeller, Henry M. Flagler, and a number of other corporations and individuals. The government charged that a violation of Secs. 1 and 2 of the Sherman Act occurred by the defendants' conspiracy to monopolize and restrain trade in crude oil, refined oil, and other petroleum products. The conspiracy was alleged to have begun through the formation of Standard of Ohio in 1870. The defendants were charged with having used Standard of Ohio as a means to obtain from the railroads large preferential rates and rebates over competing oil companies. The advantage of preferential railroad rates was alleged to have been used by Standard of Ohio to force smaller competitors to join their company, or alternatively, to drive these independents out of business. In addition to the power held by Standard over the railroads, Standard also exerted considerable control over the pipelines from the eastern oil fields to the mid-western oil refineries.

The Rule of Reason

Standard Oil Company of New Jersey v. *United States*[2] became a landmark decision in the annals of antitrust history with the enunciation by Chief Justice White of the rule of reason for judging the legality of various business contracts and arrangements alleged to be in restraint of trade. The Government urged a *per se* application of Sec. 1 of the Sherman Act whereby *all* contracts or combinations in restraint of trade would be illegal. Chief Justice White, however, held that *every* contract or combina-

Study in Waste (Boston: Houghton Mifflin Company, 1925); I. M. Tarbell, *History of the Standard Oil Company*, Vols. I and II (New York: McClure, Phillips, 1904); F. J. Taylor and E. M. Welty, *Black Bonanza* (New York: McGraw-Hill Book Company, 1950); and G. S. Wolbert, Jr., *American Pipelines* (Oklahoma City: University of Oklahoma Press, 1952).

[2]221 U. S. 1 (1911).

tion in restraint of trade was not illegal; only *unreasonable* restraints of trade were unlawful under the Sherman Act. In the words of the Court,

> In substance, the propositions urged by the government are reducible to this: That the language of the statute embraces every contract, combination, etc., in restraint of trade, and hence its text leaves no room for the exercise of judgment, but simply imposes the plain duty of applying its prohibitions to every case within its literal language. The error involved lies in assuming the matter to be decided. This is true because, as the acts which may come under the classes stated in the 1st section and the restraint of trade to which that section applies are not specifically enumerated or defined, it is obvious that judgment must in every case be called into play in order to determine whether a particular act is embraced within the statutory classes, and whether, if the act is within such classes, its nature or effect causes it to be a restraint of trade within the intendment of the act.
>
> If the criterion by which it is to be determined in all cases whether every contract, combination, etc., is a restraint of trade within the intendment of the law, is the direct or indirect effect of the acts involved, then of course the *rule of reason* becomes the guide, and the construction which we have given the statute, instead of being refuted by the cases relied upon, is by those cases demonstrated to be correct. This is true, because as the construction which we have deduced from the history of the act and the analysis of its text is simply that in every case where it is claimed that an act or acts are in violation of the statute the *rule of reason*, in the light of the principles of law and the public policy which the act embodies, must be applied.[3]

The Per Se *Doctrine*

Justice Harlan dissented in part from the majority opinion in the *Standard Oil* case. Harlan maintained that the arguments in favor of a rule of reason interpretation of Sec. 1 of the Sherman Act had been expressly rejected by the Supreme Court fifteen years earlier in the *Trans-Missouri Freight Association* case.[4] This case involved the validity under the Sherman Act of an agreement between numerous railroad companies for the formation of an association whose purpose was the maintenance of reasonable rates and regulations for member carriers.

Justice Peckham, speaking for the majority in the *Trans-Missouri* case, rejected the plea for the establishment of a rule of reason in the interpretation of the Sherman Act. The concept of *per se*, which is commonly treated as the antithesis of the rule of reason, emerges from the following passage in Justice Peckham's opinion:

> This agreement so made, the government alleges, is illegal as being in restraint of trade, and was entered into between the companies for the purpose of enhancing the freight rates. The companies, while denying the illegality of the agreement or its purpose to be other than to maintain reasonable rates, yet allege that without some

---

[3]*Ibid.*, pp. 63 66; italics added.

[4]*United States* v. *Trans-Missouri Freight Assn.*, 166 U. S. 290 (1896).

such agreement the competition between them for traffic would be so severe as to cause great losses to each defendant and possibly ruin the companies represented in the agreement.[5] What is the meaning of the language as used in the statute, that "every contract, combination in the form of trust or otherwise, or conspiracy in restraint of trade or commerce among the several States or with foreign nations, is hereby declared to be illegal?" Is it confined to a contract or combination which is only in unreasonable restraint of trade or commerce, or does it include what the language of the act plainly and in terms covers, all contracts of that nature?[6]

. . . The arguments which have been addressed to us against the inclusion of all contracts in restraint of trade, as provided for by the language of the act, have been based upon the alleged presumption that Congress, notwithstanding the language of the act, could not have intended to embrace all contracts, but only such contracts as were in unreasonable restraint of trade. Under these circumstances we are, therefore, asked to hold that the act of Congress excepts contracts which are not in unreasonable restraint of trade, and which only keep rates up to a reasonable price, notwithstanding the language of the act makes no such exception. In other words, we are asked to read into the act by way of judicial legislation an exception that is not placed there by the law-making branch of the government, and this is done upon the theory that the impolicy of such legislation is so clear that it cannot be supposed Congress intended the natural import of the language it used. This we cannot and ought not to do.[7]

The *Trans-Missouri* case was basically a price-fixing case and, consequently, might have been disposed of by the Court on the basis that conspiracies among competitors to fix prices are by their inherent nature unreasonable restraints of trade, *i.e.*, no reason exists which could justify the fixing of prices.[8] Justice Peckham, however, believed that a decision as to the reasonableness of a contract necessitated a judgment as to the level of prices resulting from the contract. This type of inquiry, Justice Peckham foresaw, would open the floodgates of evidence and create considerable uncertainty as to the import of the Sherman Act and the legality of business conduct. In his words,

There is another side to this question, however, and it may not be amiss to refer to one or two facts which tend to somewhat modify and alter the light in which the subject should be regarded. If only that kind of contract which is in unreasonable restraint of trade be within the meaning of the statute, and declared therein to be illegal, it is at once apparent that the subject of what is a reasonable rate is attended with great uncertainty. What is a proper standard by which to judge the fact of reasonable rates? Must the rate be so high as to enable the return for the whole business done to amount to a sum sufficient to afford the shareholder a fair and reasonable profit upon his investment? If so, what is a fair and reasonable profit?

[5]*Ibid.*, p. 327.

[6]*Ibid.*

[7]*Ibid.*, p. 340.

[8]Cf. *Chicago Board of Trade* v. *United States*, 246 U. S. 231 (1918).

That depends sometimes upon the risks incurred, and the rate itself differs in different localities: which is the one to which reference is to be made as the standard? Or is the reasonableness of the profit to be limited to a fair return upon the capital that would have been sufficient to build and equip the road, if honestly expended? Or is still another standard to be created, and the reasonableness of the charges tried by the cost of carriage of the article and a reasonable profit allowed on that? And in such case would contribution to a sinking fund to make repairs upon the roadbed and renewal of cars, etc., be assumed as a proper item?[9]

The Dichotomy of the Rule of Reason and the Per Se Doctrine

Professor Handler, observing the importance of the *Trans-Missouri* and *Standard Oil* cases in the development of the rule of reason, states: "Peckham, of course, had the best of the argument from the standpoint of the statute's wording. 'Every' plainly means all and not some. His literal reading, however, would have made the statute inadministrable, as he himself soon learned with more experience in Sherman Act litigation. . . . White's practical statesmanship foresaw the need for flexibility to adopt a statute of general application to changing circumstances. Despite his dubious scholarship and rhetoric, his was the interpretation that gave viability to the law."[10]

Both the *per se* doctrine and the rule of reason are essential elements in the interpretation of our present antitrust laws. "Antitrust reflects," in the words of Professor Oppenheim, "the never-ending conflict between the desire for certainty and the desire for flexibility that is as old as the processes of the law itself."[11] The *per se* doctrine offers greater certainty to the antitrust laws, but sacrifices the vital elements of flexibility which are associated with the rule of reason. The methodologies of the two approaches have been distinguished by Professor Oppenheim as follows: "Whereas a per se rule immediately brands the operative fact embraced by it as unreasonable, the Rule of Reason opens the way to reliance upon a broad range of discretion in weighing the evidence of defenses of justification compatible with the purposes of the antitrust statutes. The Rule of Reason operates through a process of inclusion and exclusion in a case-by-case consideration of all the facts. The per se illegality doctrine operates by converting predetermined single-fact categories into fixed rules of law."[12]

[9]166 U. S. 290, 331 (1896).

[10]"The Judicial Architects of the Rule of Reason," in *Antitrust in Perspective* (New York: Columbia University Press, 1957), p. 11.

[11]S. C. Oppenheim, "Federal Antitrust Legislation: Guideposts to a Revised National Antitrust Policy," *Michigan Law Review*, Vol. L (June, 1952), 1149.

[12]*Ibid.*, pp. 1151–52.

The rule of reason does not lend itself to precise definition. A number of justices and legal writers have disagreed as to whether the Sherman Act gave new substance to the law or merely codified the existing common law with regard to ancillary and nonancillary restraints of trade.[13] An ancillary restraint is subordinate to the main lawful purpose of a larger transaction. For example, a contract for the sale of a business or professional practice often includes an ancillary agreement that the seller will not establish a nearby business to compete with the buyer until a number of years elapses. A nonancillary restraint refers to a transaction in which the primary purpose is to eliminate or restrict competition, such as a price-fixing agreement.

Judge Taft in the *Addyston Pipe* case[14] maintained that the rule of reason was applied at common law only to ancillary restraints upon competition. In contrast, Justice White in the *Standard Oil* case of 1911 maintained that the rule of reason applied both to ancillary and nonancillary restraints and only unreasonable restraints were illegal. Although the Taft version of the rule of reason appears to be established as the existing state of the law, it can be argued that the Taft and White versions "come to the same thing if it is believed — as modern supporters of antitrust usually do believe — that any conduct that is *significantly anticompetitive* is *ipso facto* unreasonable in White's sense."[15]

The Specific Intent to Monopolize

The *Standard Oil* decision is also significant for its analysis of the prerequisite legal elements for monopolization. Section 2 of the Sherman Act provides in part:

> Every person who shall monopolize, or attempt to monopolize, or combine or conspire with any other person or persons, to monopolize any part of the trade or commerce among the several States, or with foreign nations, shall be guilty of a misdemeanor . . .

[13]See S. C. Oppenheim, *Federal Antitrust Laws—Cases and Comments* (St. Paul, Minn.: West Publishing Company, 1959), pp. 1–8.

[14]*United States* v. *Addyston Pipe & Steel Co.*, 85 F. 271 (6th Cir., 1898), modified and affirmed 175 U. S. 211 (1899). Also see W. H. Taft, *The Antitrust Act and the Supreme Court* (New York: Harper & Row, Publishers, 1914).

[15]A. D. Neale, *The Antitrust Laws of the U. S. A.* (London: Cambridge University Press, 1960), p. 20; and United States, *Report of the Attorney General's National Committee to Study the Antitrust Laws* (Washington, D.C.: Government Printing Office, 1955), p. 11. Cf. J. C. Peppin, "Price Fixing Agreements Under the Sherman Antitrust Law," *California Law Review*, Vol. XXVIII (1940), 677.

Chief Justice White, in contrasting the abusive market practices of Standard Oil with "advancing the development of business power by usual methods," implied that the positive drive for monopolization rather than the market structure of monopoly was condemned by the Sherman Act.[16] The presence of this positive drive can be found by examining the intent and purpose of the defendants' acts. In the following passage, Chief Justice White attempts to document the finding that the defendants had a specific intent to monopolize the oil industry:

> ... the unification of power and control over petroleum and its products which was the inevitable result of the combining in the New Jersey corporation by the increase of its stock and the transfer to it of the stocks of so many other corporations, aggregating so vast a capital, gives rise, in and of itself, in the absence of countervailing circumstances, to say the least, to the prima facie presumption of intent and purpose to maintain the dominancy over the oil industry, not as a result of normal methods of industrial development, but by new means of combination which were resorted to in order that greater power might be added than would otherwise have arisen had normal methods been followed, the whole with the purpose of excluding others from the trade, and thus centralizing in the combination a perpetual control of the movements of petroleum and its products in the channels of interstate commerce. ... the acquisition here and there which ensued of every efficient means by which competition could have been asserted, the slow but resistless methods which followed by which means of transportation were absorbed and brought under control, the system of marketing which was adopted by which the country was divided into districts and the trade in each district in oil was turned over to a designated corporation within the combination, and all others were excluded, all lead the mind to a conviction of a purpose and intent which we think is so certain as practically to cause the subject not to be within the domain of reasonable contention.[17]

Legal and Economic Concepts of Monopoly

Justice White, in speaking for the majority in the *Standard Oil* case, found that Standard Oil had violated both Sec. 1 of the Sherman Act by combining or forming a conspiracy in restraint of trade, and Sec. 2 by an attempt to monopolize and actual monopolization. The analysis of Justice White with respect to the meaning of monopoly and the legal prerequisites for a finding of an attempt to monopolize is fundamental for an understanding of subsequent judicial interpretations of the Sherman Act.

Justice White was primarily concerned with restrictions on competition rather than technical or abstract definitions of monopoly. If an act has the same effect as monopoly granted by a sovereign power, the act, in the opinion of White, should be treated as "amounting to monopoly." The

[16]Neale, *The Antitrust Laws of the U. S. A.*, p. 103.
[17]221 U. S. 1, 75–77 (1911).

existence of monopoly should be found by examining the abuses which have been associated traditionally with government granted monopolies. In his words,

It is remarkable that nowhere at common law can there be found a prohibition against the creation of monopoly by an individual. This would seem to manifest, either consciously or intuitively, a profound conception as to the inevitable operation of economic forces and the equipose or balance in favor of the protection of the rights of individuals which resulted. That is to say, as it was deemed that monopoly in the concrete could only arise from an act of sovereign power, and, such sovereign power being restrained, prohibitions as to individuals were directed not against the creation of monopoly, but were only applied to such acts in relation to particular subjects as to which it was deemed, if not restrained, some of the consequences of monopoly might result. . . . In other words, here as had been the case in England, practical common sense caused attention to be concentrated not upon the theoretically correct name to be given to the condition or acts which gave rise to a harmful result, but to the result itself and to the remedying of the evils which it produced.[18]

In the *Standard Oil* case the Court presented only a limited analysis of the structure of the oil industry and the market position held by Standard Oil in the refined, crude and broad petroleum field. The Court mentioned that by the end of the first period, 1870–82, or approximately thirty years before the writing of the opinion in the case — and before the passage of the Sherman Act — Standard of Ohio had obtained "mastery over the oil industry, controlling 90 per cent of the business, and was thus able to fix the price of crude and refined petroleum."[19] Nevertheless, the Court conceded that Standard controlled only a "very small percentage of the crude oil produced."[20] Standard Oil's market power existed in the refined oil market; this power, maintained the Court, permitted the company to control the crude oil market despite the fact that Standard produced very little crude oil. In the words of Chief Justice White:

The inference that no attempt to monopolize could have been intended, and that no monopolization resulted from the acts complained of, since it is established that a very small percentage of the crude oil produced was controlled by the combination, is unwarranted. As substantial power over the crude product was the inevitable result of the absolute control which existed over the refined product, the monopolization of the one carried with it the power to control the other; and if the inferences which this situation suggests were developed, which we deem unnecessary to do, they might well serve to add additional cogency to the presumption of intent to monopolize which we have found arises from the unquestioned proof on other subjects.[21]

[18]*Ibid.*, p. 55.
[19]*Ibid.*, p. 33.
[20]*Ibid.*, p. 77.
[21]*Ibid.*

The Court concluded that Standard Oil had monopolized the crude and refined oil markets. But note that the Court did not follow a purely economic concept of monopoly in the sense of a company in control of all the output of an industry. Rather, the Court employed a legalistic concept of monopoly which was related to predatory market practices. The distinction between economic and legal concepts of monopoly during this period has been noted by Professor Mason: "By monopoly, however, the courts did not mean control of the market but restriction of competition. . . . If the manifestation of the intention to limit the competition of outsiders took the form of overt acts such as local price discrimination, espionage, or securing of railway rebates, the courts could find evidence of restrictions directly relevant to their conception of monopoly. As a matter of fact it is clear that this was the direction taken in the judicial application of the rule of reason. The size of the combination or its share of total output of a product became important only when accompanied by predatory practices affecting the freedom of others to compete."[22]

Note on the American Tobacco Case (1911)

In *United States* v. *American Tobacco Company*,[23] a companion case to *Standard Oil*, the Supreme Court condemned the "tobacco trust" on the grounds that its existence violated the Sherman Act. In 1890 a trust was formed composed of five concerns which had formerly competed fiercely in the manufacture, distribution and sale of 95 per cent of all domestic cigarettes. The trust attempted to extend its operations by engaging in ruthless price competition in the plug tobacco field until it was able, in 1898, to acquire five large plug manufacturers. Thereafter, the trust expended over fifty million dollars purchasing thirty competing firms, which on being acquired were immediately shut down. Chief Justice White, in speaking for the Court again, reiterated the *Standard Oil* rule that wrongful purpose or intent must be established in addition to market power for a violation of the Sherman Act monopolization provision. In his words,

Indeed, the history of combination is so replete with the doing of acts which it was the obvious purpose of the statute to forbid, so demonstrative of the existence

---

[22]E. S. Mason, "Monopoly in Law and Economics," *Yale Law Journal*, Vol. XLVII (November, 1937), 34–49; reprinted in his *Economic Concentration and the Monopoly Problem* (Cambridge, Mass.: Harvard University Press, 1957), p. 342.

[23]211 U. S. 106 (1911). See W. H. Nicholls, *Price Policies in the Cigarette Industry* (Nashville, Tenn.: Vanderbilt University Press, 1951), pp. 26–32; R. Cox, *Competition in the American Tobacco Industry, 1911–1932* (New York: Columbia University Press, 1933); and R. B. Tennant, *The American Cigarette Industry* (New Haven: Yale University Press, 1950).

from the beginning of a purpose to acquire dominion and control of the tobacco trade, not by the mere exertion of the ordinary right to contract and to trade, but by methods devised in order to monopolize the trade by driving competitors out of business, which were ruthlessly carried out upon the assumption that to work upon the fears or play upon the cupidity of competitors would make success possible. We say these conclusions are inevitable, not because of the vast amount of property aggregated by the combination, not because, alone, of the many corporations which the proof shows were united by resort to one device or another. Again, not alone because of the dominion and control over the tobacco trade which actually exists, but because we think the conclusion of wrongful purpose and legal combination is overwhelmingly established by the following considerations: (a) By the fact that the very first organization or combination was impelled by a previously existing fierce trade war, . . . (b) Because, immediately after that combination and the increase of capital which followed, the acts which ensued justify the inference that the intention existed to use the power of the combination as a vantage ground to further monopolize the trade in tobacco by means of trade conflicts designed to injure others, either by driving competitors out of business or compelling them to become parties to a combination, — a purpose whose execution was illustrated by the plug war which ensued and its results, by the snuff war which followed and its results, and by the conflict which immediately followed the entry of the combination in England, and the division of the world's business by the two foreign contracts which ensued. . . . (d) By the gradual absorption of control over all the elements essential to the successful manufacture of tobacco products, and placing such control in the hands of seemingly independent corporations serving as perpetual barriers to the entry of others into the tobacco trade. (e) By persistent expenditure of millions upon millions of dollars in buying out plants, not for the purpose of utilizing them, but in order to close them up and render them useless for the purposes of trade. (f) By the constantly recurring stipulations, . . . by which numbers of persons, whether manufacturers, stockholders, or employees, were required to bind themselves, generally for long periods, not to compete in the future.[24]

[24]221 U. S. 106, 181–83.

CHAPTER FIVE

The United States Steel Case (1920)

In *United States* v. *U.S. Steel Corp.*[1] the Government charged U.S. Steel with monopolizing the iron and steel industry by bringing under control in 1901 approximately 180 independent concerns accounting for about 50 per cent of the national iron and steel output. It was argued on behalf of U.S. Steel that the corporation was not formed with the purpose to monopolize trade or restrict competition, but rather it was the natural response to the metallurgical methods of making and handling steel. Vertical integration, or the continuity in the processes of the industry from ore mines to the finished product, as well as plant specialization, whereby one plant makes a single product continuously rather than 20 or 50 products, offered mutual advantages to the member firms. A further purpose of the organization was the building up of export trade in iron and steel which heretofore involved sporadic dumping of products upon foreign markets. The Supreme Court found that U.S. Steel had not violated the

[1]251 U. S. 417 (1920). For background information on the iron and steel industry, see S. Whitney, *Antitrust Policies: American Experience in Twenty Industries*, (New York: Twentieth Century Fund, 1958), Chap. 5; W. Adams, ed., *The Structure of American Industry*, Chap. 5. Earlier literature on the formative years of U. S. Steel can be found in U. S. Bureau of Corporations, *Report on the Steel Industry*, 3 vols. (Washington D.C.: Government Printing Office, 1912–13); *Report of Special Committee to Investigate Violations of the Antitrust Act of 1890: Investigation of the United States Steel Corporation*, 62nd Cong., 2nd Sess., House Report Docket No. 1127 (Washington, D.C.: Government Printing Office, 1912); A. Berglund, *The United States Steel Corporation* (New York: Columbia University Press, 1907), and E. McCallum, *The Iron and Steel Industry in the United States* (London: P.S. King & Son, 1931).

monopolization provisions of the Sherman Act by its formation or subsequent conduct. The case was therefore dismissed.

Justice McKenna of the Supreme Court noted that U.S. Steel employed none of the abusive trade practices which were alleged to exist in the earlier *Standard Oil* and *Tobacco* cases. In his words,

> It resorted to none of the brutalities or tyrannies that the cases illustrate of other combinations. It did not secure freight rebates; it did not increase its profits by reducing the wages of its employees — whatever it did was not at the expense of labor; it did not increase its profits by lowering the quality of its products, nor create an artificial scarcity of them; it did not oppress or coerce its competitors — its competition, though vigorous, was fair; it did not undersell its competitors in some localities by reducing its prices there below those maintained elsewhere, or require its customers to enter into contracts limiting their purchases or restricting them in resale prices; it did not obtain customers by secret rebates or departures from its published prices; there was no evidence that it attempted to crush its competitors or drive them out of the market, nor did it take customers from its competitors by unfair means, and in its competition it seemed to make no difference between large and small competitors.[2]

The Abuse Theory of Monopoly

With substantial evidence showing the absence of abusive market practices, the foundation was laid for the Court to enunciate the so-called "abuse theory," namely, in the absence of abusive market practices the law does not make mere size an offense. In the words of Justice McKenna,

> Competition consists of business activities and ability — they make its life; but there may be fatalities in it. Are the activities to be encouraged when militant, and suppressed or regulated when triumphant, because of the dominance attained? To such paternalism the government's contention, which regards power, rather than its use, the determining consideration, seems to conduct. . . . We have pointed out that there are several of the government's contentions which are difficult to represent or measure, and the one we are now considering — that is, the power is ''unlawful regardless of purpose'' — is another of them. It seems to us that it has for its ultimate principle and justification that strength in any producer or seller is a menace to the public interest and illegal, because there is potency in it for mischief. . . . The corporation is undoubtably of impressive size, and it takes an effort of resolution not to be affected by it or to exaggerate its influence. But we must adhere to the law, and the law does not make mere size an offense, or the existence of unexerted power an offense. It, we repeat, requires overt acts, and trusts to its prohibition of them and its power to repress or punish them.[3]

[2]251 U.S. 417, 440–41.

[3]*Ibid.*, pp. 450–51.

The Prerequisite Market Power
for Monopolization

Despite the above pronouncements, the *U.S. Steel* case was not decided technically in terms of the "abuse theory." Rather, the decision in the case turned on the finding that U.S. Steel lacked the necessary market power for monopolization.[4] The Court noted that "whatever there was of wrong intent could not be executed" because U.S. Steel was unable *by itself* to control steel prices. Illegal conspiratorial conduct, such as pools, and industry gatherings called "Gary Dinners," which were given by E. H. Gary while he was president of U.S. Steel, were offered as evidence by U.S. Steel for showing that it was not a monopoly and, consequently, had to persuade rather than coerce its competitors in order to control steel prices. In the words of the Court,

> Monopoly, therefore, was not achieved, and competitors had to be persuaded by pools, associations, trade meetings, and through the social form of dinners, all of them, it may be, violations of the law, but transient in their purpose and effect. They were scattered through the years from 1901 (the year of the formation of the corporation) until 1911, but after instances of success and failure were abandoned nine months before this suit was brought.[5]

The District Court opinion of Judge Bufferton in the *U.S. Steel* case offered considerable evidence showing the declining market position of U.S. Steel during the period 1901 to 1911.[6] The share of the national steel business accounted for by U.S. Steel fell from 50.1 to 40.9 per cent. In six major steel product markets the following changes occurred:

> TOTAL FINISHED ROLLED PRODUCTS. In 1901, when the Steel Company was formed, the total finished roll product of the United States was 13,000,000 tons. This was substantially divided between 49.9 per cent made by competitors, and 50.1 per cent by the Steel Company. While both together have since increased the nation's product from 13,000,000 to 19,000,000 tons, yet of this 6,000,000 increase its competitors produced 3,400,000 tons to the Steel Company's 2,600,000 tons.[7]

> STEEL INGOTS. . . . while in 1901, of the 13,000,000 tons of total American ingot production, the competitors of the Steel Company only made 4,500,000 tons, as against the Steel Company's 8,500,000, yet by 1911, in the country's vast increase from 13,000,000 to 24,000,000 tons, the competitors had increased their production

[4]A. D. Neale, *The Antitrust Laws of the U. S. A.*, p. 109.

[5]251 U. S. 417, 444–45.

[6]223 F. 55 (1915).

[7]*Ibid.*, p. 65.

by 6,500,000 tons, while the Steel Company had only increased 4,500,000. In other words, while the Steel Company produced in 1901, 66 per cent of the country's ingot production, it was producing but 54 per cent in 1911.[8]

PIG IRON. In 1911, out of a total cast of 22,000,000 tons of pig iron . . . only 12,000,000 or 54.8 per cent, were made by competitors of the Steel Company, as against 9,000,000, or 56.8 per cent, made by such competitors in 1901, out of a total of 16,000,000 — a decrease of 2 per cent.[9]

WIRE NAILS. When the Steel Corporation was formed in 1901, of the 9,000,000 kegs of wire nails then made in the United States, the competitors of the Steel Corporation made 3,000,000 kegs, and the Steel Corporation 6,000,000. By 1911, the country's production had grown to 13,000,000, but of the 3,500,000 of increase the Steel Corporation made 1,000,000 as against its competitors making 2,500,000.[10]

STRUCTURAL STEEL. In the important item of structural steel, used in bridges, steel framed buildings, steel car frames, etc., the steel corporation's competitors produced about 67 per cent, and the Steel Corporation 33 per cent. . . . the Steel Company was in 1911 making relatively less structural articles of this country's consumption than it was in 1901.[11]

STEEL RAILS. In 1901, the competitors of the Steel Company made 1,100,000 tons of steel rails and the Steel Company 1,700,000. In 1911, its competitors made 1,200,000 tons, an increase of 100,000 tons, while the Steel Company made 1,600,000 tons, a decrease of 100,000 tons.[12]

"These conclusions," wrote Judge Bufferton, "show a strong trend away from any monopolistic absorption or trade-restraining control of iron and steel manufacture or markets of the United States by the Steel Corporation. On the contrary, these figures show a strong trend in that manufacture and market toward an even greater absorption thereof by the virile and growing competitors of the Steel Company."[13] Judge Woolley, in a separate opinion, agreed that "the power of the corporation is not commensurate with its size; and that the size and the consequent power of the corporation are not sufficient to retard prosperous growth of efficient competitors."[14]

Injury to Competitors Versus Injury to Competition

In the U.S. Steel case there was abundant evidence of injury to competition, such as price fixing, but the record was devoid of evidence showing

[8]Ibid.
[9]Ibid., p. 66.
[10]Ibid.
[11]Ibid.
[12]Ibid.
[13]Ibid., p. 67.
[14]Ibid., p. 65.

that any competitors had been injured. Illegal collusive arrangements tended to protect the smaller steel producers by allocating territories to them and allowing them to charge higher prices. It could be argued that the sympathetic attitude of the Supreme Court toward U.S. Steel was a reflection of their concern with injury to competitors, of which there was none, rather than injury to competition, of which there was ample evidence.

U.S. Steel did not attempt to drive out independent concerns from its industry. In fact, the business policy of U.S. Steel against directly injuring its competitors accounts in large part for the decline in market position of the various combinations absorbed by the parent company. For example, the American Tin Plate Company produced 95 per cent of all the tin plate in the United States in 1899 before it was merged into the U.S. Steel Corporation. The market control of the Plate Company gradually decreased thereafter until in 1912 its proportion of the manufactured tin plate output was 53.7 per cent. "After it was absorbed by the corporation, it ceased to rely upon its own power to fix and maintain prices, complete as was its power at first, and, like the other subsidiaries, was forced to cooperate with its competitors."[15] The gradual reduction in the market position of U.S. Steel in the decades following its formation provided the Supreme Court in 1920 with a rationale for dismissing the monopolization charge against U.S. Steel.

[15]*Ibid.*, p. 70. For an analysis of subsequent developments in the tin plate market, see J. W. McKie, *Tin Cans and Tin Plate* (Cambridge, Mass.: Harvard University Press, 1959).

CHAPTER SIX

The Alcoa Case (1945)

The Aluminum Company of America was organized in 1888 and acquired in the following year the patent on the Hall process for the commercial production of aluminum.[1] In 1903 Alcoa acquired the Bradley patent for smelting aluminum without the use of external heat. By 1909 both of these patents had expired. During this period, Alcoa obtained several contracts binding electrical power companies not to sell power to anyone else for the manufacture of aluminum. The company also entered into cartel arrangements with foreign aluminum producers to limit aluminum imports into the United States. A consent decree between Alcoa and the United States government in 1912 enjoined Alcoa from engaging in the above restrictive agreements.

---

[1]For background information on the aluminum industry, see D. H. Wallace, *Market Control in the Aluminum Industry* (Cambridge, Mass.: Harvard University Press, 1937); *Report of United States Attorney General on Aluminum, Industry and Post-War Conversion* (Washington, D.C.: Government Printing Office, 1945); (Aluminum Industry), *Fifth Report of the United States Attorney General*, Senate Doc. No. 94, 79th Congress, 1st Sess. (Washington, D.C.: Government Printing Office, 1945); *Joint Hearings on Aluminum Plant Surplus Property Disposal* (Committee on Military Affairs, Small Business Committee and Special Committee on Post-War Policy and Planning, U. S. Senate, 79th Congress, 1st Sess. (Washington, D.C.: Government Printing Office, 1945); U. S. Tariff Commission, *Aluminum*, War Changes in Industry Series, Report No. 14 (Washington, D.C.: Government Printing Office, 1946); L. A. Doyle, "Industrial Economic Problems in the Post-War Aluminum Market in the U. S.," *Journal of Industrial Economics*, Vol. I (July, 1953), 212–30; and C. Muller, "The Aluminum Monopoly and the War," *Political Science Quarterly*, Vol. LX (March, 1945), 14–43.

Definition of the Market

In *United States* v. *Aluminum Company of America*,[2] the Government charged Alcoa with monopolizing the following markets: bauxite, water power, alumina, virgin aluminum (pig and ingot), castings, cooking utensils, pistons, extrusions and structural shapes, foil, miscellaneous fabricated articles, sheet and cable. Judge Caffey in the District Court found that Alcoa had not monopolized any of these markets. Judge Learned Hand, in the Court of Appeals, which was sitting as a court of last resort since the Supreme Court did not have a sufficient number of justices who were qualified to hear the case, reversed the District Court and held that Alcoa had monopolized the virgin aluminum ingot market.

Judge Hand rested his finding that Alcoa was a monopoly primarily on a market definition which showed Alcoa holding 90 per cent of the virgin aluminum ingot market. Judge Caffey, on the other hand, employed a market definition under which Alcoa was found to hold only 33 per cent of the market. The difference between market definitions was vital to Judge Hand's approach to monopoly whereby a company with a market share of 90 per cent was a monopoly, with 60 per cent was probably not a monopoly, and with 33 per cent was not a monopoly. In the words of Judge Hand,

There are various ways of computing "Alcoa's" control of the aluminum market — as distinct from its production — depending upon what one regards as competing in that market. The judge figured its share — during the years 1929–1938, inclusive — as only about thirty-three per cent; to do so he included "secondary," and excluded that part of "Alcoa's" own production which it fabricated and did not therefore sell as ingot. If, on the other hand, "Alcoa's" total production, fabricated and sold, be included, and balanced against the sum of imported "virgin" and "secondary," its share of the market was in the neighborhood of sixty-four per cent for that period. The percentage we have already mentioned — over ninety — results only if we both include all "Alcoa's" production and exclude "secondary." That per-

[2] 148 F. 2nd 416 (2nd Cir., 1945). See generally, W. Adams, "The Aluminum Case: Legal Victory — Economic Defeat," *American Economic Review*, Vol. XLI (December, 1951), 915–22; E. Rostow, "The Sherman Act: A Positive Instrument of Progress," *University of Chicago Law Review*, Vol. XVI (June, 1947), 567–600, and "Monopoly under the Sherman Act: Power or Purpose?" *Illinois Law Review*, Vol. XLIII (January–February, 1949) 745–93; E. Johnston and J. Stevens, "Monopoly or Monopolization — A Reply to Professor Rostow," *ibid.*, Vol. XLIV (July–August, 1949), 269–97; J. V. Krutilla, "Aluminum — A Dilemma for Antitrust Aims?" *Southern Economic Journal*, Vol. XXII (October, 1955), 164–77; Comment, "Vertical Integration in Aluminum: A Bar to Effective Competition," *Yale Law Review*, Vol. LX (February, 1951), 294–310; Comment, *Columbia Law Review*, Vol. XLV (July, 1945), 655–59; *Yale Law Review*, Vol. LIV (September, 1945), 860–68; and M. J. Peck, *Competition in the Aluminum Industry, 1945–1958* (Cambridge, Mass.: Harvard University Press, 1961).

centage is enough to constitute a monopoly; it is doubtful whether sixty or sixty-four per cent would be enough; and certainly thirty-three per cent is not. Hence it is necessary to settle what we shall treat as competing in the ingot market.[3]

The three methods of defining the aluminum market have been reduced to formulas in the table.

Sources of Aluminum Ingot

(1) Open market virgin ingot   (3) Secondary or scrap ingot
(2) Alcoa's own use virgin ingot   (4) Imported virgin and secondary ingot

Computation of Alcoa's Market Share of Ingot

Judge Caffey's formula: $$\frac{(1) + (3)}{(1) + (3) + (4)} = 33\%$$

Judge Hand's formula: $$\frac{(1) + (2)}{(1) + (2) + (4)} = 90\%$$

A third formula: $$\frac{(1) + (2)}{(1) + (2) + (3) + (4)} = 64\%$$

Judge Caffey noted that for certain purposes virgin aluminum ingot received "active competition" not only from secondary ingot and imports, but from stainless steel, lead, nickel, tin, zinc, and copper.[4] This finding supported his conclusion that Alcoa did not hold a monopoly. Judge Hand reversed this finding in the Court of Appeals by employing a narrower market definition. Finally, Judge Knox, in a subsequent hearing in 1950 on the remedial action in the Alcoa case, followed a broader market definition than even Judge Caffey had used. Judge Knox maintained that the applicable aluminum market should not be virgin ingot, nor virgin and secondary ingot, but the market for all aluminum products: ingot as well as fabricated items. The reason given by Judge Knox for this broader market definition was the recent entry of two fully integrated aluminum producers: Reynolds Metals Company and Kaiser Aluminum and Chemical Corporation. In the words of Judge Knox,

Thus, in the aluminum industry, competition manifests itself in the market for fabricated aluminum products rather than in that for pig and ingot. In determining the relative shares of the market among Alcoa, Reynolds and Kaiser, the integration of these producers requires "market" to be a broad concept, unrelated to any particular aluminum product. Aluminum can be sold in the form of pig or ingot, or as a semi-fabricated or fully fabricated article. It is with reference to the totality of the markets for these products that the relative shares of the three integrated producers must be considered.[5]

[3]148 F. 2nd 416, 424 (1945).
[4]44 F. Supp. 97, 165 (1941).
[5]91 F. Supp. 333, 356 (1950).

OWN-USE PRODUCTION. In the *Alcoa* case the District Court excluded the amount of ingot which Alcoa produced for its own use in its fabricating plant. However, Judge Hand in the Court of Appeals maintained that even though the own-use ingot production never reached the open market it still had an effect on this market. The more fabricated products Alcoa sold, the fewer products the independent aluminum fabricators could sell, and their demand for ingots would correspondingly be lower. In the words of Judge Hand,

> That part of its production which "Alcoa" itself fabricates, does not of course ever reach the market as ingot . . . However, . . . the ingot fabricated by "Alcoa", necessarily had a direct effect upon the ingot market. All ingot — with trifling exceptions — is used to fabricate intermediate, or end, products; and therefore all intermediate, or end, products which "Alcoa" fabricates and sells, pro tanto reduce the demand for ingot itself. The situation is the same, though reversed, as in *Standard Oil Company v. United States*, . . . where the court answered the defendants' argument that they had no control over the crude oil by saying that "as substantial power over the crude product was the inevitable result of the absolute control which existed over the refined product, the monopolization of the one carried with it the power to control the other." We cannot agree that the computation of the percentage of "Alcoa's" control over the ingot market should not include the whole of its ingot production.[6]

SECONDARY INGOT PRODUCTION. The Court of Appeals concluded that aluminum scrap, or secondary ingot, competed with virgin ingot, and thereby set an upper price ceiling on the amount that could be charged for virgin ingot.

> As to "secondary", as we have said, for certain purposes the industry will not accept it at all; but for those for which it will, the difference in price is ordinarily not very great; the judge found that it was between one and two cents a pound, hardly enough margin on which to base a monopoly. . . . At any given moment therefore "secondary" competes with "virgin" in the ingot market; further, it can, and probably does, set a limit or "ceiling" beyond which the price of "virgin" cannot go, for the cost of its production will in the end depend only upon the expense of scavenging and reconditioning. It might seem for this reason that in estimating "Alcoa's" control over the ingot market, we ought to include the supply of "secondary", as the judge did.[7]

Nevertheless, the court refused to include secondary ingot in its computation of Alcoa's share of the ingot market. The theory of the court was based on the fact that the secondary ingot was derived from ingot originally produced by Alcoa:

[6]148 F. 2nd 416, 424 (1945).

[7]*Ibid.*

Thus, in the case at bar "Alcoa" always knew that the future supply of ingot would be made up in part of what it produced at the time, and, if it was far sighted as it proclaims itself, that consideration must have had its share in determining how much to produce. How accurately it could forecast the effect of present production upon the future market is another matter. Experience, no doubt, would help; but it makes no difference that it had to guess; it is enough that it had an inducement to make the best guess it could, and that it would regulate that part of the future supply, so far as it should turn out to have guessed right. The competition of "secondary" must therefore be disregarded, as soon as we consider the position of "Alcoa" over a period of years; it was as much within "Alcoa's" control as was the production of the "virgin" from which it had been derived. This can be well illustrated by the case of a lawful monopoly: e.g., a patent or a copyright. The monopolist cannot prevent those to whom he sells from reselling at whatever prices they please.[8]

Evidence that Alcoa could foresee that the virgin ingot it produced today would return to the market as secondary ingot in the next five to twenty-five years does not establish that Alcoa had effective control over the aluminum scrap market. Judge Caffey noted in his opinion the following finding made by a Federal Trade Commissioner in 1929: "The record shows that respondent (Alcoa) never attempted to monopolize the scrap market; that it is impossible to do so, the scrap market being so scattered and diversified and in such available quantities that one concern, no matter how large its purchases, could never corner the said market."[9] Judge Hand in the opinion of the Court of Appeals found that if secondary ingot had been included, Alcoa's market share would have been reduced from 90 per cent to between 60 and 64 per cent for the period 1929–38. The decision of Judge Hand to exclude secondary aluminum ingot from his market definition was the pivotal factor in his finding that Alcoa held a 90 per cent market share and was a monopoly.

In 1950 Judge Knox wrote an opinion on whether divestiture of Alcoa's assets was still an appropriate remedy in view of the changed industry conditions, namely the entry of Kaiser and Reynolds Metals as primary aluminum producers. Judge Knox found that secondary aluminum should now be properly included in the applicable market definition because Alcoa no longer held exclusive control over the domestic supply of virgin aluminum. In the words of Judge Knox,

Now, all three producers contribute to the production of aluminum for fabricated articles which, in due time, will return to the market as old scrap. . . . Alcoa's loss of exclusive control of production during the war and postwar period warrants the inclusion of secondary recovered from old scrap as an independent source of aluminum. Such secondary has been shown to be competitive with primary metal.[10]

[8]*Ibid.*, p. 425.
[9]44 F. Supp. 97, 107 (1941).
[10]91 F. Supp. 333, 357 (1950).

Judge Knox implicitly accepted Judge Hand's conclusion that the control of virgin aluminum implies control of secondary aluminum returning to the market in subsequent years. But the proper test, it could be argued, should have been whether Alcoa had actual control over the prices or output of the approximately fifty firms in the secondary aluminum market.

IMPORTED INGOT. The remaining 10 per cent of the aluminum ingot market, which Alcoa did not hold, was accounted for by imports. The Court of Appeals included imports in its definition of the ingot market because it found that this source of supply of ingot was directly competitive and placed a limit on the prices which Alcoa could charge. In the words of Judge Hand,

> It is entirely consistent with the evidence that it was the threat of greater foreign imports which kept "Alcoa's" prices where they were, and prevented it from exploiting its advantage as sole domestic producer; indeed, it is hard to resist the conclusion that potential imports did put a "ceiling" upon those prices. Nevertheless, within the limits afforded by the tariff and the cost of transportation, "Alcoa" was free to raise its prices, as it chose, since it was free from domestic competition, save as it drew other metals into the market as substitutes.[11]

The Alcoa Test of Monopolization

The *Alcoa* case is considered an antitrust landmark decision because of its unusual emphasis on market structure rather than on the abusive market practices of the defendant. The decision appeared to reject the older "abuse theory," in which an illegal attempt to monopolize was inferred from the defendant's predatory conduct. In its place, the Court of Appeals accepted a "structure test," in which corporate size is largely the determining factor. It is questionable that the reasoning of Judge Hand, and the change in antitrust doctrine, was in fact this abrupt. Alternatively, it could be argued that Judge Hand, rather than rejecting the "abuse theory," extended the meaning of the term "abuse" to include acts which, taken alone, would generally be considered "honestly industrial," but which in the aggregate showed "no motive except to exclude others and perpetuate its hold upon the ingot market." In the words of Judge Hand,

> "Alcoa's" size was "magnified" to make it a "monopoly"; indeed, it has never been anything else; and its size, not only offered it an "opportunity for abuse," but it "utilized" its size for "abuse," as can easily be shown.
> ... There were at least one or two abortive attempts to enter the industry, but "Alcoa" effectively anticipated and forestalled all competition, and succeeded in holding the field alone. True, it stimulated demand and opened new uses for the

[11]148 F. 2nd 416, 426 (1945).

metal, but not without making sure that it could supply what it had evoked. There is no dispute as to this; "Alcoa" avows it as evidence of the skill, energy and initiative with which it has always conducted its business; as a reason why, having won its way by fair means, it should be commended, and not dismembered. We need charge it with no moral derelictions after 1912; we may assume that all it claims for itself is true. The only question is whether it falls within the exception established in favor of those who do not seek, but cannot avoid, the control of a market. It seems to us that that question scarcely survives its statement. It was not inevitable that it should always anticipate increases in the demand for ingot and be prepared to supply them. Nothing compelled it to keep doubling and redoubling its capacity before others entered the field. It insists that it never excluded competitors; but we can think of no more effective exclusion than progressively to embrace each new opportunity as it opened, and to face every newcomer with new capacity already geared into a great organization, having the advantage of experience, trade connections and the elite of personnel. Only in case we interpret "exclusion" as limited to manoeuvers not honestly industrial, but actuated solely by a desire to prevent competition, can such a course, indefatigably pursued, be deemed not exclusionary.[12]

The "Absence of Specific Intent" Defense

In the *Standard Oil of New Jersey* case the alleged offense was an *attempt* to monopolize, since Standard Oil had not completely achieved a monopoly. Justice White sought to establish through Standard's corporate history of alleged ruthless market practices the existence of a "specific intent" to monopolize the petroleum industry. The defendant officers of Standard Oil were found to have possessed the required "specific intent," for their actions showed that they intended to commit the specific crime of monopolization.

In the *Alcoa* case, however, the alleged offense was not an *attempt* to monopolize but *actual* monopolization. The proof of intent was less demanding than in the *Standard Oil* case, since the acts of the defendants did not fall short of achieving an actual monopoly. The prerequisite legal intent in Alcoa was a "general intent" or a "deliberateness" to maintain its monopoly position.[13] The general intent requirement has little analytical content and is almost perfunctory in nature, since this type of intent is objectively presumed where the defendant holds an actual monopoly. However, the requirement for a general intent is not devoid of meaning. It can serve as a safety valve to exclude obvious cases where a monopoly was not intended. For example, a vendor who places a new product upon the market, and who has as yet to face competition from a seller of identical

---

[12]*Ibid.*, p. 431.

[13]United States, *Report of the Attorney General's National Committee to Study the Antitrust Laws*, p. 43.

goods, should not be adjudged a violator of the Sherman Act as he lacks the "general intent" to monopolize.[14]

The importance of the passage which follows lies in the change in emphasis by Judge Hand from the concept of specific intent, which required proof of abusive market practices, to the concept of monopoly and business size taken by itself. Judge Hand thereby laid the foundation for the "structure theory" of the law of monopoly. Under this approach the intent of the defendant is de-emphasized and the market power of the defendant becomes the determining factor. According to Judge Hand,

> We disregard any question of "intent." . . . conduct falling short of monopoly, is not illegal unless it is part of a plan to monopolize, or to gain such other control of a market as is equally forbidden. To make it so, the plaintiff must prove what in the criminal law is known as "specific intent"; an intent which goes beyond the mere intent to do the act. . . . In order to fall within §2, the monopolist must have both the power to monopolize, and the intent to monopolize. To read the passage as demanding any "specific intent," makes nonsense of it, for no monopolist monopolizes unconscious of what he is doing. So here, "Alcoa" meant to keep, and did keep, the complete exclusive hold upon the ingot market with which it started. That was to "monopolize" that market, however innocently it otherwise proceeded.[15]

The general intent required for a charge of monopolization is a conclusion based on the *deliberateness* of the defendant's actions in acquiring, maintaining, and using the monopoly power. This deliberateness is clearly shown if monopoly has been established or maintained by illegal means under Sec. 1 of the Sherman Act. However, the requisite degree of deliberateness has been found where defendant's acts were legal in themselves but nevertheless had an exclusionary effect on competitors or potential entrants.[16]

[14] G. E. Hale and R. D. Hale, *Market Power: Size and Shape Under the Sherman Act*, Trade Regulation Series, S. C. Oppenheim, ed. (Boston: Little, Brown & Company, 1958), p. 770.

[15] 148 F. 2nd 416, 431–32 (1945).

[16] For example, the former practice of the Big Three cigarette manufacturers (American Tobacco, Liggett & Meyers, and R. J. Reynolds) to bid up at auction the cheaper grades of tobacco in order to exclude potential competitors from maufacturing cheaper cigarettes was not illegal in itself; yet coupled with the Big Three's 68 per cent of the U. S. cigarette production, and 80 per cent of the burley blend cigarette market, it served as evidence of a deliberate purpose to exclude competition and monopolize. Furthermore, the Supreme Court added, ". . . neither proof of exertion of the power to exclude nor proof of actual exclusion of existing or potential competitors is essential to sustain a charge of monopolization." See *American Tobacco Co.* v. *United States*, 328 U. S. 781, 813–15 (1946). Compare *United States* v. *Griffith*, 334 U. S. 100, 107 (1948) with *United States* v. *Cresent Amusement Co.*, 323 U. S. 173 (1944).

The "Good Trust" Defense

An important part of the defense presented in the *Alcoa* case was that Alcoa, even if it were a monopoly, had not abused its power. Alcoa claimed that it never received more than a "fair profit" from its activities. The District Court found that over the half century of its existence, Alcoa's profits upon capital invested, after payment of income taxes, had been about ten per cent.[17] Relying upon the *U.S. Steel* case, the defense argued that the absence of market abuses constituted a defense to monopoly. Judge Hand rejected this argument on the grounds that "it is no excuse for 'monopolizing' a market that the monopoly has not been used to extract from the consumer more than a 'fair' profit."[18] In the following passage the so-called "good trust" defense is rejected by the Court:

> True, it might have been thought adequate to condemn only those monopolies which could not show that they had exercised the highest possible ingenuity, had adopted every possible economy, had anticipated every conceivable improvement, stimulated every possible demand. No doubt, that would be one way of dealing with the matter, although it would imply constant scrutiny and constant supervision, such as courts are unable to provide. Be that as it may, that was not the way that Congress chose; it did not condone "good trusts" and condemn "bad" ones; it forbade all.[19]

Monopoly "Thrust Upon" the Defendant

Judge Hand stated in the *Alcoa* opinion that under some circumstances monopoly power can be innocently acquired; for example, where a change in tastes leaves only one producer remaining in the market. Since the Sherman Act condemns "monopolization" rather than "monopoly in the concrete," the antitrust laws are not violated where monopoly power is *thrust upon* the defendant. In the words of Judge Hand,

> It does not follow because "Alcoa" had such a monopoly, that it "monopolized" the ingot market: it may not have achieved monopoly; monopoly may have been thrust upon it. If it had been a combination of existing smelters which united the whole industry and controlled the production of all aluminum ingot, it would certainly have "monopolized" the market. . . . It is unquestionably true that from the very outset the courts have at least kept in reserve the possibility that the origin of monopoly may be critical in determining its legality; and for this they had warrant in some of the congressional debates which accompanied the passage of the act. . . . This notion has usually been expressed by saying that size does not determine guilt; that there must be some "exclusion" of competitors; that the growth must be some-

[17]148 F. 2nd 416, 427 (1945).

[18]*Ibid.*

[19]*Ibid.*

thing else than "natural" or "normal"; that there must be a "wrongful intent," or some other specific intent; or that some "unduly" coercive means must be used. At times there has been emphasis upon the active verb, "monopolize," as the judge noted in the case at bar. . . . What engendered these compunctions is reasonably plain; persons may unwittingly find themselves in possession of a monopoly, automatically so to say: that is, without having intended either to put an end to existing competition, or to prevent competition from arising when none existed; they may become monopolists by force of accident.

. . . A market may, for example, be so limited that it is impossible to produce at all and meet the cost of production except by a plant large enough to supply the whole demand. Or there may be changes in taste or in cost which drive out all but one purveyor. A single producer may be the survivor out of a group of active competitors, merely by virtue of his superior skill, foresight and industry.[20]

According to Judge Hand, a defendant who survives "merely by virtue of his superior skill, foresight and industry" is not guilty of monopolization. Yet the findings given by Judge Hand for establishing the illegal monopolization of the virgin aluminum ingot market come rather close to the very factors which are considered to be within the realm of defensible monopoly. For example, is it not *foresight* to "anticipate increases in the demand for ingot and be prepared to supply them," or "to embrace each new opportunity as it opened?" Is it not *skill* to have "the advantage of experience" and the "elite of personnel"? Is it not *industry* to "double and redouble capacity"? Yet each of these factors was used by Judge Hand to establish the finding that Alcoa consciously obtained monopoly and was guilty of monopolization.

Note on the United Shoe Machinery Case (1953)

United Shoe successively defended in 1918 a monopolization charge stemming from its merger with approximately 50 companies holding complementary shoe machinery patents.[21] It had been forced in 1922 to revise its leasing methods to eliminate "tying clauses" relating to supplies used in the shoe manufacturing machines,[22] and in 1953 was unsuccessful in defending a charge that it had monopolized the shoe machinery market in violation of Sec. 2 of the Sherman Act.[23] The leases of United Shoe in

[20]148 F. 2nd 416, 429–30 (1945).

[21]*United States* v. *United Shoe Machinery Co. of New Jersey*, 247 U. S. 32 (1918).

[22]*United Shoe Machinery Corp.* v. *United States*, 258 U. S. 451 (1922).

[23]110 F. Supp. 295 (D.C. Mass., 1953), affirmed *per curiam*, 347 U. S. 521 (1954). For a detailed economic analysis of the case, see C. Kaysen, *United States* v. *United Shoe Machinery Corporation*, Harvard Economic Studies No. 99 (Cambridge, Mass.: Harvard University Press, 1956). Also see L. S. Keyes, "The Shoe Machinery Case and the Problem of the Good Trust," *Quarterly Journal of Economics*, Vol. LXVIII (May, 1954), 287–304.

1953 took account of the judgment in the earlier case, and the mergers involved in its formation of the company were judged in 1918 to be legal. Therefore, the District Court in 1953 could not base its decision on the finding that United Shoe's conduct was an illegal restraint of trade reflecting the necessary intent for monopolization. On the other hand, the District Court was not of the opinion that United Shoe owed its monopoly *solely* to the "superior skill, foresight and industry" or to superior products, natural advantages, technological efficiency, or scientific research. United Shoe fit into an intermediate category, "where the causes of an enterprise's success were neither common law restraints of trade, nor the skill with which the business was conducted, but rather some practice which without being predatory, abusive, or coercive was in economic effect exclusionary."[24]

The record of United Shoe's performance in terms of efficient service, exceptional innovation, and absence of predatory conduct was outstanding. The company spent over $3 million annually on research and succeeded in producing several thousands of patented machines. The company's market position was not attributable primarily to these patents. United did not secure a monopoly profit: it earned in the period 1925–49 about 10 per cent net, after taxes, on invested capital. In finding that United Shoe's market power did not rest on predatory practices, the District Court noted that "probably few monopolies could produce a record so free from any taint of that kind of wrongdoing."[25] Nevertheless, United Shoe was found to have monopolized the shoe machinery market, in which it accounted for between 75 and 80 per cent, because it maintained its market position by legal, although not economically inevitable, market practices. That is, United Shoe was found to have engaged in market practices which would be legally permissive if practiced by a firm in a competitive market structure, but illegal if employed by a company maintaining a monopoly control of a market.

Judge Wyzanski, in a voluminous opinion, found that United Shoe engaged in a number of leasing arrangements which, although legal in themselves, tended to exclude competition. For example, United Shoe leased but did not sell its major machines; it required a ten-year lease; the lessee was obligated to use United Shoe's machinery at full capacity before using a competitive manufacturers' machine for the same operation, and service was provided at no additional charge with the result that an entrant to the industry would also have to provide servicing to remain competitive with United Shoe. Judge Wyzanski found that these practices were "honestly industrial" but nevertheless, in his words,

[24]110 F. Supp. 295, 341.
[25]*Ibid.* p. 345.

... they are not practices which can be properly described as the inevitable consequences of ability, natural forces, or law. They represent something more than the use of accessible resources, the process of invention and innovation, and the employment of those techniques of employment, financing, production, and distribution, which a competitive society must foster. They are contracts, arrangements, and policies which, instead of encouraging competition based on pure merit, further the dominance of a particular firm. In this sense, they are unnatural barriers; they unnecessarily exclude actual and potential competition; they restrict a free market. . . .

The violation with which United is now charged depends not on moral considerations, but on solely economic considerations. United is denied the right to exercise effective control of the market by business policies that are not the inevitable consequences of its capacities or its natural advantages. That those policies are not immoral is irrelevant.[26]

In summary, Judge Wyzanski required a higher standard of conduct for a company possessing a monopoly or dominant market position than for a company in a more competitive market structure. Unless its conduct was in every conceivable manner beyond reproach, a company possessing a monopoly would be vulnerable to a charge that it deliberately maintained its position by practices which tended to exclude actual or potential competitors from entering its industry.

[26]*Ibid.*, pp. 344-45.

CHAPTER SEVEN

The Cellophane Case (1956)

In *United States* v. *E. I. du Pont de Nemours & Company* the Supreme Court faced the single legal issue of whether du Pont had monopolized the cellophane market in violation of Sec. 2 of the Sherman Act.[1] The Government did not attempt to show that du Pont was guilty of an *attempt* to monopolize interstate commerce in cellophane. Consequently, the Government had to prove a high degree of market power.

During the period relevant to the case, du Pont produced almost 75 per cent of the cellophane sold in the United States, which constituted less than 20 per cent of the sales of all flexible packaging materials. If the Government could establish that the relevant market was cellophane, the 75 per cent market share of du Pont would probably have been sufficient for establishing its monopolization charge. However, if the Government failed to convince the Court that cellophane was a distinct and separate product market, the applicable market would cover the broader product sphere of all flexible packaging materials, including such items as aluminum foil, glassine, Saran, and polyethylene. Du Pont's share of this latter

[1]351 U. S. 377 (1956). See Symposium, "Impact of the Cellophane Case on Section 2 of the Sherman Act and Section 7 of the Clayton Act," *Antitrust Bulletin*, Vol. II (March, 1957), 435–500; J. Dirlam and I. Stelzer, "The Cellophane Labyrinth," *Antitrust Bulletin*, Vol. I (February–April, 1956,) 633–51; G. Stocking and W. Mueller, "The Celophane Case and the New Competition," *American Economic Review*, Vol. XLV (March, 1955), 29–63; D. Turner, "Antitrust Policy and the Cellophane Case," *Harvard Law Review* Vol. LXX (December, 1956), 281–318; and Note, *Columbia Law Review*, Vol. LIV (April, 1954), 580–603.

market was only 20 per cent, a figure which would be insufficient to establish the requisite market power for the asserted monopolization charge.

Judge Leahy in the District Court held that the relevant market was flexible wrapping materials. Competition from other flexible wrapping materials was found to have prevented du Pont from possessing monopoly power over the market for cellophane. Justice Reed, writing the majority opinion of the Supreme Court, affirmed Judge Leahy's decision and summarized the issues facing the Court as follows:

The Government asserts that cellophane and other wrapping materials are neither substantially fungible nor like priced. For these reasons, it argues that the market for other wrappings is distinct from the market for cellophane and that the competition afforded cellophane by other wrappings is not strong enough to be considered in determining whether du Pont has monopoly power.... The ultimate consideration in such a determination is whether the defendants control the price and competition in the market for such part of trade or commerce as they are charged with monopolizing. Every manufacturer is the sole producer of the particular commodity it makes but its control in the above sense of the relevant market depends upon the availability of alternative commodities for buyers: i.e., whether there is a cross-elasticity of demand between cellophane and the other wrappings. The interchangeability is largely gauged by the purchase of competing products for similar uses considering the price, characteristics and adaptability of the competing commodities. The court below found that the flexible wrappings afforded such alternatives. This Court must determine whether the trial court erred in its estimate of the competition afforded cellophane by other materials.[2]

Definition of the Market

A product market is a relative term, encompassing at one extreme all products in the economy which compete for the consumer dollar, and at the other extreme, excluding all but one product which is deemed physically or economically distinct. In the passage below, Supreme Court Justice Reed describes the problem of ascertaining the relevant market for cellophane:

Determination of the competitive market for commodities depends on how different from one another are the offered commodities in character or use, how far buyers will go to substitute one commodity for another. For example, one can think of building materials as in commodity competition but one could hardly say that brick competed with steel or wood or cement or stone in the meaning of Sherman Act litigation; the products are too different. This is the inter-industry competition emphasized by some economists. . . . where there are market alternatives that buyers may readily use for their purposes, illegal monopoly does not exist merely because the product said to be monopolized differs from others. If it were not so, only physically identical products would be a part of the market. To accept the Govern-

2351 U. S. 377, 381 (1956).

ment's argument, we would have to conclude that the manufacturers of plain as well as moistureproof cellophane were monopolists, and so with films such as Pliofilm, foil, glassine, polyethylene and Saran, for each of these wrapping materials is distinguishable. These were all exhibits in the case. New wrappings appear, generally similar to cellophane, is each a monopoly? What is called for is an appraisal of the "cross-elasticity" of demand in the trade.[3]

The Reasonable Interchangeability Test

The use of the term "cross-elasticity" of demand by the Supreme Court marks a high point in the use of theoretical economic concepts in judicial antitrust opinions. Cross-elasticity of demand indicates the percentage of change in the quantity demanded of a particular product for a very small percentage of change in the price of another good — all other things remaining equal. The concept of cross-elasticity of demand cannot be used exclusively to define a relevant market unless price is the only important economic variable. The Supreme Court in the *Cellophane* case examined also the qualities and end-uses of products which were related or "reasonably interchangeable" with cellophane. In the words of Justice Reed,

> The "market" which one must study to determine when a producer has monopoly power will vary with the part of commerce under consideration. The tests are constant. That market is composed of products that have *reasonable interchangeability* for the purposes for which they are produced — price, use and qualities considered.[4]

The analysis of the Court of the interchangeability of cellophane in terms of price, use, and quality are examined separately below.

PRICE. Justice Reed agreed with the District Court that the "great sensitivity of customers in the flexible packaging markets to price and quality changes" prevented du Pont from possessing monopoly power over price. Cellophane was found to have a high cross-elasticity of demand with other flexible wrapping materials, and therefore was considered part of this broader market:

> An element for consideration as to cross-elasticity of demand between products is the responsiveness of the sales of one product to price changes of the other. If a slight decrease in the price of cellophane causes a considerable number of customers of other flexible wrappings to switch to cellophane, it would be an indication that a high cross-elasticity of demand exists between them; that the products compete in the same market.[5]

[3]*Ibid.*, p. 394.
[4]*Ibid.*, p. 404.
[5]*Ibid.*, p. 400.

In an appendix to the Supreme Court majority opinion, Justice Reed included a price list of flexible wrapping materials. The price range in 1949 was from less than one cent per 1000 square inches for bleached greaseproof paper to six cents per 1000 square inches for Saran. Both products were included by the Supreme Court in the same relevant market for flexible wrapping materials, even though the price of the latter product is more than six times the price of the former.

TABLE 7–1

1949 AVERAGE WHOLESALE PRICES OF FLEXIBLE WRAPPING MATERIALS

	Price Per 1000 Square Inches
1. Saran	$.061
2. Polyethylene	.054
3. Pliofilm	.038
4. Cellulose acetate	.033
5. Moistureproof cellophane	.023
6. Plain cellophane	.021
7. Aluminum foil	.018
8. Vegetable parchment	.014
9. Plain waxed sulfite	.011
10. Bleached glassine	.010
11. Bleached greaseproof	.009

The dissent in the *Cellophane* case, written by Chief Justice Warren, maintained that cellophane had a low cross-elasticity of demand with other flexible wrapping materials because (1) cellophane had a considerably higher price than most of the other flexible wrapping materials, and (2) producers of these other materials did not respond with lower prices when du Pont lowered its cellophane price. In the dissenting words of Chief Justice Warren,

. . . from 1924 to 1932 du Pont dropped the price of plain cellophane 84%, while the price of glassine remained constant. And during the period 1933–1946 the prices for glassine and waxed paper actually increased in the face of a further 21% decline in the price of cellophane. If "shifts of business" due to "price sensitivity" had been substantial, glassine and waxed paper producers who wanted to stay in business would have been compelled by market forces to meet du Pont's price challenge. . . . That producers of glassine and waxed paper remained dominant in the flexible packaging materials market without meeting cellophane's tremendous price cuts convinces us that cellophane was not in effective competition with their products. During the period covered by the complaint (1923–1947) cellophane enjoyed phenomenal growth. . . . Yet throughout this period the price of cellophane was far greater than that of glassine, waxed paper or sulphite paper. . . . in 1929 cellophane's price was seven times that of glassine, in 1934, four times, and in 1949 still more than twice glassine's price. . . . cellophane had a similar price relation to waxed paper and . . . sulfite paper sold at even less than glassine and waxed paper. We cannot believe that buyers, practical businessmen, would have bought cellophane in increasing amounts over a quarter of a century if close substitutes were available from one-seventh to one-half cellophane's price. That they did so is testimony to cellophane's distinctiveness.[6]

The fundamental consideration in cross-elasticity of demand is the responsiveness of the sales of one product to price changes in the other. Implicit in this relationship is the *ceteris paribus* assumption that "other things remain equal." In the absence of such an assumption, it may not be possible to ascertain whether the demand for a product such as cellophane is responding to price changes in related products or is reacting on its own merits to more intensive salesmanship, promotion campaigns, general market acceptance, or a growth in the needs of its customers. The latter factor is cited in the passage below from the Supreme Court majority opinion as an explanation for the increased demand for cellophane.

It could not be said that this immense increase in use was solely or even largely attributable to the superior quality of cellophane or to the technique or business acumen of du Pont, though doubtless these factors were important. The growth was a part of the expansion of the commodity-packaging habits of business, a by-product of general efficient competitive merchandising to meet modern demands.[7]

Since cross-elasticity of demand varies with price, a high or low cross-elasticity of demand may be a function of the level at which a monopolistic firm sets its price. A monopolist would maximize profit by raising its price up to the point where a slight additional rise would cause large-scale substitution of alternative products. At this price level cross-elasticity of demand would be high. But cross-elasticity of demand might be very low at prices equal to or slightly above normal long-run cost. In this context a finding of high cross-elasticity of demand may mean that monopoly power has been exercised by raising price to the profit maximizing point. The use of evidence showing a high cross-elasticity of demand as indicating an absence of monopoly power would be erroneous in this situation.

Professor J. M. Clark has observed that a high cross-elasticity of demand should not be considered an equivalent to competition: "Despite the wonders of applied science in creating synthetic substitutes, it has not made all substitutes fully interchangeable, nor rendered substitution in general equivalent to competition as a dependable and effective protection to the buyer. If competition does not exist in a given case, effective sub-

[6]*Ibid.*, pp. 416–18.
[7]*Ibid.*, p. 385.

stitution helps. But it is not safe to generalize that substitution between products renders unimportant the preservation of competition . . . ."[8]

Only in the abstract world of economic theory can forces other than a change in the price of another good be held constant. Since the economic concept of cross-elasticity of demand presupposes such strict conditions as "other things remaining equal," it is open to the danger that standard theoretical conclusions may be drawn when the concept is utilized in examining empirical data. In contrast, the legal concept of "reasonable interchangeability," which considers factors other than price, such as quality and type of end-use, appears as a more suitable analytical tool for a court to employ in defining relevant product markets.

QUALITY. The quality or physical characteristics of related products must be taken into consideration in evaluating their degree of reasonable interchangeability. The Supreme Court specifically rejected in the *Cellophane* case the argument by the Government that products have to be substantially fungible or physically identical to be in the same relevant market. The proper test, stated the Court, is whether there exists "market alternatives that buyers may readily use for their purposes."

The Court found that 80 per cent of the cellophane made by du Pont is sold for packaging in the food industry. A commercially suitable packaging material for fresh vegetables must be transparent so that a customer can examine the quality of the product. It must also have a low permeability to gases so that the enclosed product will not be contaminated by surrounding products with strong odors; and, finally, the packaging material must have a low moisture permeability to retain the freshness of the produce. Moistureproof cellophane, pliofilm, plain glassine, and Saran have the above qualities. But other flexible wrapping materials, such as aluminum foil, are completely opaque and cannot serve as an "alternative source of supply" for the packaging requirements of fresh produce retailers. The degree of physical differences existing between products included in the same relevant market by the Supreme Court in the *Cellophane* case can be observed in Table 7-2, which contrasts three of the more than ten types of flexible wrapping materials included by the Court in the relevant product market.

END-USE. The relative importance of different physical characteristics can be observed from the end-uses of products. The interchangeability of flexible wrapping materials was discussed by the Court in terms of the

[8]J. M. Clark, *Competition as a Dynamic Process* (Washington, D.C.: Brookings Institution, 1961), p. 107.

TABLE 7–2

PHYSICAL PROPERTIES OF SELECTED FLEXIBLE PACKAGING MATERIALS

	Moistureproof Cellophane	Plain Glassine	Aluminum Foil
1. Heat sealability	Yes	Yes	No
2. Printability	Yes	Yes	Yes
3. Tear strength	Low	Good	Low
4. Bursting strength	High	Low	Low
5. Water absorption	High	High	Nil
6. Permeability to gases	Very low	Low	Very low
7. Wrapping machine running qualities	O.K.	O.K.	O.K.
8. Dimensional change with humidity difference	Large	Moderate	None
9. Moisture permeability	Low to medium	High	Very low
10. Clarity	Highly transparent	Commercially transparent to opaque	Opaque

classification of sales made by 19 converters of these materials. The sales of the converters were divided into categories, such as bakery products, candy, fresh produce, snacks, and meat and poultry. The Supreme Court summarized, in the passage below, the competition which cellophane faces:

In determining the market under the Sherman Act, it is the use or uses to which the commodity is put that control. The selling price between commodities with similar uses and different characteristics may vary, so that the cheaper product can drive out the more expensive. Or, the superior quality of higher priced articles may make dominant the more desirable. Cellophane costs more than many competing products and less than a few. . . . It may be admitted that cellophane combines the desirable elements of transparency, strength and cheapness more definitely than any of the others. . . . But, despite cellophane's advantages it has to meet competition from other materials in every one of its uses. . . . cellophane furnishes less than 7% of wrappings for bakery products, 25% for candy, 32% for snacks, 35% for meats and poultry, 27% for crackers and biscuits, 47% for fresh produce, and 34% for frozen foods. Seventy-five to eighty per cent of cigarettes are wrapped in cellophane. . . . Thus, cellophane shares the packaging market with others. The over-all result is that cellophane accounts for 17.9% of flexible wrapping materials, measured by the wrapping surface.[9]

In summary, the Supreme Court concluded after an examination of the price, quality, and end-use of cellophane that a reasonable interchangeability existed between this product and other flexible wrapping materials. Consequently, the relevant market was not cellophane, but the broader

[9]351 U. S. 377, 395 (1956).

market of flexible wrapping materials. The fact that duPont accounted for 75 per cent of the cellophane sales in the United States was not controlling. The paramount finding was that duPont accounted for less than 20 per cent of the relevant market of flexible wrapping materials. The latter percentage was deemed insufficient by the Court to establish the requisite market power for the monopolization charge.

Note on the Grinnell Case (1966)

The *Cellophane* doctrine of reasonable interchangeability was applied a decade later by the Supreme Court in *United States* v. *Grinnell Corp.*[10] The Court held that Grinnell and its affiliated subsidiary companies unlawfully monopolized, in violation of Sec. 2 of the Sherman Act, the "accredited central station protective service business" (fire and burglar alarm systems) by controlling 87 per cent of this line of commerce.

The defendants argued unsuccessfully that the different central station services were so diverse that they could not be included in the same relevant market. For instance, burglar alarm services should not be considered reasonably interchangeable with fire alarm systems. Furthermore, the defendants urged that protective services other than those of the central station variety shoud be included in the market definition. For example, Grinnell faced competition, in some degree, from local alarms, systems directly connected to police and fire stations, telephone connected services, automatic proprietary systems confined to one site, and watchmen.

The Supreme Court, in rejecting the contentions of the defendants, found that these other protective services should not be included in the relevant market, since they were not reasonably interchangeable with accredited central station protective services. Watchmen services were deemed more costly and less reliable. Systems that set off an audible alarm at the site were cheaper, but less reliable, since the local ringing of an alarm may not attract the needed attention and help. Proprietary systems can be used only by very large businesses. Most cities with an accredited central station do not permit direct, connected service between private businesses and municipal police or fire departments.

A more controversial aspect of the relevant market analysis of the Court concerned whether accredited, as distinguished from nonaccredited, service is a separate line of commerce. The majority of the Court found that central station protective services, which are "accredited" by insurance companies, are of better quality and tend to give larger discounts to their

[10]384 U. S. 563 (1966).

policy holders. The accredited central station is located in a building of approved design, provided with an emergency lighting system and two alternative main power sources, manned constantly by a minimum number of operators, and provided with a direct line to fire and police departments.

In a strongly worded dissent, Justice Fortas stated the product market definition selected by the majority was "... Procrustean — that it has tailored the market to the dimensions of the defendants.... This Court now approves this strange red-haired, bearded, one-eyed man-with-a-limp classification." There is no pretense by the majority, in the dissenting opinion of Justice Fortas, that the accredited central service protective stations furnish "peculiar services for which there is no alternative in the market place, on either a price or functional basis." The differentials in insurance discounts may affect the relative cost to the consumer for the competing modes of protection, but there was no proof that it resulted in eliminating the competing services from the category of those to which the purchaser can practically turn for supplies. Therefore, Justice Fortas concluded, "... this sort of exclusion of the supposedly not-quite-so-attractive service from the basic definition of the kinds of business and service against which defendant's activity will be measured, is entirely unjustified on this record."

But the majority of the Supreme Court believed otherwise: "There are, to be sure, substitutes for the accredited central station service. But none of them appears to operate on the same level as the central station service so as to meet the interchangeability test of the *du Pont* case."

CHAPTER EIGHT

Monopoly Indexes

The Measurement of Monopoly Power

Changes in the structure of industrial sectors of our economy are important because the allocation of resources in an economy may be unfavorably affected if important industries are monopolized. The higher price or restricted supply of the monopolized industry may alter adversely the distribution of the resources of this industry relative to other industries. One purpose of a monopoly index is to help economists and public policy makers recognize changes in market structures which are deemed undesirable.

The basic heterogeneity of competition in the United States makes the identification of monopoly power by a select number of salient characteristics difficult. If nonquantitative factors are deemed essential for measuring monopoly power, one will not be able to construct a suitable scale of monopoly power or a "competitive thermometer." The forces of monopoly may be so complex and nonquantifiable that they cannot be characterized by a single number for an industrial sector.[1]

The basic problem in developing an index for measuring monopoly power is finding a set of variables that will describe uniquely different degrees of monopoly power. Control of price or supply, and conditions of entry are important factors which, directly or indirectly, must be considered. Thus, monopoly indexes have taken into account slopes and the elasticity of

---

[1] J. P. Miller, "Measures of Monopoly Power and Concentration: Their Economic Significance," *Business Concentration and Price Policy*, p. 119.

demand curves, rates of profits, degree of product substitution, marginal costs, and related conditions of supply.

Professor Lerner defines a monopolist as a firm with a downward sloping demand curve. In contrast, Professor Chamberlin observes that a firm with a declining demand curve may face competition from other firms with similar, although not identical, products. All products have some type of substitutes, either close or imperfect. This continuum of substitute products results in all industries shading into each other; therefore, the case of pure monopoly, in which by definition all substitutes are excluded, is impossible. Professor Chamberlin concludes that unless a firm controlled all products in an economy, it could not be a pure monopolist. Other economists, however, have not abandoned the concept of an industry: close, competitive substitute products, which serve as practical alternative sources of supply for customers, are classified in the same industry.[2]

The Lerner Index

Professor Lerner proposed as a measure of monopoly power the following index:[3]

$$\text{Lerner index} = \frac{\text{Price} - \text{Marginal cost}}{\text{Price}}$$

The degree of monopoly power in the Lerner index depends upon the divergence between price and marginal cost. In pure and perfect competition, price is equal to marginal cost for each product in the economy, and the Lerner index is equal to zero. For a costless output, with zero marginal cost, the index equals unity, indicating the ability of a seller to charge a price for a free good.[4] In the case of overproduction, marginal cost may exceed price and the index will have a negative value. The index defines monopoly in terms of the slope of a demand curve. This is seen clearly where the profit maximizing firm is in equilibrium: marginal revenue is

---

[2]Compare A. P. Lerner, "The Concept of Monopoly and the Measurement of Monopoly Power," *Review of Economic Studies*, Vol. I (June, 1934), 157–75; E. H. Chamberlin, "Measuring the Degree of Monopoly and Competition," *Monopoly and Competition and Their Regulation*, Papers and Proceedings of A Conference Held by the International Economic Association, E. H. Chamberlin, ed. (London, 1954); reprinted in his *Towards A More General Theory of Value*, p. 83; and M. Olson and D. McFarland, "The Restoration of Pure Monopoly and the Concept of the Industry," *Quarterly Journal of Economics*, Vol. LXXVI (November, 1962), 623.

[3]Lerner, "The Concept of Monopoly."

[4]S. Weintraub, *Price Theory* (New York: Pitman Publishing Corporation, 1949), p. 146.

equal to marginal cost, and the Lerner index is equal to the inverse of the elasticity of demand,

$$\frac{\text{Price}}{\text{Price} - \text{Marginal revenue}}$$

Professor Lerner was primarily interested in obtaining an index of monopoly which would reflect not the measure of tribute individuals could obtain from others by virtue of being in a monopolistic position, but rather the divergence of the economy from the "social optimum that is reached in perfect competition." Since the Lerner index is essentially static, it does not indicate whether the present deviation of marginal cost from price and the present alteration in the allocation of resources are a worthwhile cost to pay for possible innovation or new plant construction. Either of the latter advances could be expected to leave society on an even higher level of economic development in the longer run.[5] Furthermore, the theory of second best, discussed in Chap. 3, questioned the validity of viewing in isolation the equality of price and marginal cost in one industry as evidence of an optimum allocation of resources.

The Lerner index does not reveal whether the level of marginal costs is a reflection of superior efficiency, which takes advantage of the existing body of knowledge and fosters further technical development, or, in contrast, a reflection of anachronistic methods of production in plants of uneconomic size and purchasing practices which exploit suppliers.[6] Application of the Lerner index is also affected by changes over time in the ratio of capital to labor in an industry.[7] Despite these shortcomings, as well as the difficult problem of obtaining even an approximation of marginal cost over the applicable range of output, there have been several attempts toward the application of this index.[8]

[5]Schumpeter, *Capitalism, Socialism and Democracy*, Chap. 8.

[6]Miller, "Measures of Monopoly Power and Concentration," p. 124.

[7]See R. H. Whitman, "A Note on the Concept of 'Degree on Monopoly,'" *Economic Journal*, Vol. LI (June-September, 1941), 261–70. Reply by M. Kalecki, "'Degree of Monopoly' — A Comment," *The Economic Journal*, Vol. LII (April, 1942), 121–27; and P. T. Bauer, "A Note on Monopoly," *Economica*, Vol. VIII, New Series (May, 1941), 194–203.

[8]Professor Dunlop applied the Lerner index to selected industries to ascertain the changes in the degree of monopoly over the course of the business cycle. J. T. Dunlop, "Price Flexibility and the Degree of Monopoly," *Quarterly Journal of Economics*, Vol LIII (August, 1939), 522–33. Professor Kalecki attempted to evaluate statistically the degree of monopoly for the whole economy. M. Kalecki, "The Determinants of the Distribution of the National Income," *Econometrica*, Vol. VI (April, 1938), 97–112. For a criticism of the latter article, see F. Machlup, *The Political Economy of Monopoly* (Baltimore: Johns Hopkins University Press, 1952), p. 517.

The Bain Index

Professor Bain uses the divergence between price and *average* cost to measure monopoly power rather than the difference in the Lerner index between price and marginal cost. Professor Bain justifies his index on the grounds that it is possible to view the divergence between price and average cost as evidence, on a probability basis, of the existence of a discrepancy between price and marginal cost: "Although excess profits (a price-average cost discrepancy) are not a sure indication of monopoly, they are *if persistent*, a probable indication."[9]

In Fig. 8-1 the firm produces output OQ and charges a price OP. Assume the firm has a demand curve D and an average cost curve in position AC'. In this case a discrepancy will exist both between price and average cost (line segment AE) and between price and marginal cost (line segment AB). Professor Bain maintains that the existence of a line segment such as AE is evidence that a line segment such as AB probably exists.

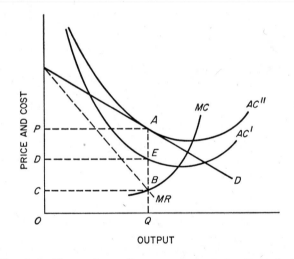

Fig. 8-1. *Monopolistic Competition and the Bain Index*

The firm will earn excess profits in Fig. 8-1, where the applicable average cost curve is AC', equal to $DEAP$ at output OQ. In other words, where a firm's price exceeds its average cost, excess profits exist. Since the Bain index depends upon the discrepancy between price and average cost, it is

[9]J. S. Bain, "The Profit Rate as a Measure of Monopoly Power," *Quarterly Journal of Economics,*, Vol. LV (February, 1941), 271–93.

utilizing a profit rate as a measure of monopoly power. The rate of profit is defined by Professor Bain as "that rate which, when used in discounting the future rents of the enterprise, equates their capital value to the cost of those assets which would be held by the firm if it produced its present output in competitive equilibrium. If this rate is greater than the rate of interest (or 'normal rate of return'), the difference may be defined as a rate of excess profit."[10]

The calculation of excess profits is performed as follows. Let R be the total annual sales revenue, and let C be the currently incurred costs for materials, wages, and salaries. Let D represent the past incurred costs allocable to the above current revenue, depreciation charges for the plant and machinery bought in previous years, and amortization expenses for stock and materials bought in prior years but used in the current year. Finally, let V be the owners' investment and i be the current interest rate for capital funds requiring the same degree of risk.[11] By definition,

$$\text{Economic excess profit} = R - C - D - i \cdot V$$

That is, excess profits are equal to total revenue less current costs, depreciation and amortization, and imputed interest on owners' investment.

"Accounting profit," on the other hand, which is generally published in the annual reports of corporations, does not deduct the imputed interest on owners' investment. Hence,

$$\text{Accounting profit} = R - C - D$$

If accounting profit just equals interest on owners' investment ($R - C - D = i \cdot V$), there will be no economic excess profits, and the price the firm charges for its product will be equal to its average cost.

Although the existence of a discrepancy between price and average cost may be grounds for inferring a probable divergence between price and marginal cost, the validity of the converse proposition is questionable. A divergence between price and marginal cost does not imply a probable difference between price and average cost. For example, in Fig. 8-1 assume that the applicable average cost curve for the firm is AC''. In this case a price-marginal cost discrepancy exists, but there is no discrepancy between price and average cost at output OQ. Hence, when the firm's average cost curve is tangent to its demand curve at its given level of output, the firm will

[10]*Ibid.*, pp. 276–77.

[11]This discussion is taken from J. S. Bain, *Industrial Organization* (New York: John Wiley & Sons, Inc. 1959), pp. 364–65.

earn no excess profits even though it may possess monopoly power in the Lerner sense that it has a downward sloping demand curve.

Professor Chamberlin has described a market structure, entitled "monopolistic competition," in which firms are relatively small, and, since little capital is required, can enter and manufacture a product very similar to products already on the market.[12] The existence of product differentiation implies that the firms in a given market do not manufacture precisely the same product, and that any monopoly power of these firms is limited by the overhanging of substitute products which can enter the market if the firm raises its price substantially. In Chamberlinian fully adjusted equilibrium, the average cost curve is at position AC'' in Fig. 8-1; price exceeds marginal cost; and price is equal to average cost.[13] Thus, there can exist a downward sloping demand curve, as well as a divergence between price and marginal cost, without a firm necessarily earning excess profits.

There are a number of other problems encountered in using the accounting rate of profit as an indicator of the degree to which monopoly power is exercised. The calculation of profit rates on the basis of book values of assets may cause profit rates to rise because of the time lag, which generally is a number of years, for book values to be adjusted to the increased demand and earnings of the firm.[14] In contrast, low rates of profit can conceal elements of monopoly if the assets of the firm are overvalued or are carried on the corporate books even though they are no longer productive. Profits may also be kept low by excessive selling costs and advertising which serve to raise barriers to entry around a strong market position of a firm. Finally, a monopoly index based on profits leaves unclear whether the profits accruing to the firm are a result of monopolistic selling practices, monopsonistic buying practices,[15] or, in contrast, superior efficiency resulting from specialized factors of production, newer manufacturing techniques, and expertise in management.[16]

[12]E. H. Chamberlin, *The Theory of Monopolistic Competition*, 7th ed. (Cambridge, Mass.: Harvard University Press, 1958).

[13]Bain, *Industrial Organization*, p. 273.

[14]F. Machlup, *The Political Economy of Monopoly*, p. 493.

[15]K. W. Rothschild, "A Further Note on the Degree of Monopoly," *Economica*, N. S., Vol. X (February, 1943), 69-71; and J. S. Bain, "Measurement of the Degree of Monopoly: A Note," *ibid.*, pp. 66–68.

[16]Professor Milton Friedman has suggested that economic rents from specialized resources or factors of production, which give rise to profits, should be capitalized into the average cost curve for the firm. An inequality between price and average cost may reflect the imperfection of the capital markets in taking into account the value of specialized resources of a firm, such as its favorable plant location. See M. Friedman, Comment on Caleb A. Smith's article, "Survey of the Empirical Evidence on Economies of Scale," in *Business Concentration and Price Policy, op. cit.*, p. 235.

The Rothschild Index

The curve dd' in Fig. 8-2 describes the conventional demand curve for a firm, whereas DD' describes the industry demand curve. The former is sometimes referred to as the "species" demand curve, and the latter as the "genus" demand curve.[17] The dd' demand curve, which assumes that

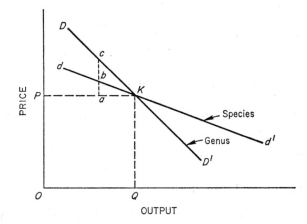

Fig. 8-2. *The Rothschild Index*

competitors hold their prices constant at the level OP, is less steep and more elastic than the demand curve DD', since a greater quantity of the product of a firm will be demanded if its competitors do not match its price reductions.

The Rothschild index measures the degree of monopoly by taking the ratio of the slope of dd' to the slope of DD'.[18] In pure competition the Rothschild index equals zero, since the demand curve for a firm will be horizontal. In pure monopoly the firm and the industry are identical, dd' coincides with DD', and the Rothschild index is equal to unity. Between zero (pure competition) and unity (pure monopoly) exist various degrees of monopoly in terms of the Rothschild index.

$$\text{Rothschild index} = \frac{\text{Slope of } dd'}{\text{Slope of } DD'} = \frac{\dfrac{ab}{aK}}{\dfrac{ac}{aK}} = \frac{ab}{ac}$$

[17]The origin of these terms is attributed to M. A. Copeland, "The Theory of Monopolistic Competition," *Journal of Political Economy*, Vol. XLII (August, 1934), 531.

[18]K. W. Rothschild, "The Degree of Monopoly," *Economica*, Vol. IX, N.S., (February 1942), 24–40.

The practicality of using slopes of different types of demand curves for the empirical evaluation of the degree of monopoly is questionable. Only if the firm has experimented in its price policy under comparable circumstances can the shape of the demand curve of the firm be estimated. Where the demand curve of the firm has shifted during the period of time considered, an econometric problem arises in identifying the demand curve.[20] Even with the benefit of econometric tools, the identification of demand curves is seldom satisfactory enough to determine the slope of a demand curve for the relevant output range.

It is doubtful that a seller will take the extreme positions of either believing that all competitors will hold their prices constant, or that all their prices will readjust to remain identical with his own. Yet these calculations are necessary for the computation of the Rothschild index. Finally, the Rothschild index of the degree of monopoly is based solely upon demand factors, to the exclusion of supply and cost conditions.

The Papandreou Index

Indexes of monopoly which employ the concept of cross-elasticity of demand for defining market structures suffer from a logical difficulty: Pure competition cannot be defined in terms of cross-elasticity of demand in a manner which keeps it distinct from its antithesis, pure monopoly.[21] Under

---

[20]T. C. Koopmans, "Identification Problems in Economic Model Construction," in W. C. Hood and T. C. Koopmans, *Studies in Econometric Method* (New York: John Wiley & Sons, Inc., 1953), and L. Klein, *A Textbook of Econometrics* (New York: Harper & Row, Publishers, 1953) Chap. 3.

[21]The use of cross-elasticities of both supply and demand in classifying market structures has been discussed in detail in the economic literature. See F. Machlup, "Monopoly and Competition: A Classification of Market Positions," *American Economic Review*, Vol. XXVII (September, 1937), 445–51, and "Competition, Pliopoly and Profit: Part I," *Economica*, N. S., Vol. IX (February, 1942), 1-24; Part II, *ibid.*, (May, 1942), pp. 153–74; R. Triffin, *Monopolistic Competition and General Equilibrium Theory* (Cambridge, Mass.: Harvard University Press, 1940); S. Weintraub, "The Classification of Market Positions: Comment," *Quarterly Journal of Economics*, Vol. LVI (August, 1942), 666–73 and E. F. Beach, "Triffin's Classification of Market Positions," *Canadian Journal of Economics and Political Science*, Vol. IX (February, 1943), 69–74; J. S. Bain, "Market Classification in Modern Price Theory," *Quarterly Journal of Economics*, Vol. LVI (August, 1942), 560–74; A. G. Papandreou, "Market Structure and Monopoly Power," *American Economic Review*, Vol. XXXIX (September, 1949), 883–97; C. M. Birch, "Papandreou's Coefficient of Penetration and Insulation," *ibid.*, Vol. LX (June, 1950), 407–10; R. L. Bishop, "Elasticities, Cross-Elasticities, and Market Relationships," *ibid.*, Vol. XLII (December, 1952), 779–803; Comments by W. Fellner and E. H. Chamberlin, *ibid.*, Vol. XLIII (December, 1953), 898–915; Reply by Bishop, *ibid.*, pp. 916–24; Comment by Hieser, *ibid.*, Vol. XLV (June, 1955), 373–82; Reply by Bishop, *ibid.*, pp. 382–86; E. H. Chamberlin, *Towards a More General Theory of Value*, pp. 84–91;

conditions of pure monopoly no firm can affect the monopolist's sales, since by definition there are no competitors in existence. However, under conditions of pure competition the sales of a given firm will also be immune from the actions of a competitor since by definition there are numerous firms — no one of which is of sufficient size to affect appreciably the sales volume of another firm in the market.

One measure of monopoly proposed by Papandreou is entitled the *coefficient of penetration*.[22] This index measures the capacity of a firm, in terms of its available supply, to penetrate the markets of its competitors by lowering its price. For example, if a firm alone lowers its price it may attract so many new customers that it will be unable to fill their demand requirements. The limitation of plant facilities may not only prevent the firm from benefiting through higher profits from an increase in demand, but may be a deterrent against the firm's penetrating the markets of many of its competitors.

Papandreou maintained that supply factors, as well as conditions of demand, must be evaluated for the determination of the degree of monopoly. Furthermore, not only must the ability of the firm to penetrate the markets of its competitors be considered, but also its ability to withstand the attacks, such as price cuts, made by its competitors. Changes in market forces must be examined in both directions: forces generated by the firm against its rivals, and forces aimed toward the firm by its rivals. The latter direction of market forces is accounted for by a *coefficient of insulation*, which measures the degree of nonresponsiveness of the sales of a firm to price reductions initiated by its competitors.

Logically, one might conclude that if enough variables could be included in an index, and all statistical difficulties for measuring cross-elasticity could be overcome, an ideal monopoly index would exist. On the other hand, Professor Chamberlin argues that the relative strength of monopoly cannot be measured. The problem of measuring monopoly is akin, in Chamberlin's words, to ascertaining the state of an individual's health. "Some aspects of health can be measured and others cannot. Among the former we have body temperature, blood pressure, metabolism, weight, etc. But these do not lend themselves to the construction of a single index of

R. W. Pfouts and C. E. Ferguson, "Market Classification Systems in Theory and Policy," *Southern Economic Journal*, Vol. XXVI (October, 1959), 111–18, "Conjectural Behavior and Classification of Oligopoly Situations," *ibid.*, Vol. XXVII (October, 1960), 139–41, and "Theory, Operationalism, and Policy: A Further Note on Market Classification," *ibid.*, Vol. XXVIII (July, 1961), 90–95; R. L. Bishop, "Market Classification Again," *ibid.*, pp. 83–90; A. Heertje, "Market Classification Systems in Theory," *ibid.*, Vol. XXVII (October, 1960), 138–39; and Olson and McFarland, "The Restoration of Pure Monopoly and the Concept of the Industry."

[22]Papandreou, "Market Structure and Monopoly Power," pp. 883–97.

health. Similarly, in economics it does not follow that because certain indices are quantitative themselves they can be averaged or in some way reduced to a single index, . . ."[23] Finally, the lack of strict formulas for defining markets, industries, or competition affords the courts an important degree of jurisprudential flexibility.

Another approach to the monopoly problem is to ascertain not the degree of monopoly in an industry at a given point of time, but the movement and generation of competitive forces, and how they affect the behavior of a selected group of firms. "Our real interest is less in the *state* of *monopoly* or *competition* than in the process of *competing* and *monopolizing*."[24] The next chapter presents an analysis of duopoly, defined as a market structure of two firms. The assumptions of one firm with respect to the behavior of a rival are shown to affect pricing and output decisions associated with the competitive process.

[23]Chamberlin, "Measuring the Degree of Monopoly and Concentration," p. 83.
[24]Miller, "Measures of Monopoly Power and Concentration," p. 123.

CHAPTER NINE

Introduction to Duopoly Theory

Writers have argued through the past decades that the concept of pure monopoly is an abstraction that does not describe the market position of any actual firm. It is difficult to conceive of a firm which possesses such economic power that it can totally exclude all potential entrants from its field, and faces virtually no substitutes for its product. The concept of pure competition, where a large number of buyers and sellers exist and any firm can sell as many units as it produces at the going market price, is also largely an abstraction. Neither of these theoretical models is particularly useful in explaining the *process of competing* whereby firms meet or undercut prices, expand or contract sales, and fight to preserve or extend a share of a market.

The duopoly and oligopoly models offer a theoretical framework for studying the strategic maneuvers of firms in changing their prices and levels of production. These models offer no single solution or strategy for a firm to follow. Prices and production levels cannot be predicted without assumptions being made as to the reaction of firms to various output and price changes initiated by its opponent. In the Cournot model each seller assumes that the output of its rival will remain constant regardless of any change it may make in its own output level. In the Bertrand model each seller assumes that the price of its rival will remain constant regardless of any change it may make in its own price. Thus, the interdependence of competitive actions on the conduct of a rival firm is ignored in both the Cournot and Bertrand models.

These two models are useful as an introduction to more complex oligopoly models where each firm within a market structure recognizes the interdependence between its own actions and the actions of its rivals, and

74

anticipates a number of possible countermoves by an opponent for each competitive move of its own.

The Cournot Duopoly Output Model

In 1838 Augustin Cournot considered the duopoly problem arising between the producers of mineral water from two neighboring springs. The two firms, or duopolists, each hold their price fixed, but compete with each other by offering for sale various amounts of the same quality of mineral water. Each of the duopolists in the Cournot model acts independently under the naïve belief that regardless what changes in output it makes, the level of output of its opponent will remain constant.[1] However, every time one of the firms sets an output level, the second firm is induced to change its output level in order to maximize profits, which in turn causes the first firm to readjust its output level. The process continues until an equilibrium position is reached and the expectation that the other will not change its output is finally correct.

The seeming obliviousness of each firm in the Cournot model to the repercussions its movements may have on the other firm has brought forth considerable criticism. The expectation that an opponent will offer no retaliation is difficult to reconcile with the rationality of profit maximization in the Cournot model. But despite its shortcomings, the Cournot model is almost indispensable as a starting point to the theory of duopoly. In the words of Professor Fellner,

A realistic approach to oligopoly problems cannot be based on Cournot's theory. Yet now, after more than a century, it is still difficult to see what is involved in an oligopoly theory without showing how the theory is related to Cournot's basic construction.[2]

[1] A. Cournot, *Researches into Mathematical Principles of the Theory of Wealth* (1838), translated by N. T. Bacon, 2nd ed. (New York: The Macmillan Company, 1927), Chap. 7; F. Machlup, *The Economics of Sellers Competition* (Baltimore: Johns Hopkins University Press, 1952), pp. 372–77; W. J. Fellner, *Competition Among the Few* (New York: Alfred A. Knopf, Inc., 1949), Chap. 2; Chamberlin, *The Theory of Monopolistic Competition*, 7th ed., Chap. 3; M. Shubik, *Strategy and Market Structure* (New York: John Wiley & Sons, Inc., 1959), p. 92; R. D. Theocharis, "On the Stability of the Cournot Solution on the Oligopoly Problem," *Review of Economic Studies*, Vol. XXVII (February, 1960), 133–34; M. McManus and R. E. Quandt, "Comments on the Stability of the Cournot Oligopoly Model," *ibid.*, Vol. XXVIII (February, 1961), 136–39; F. H. Hahn, "The Stability of the Cournot Oligopoly Solution," *ibid.*, Vol. XXIX (October, 1962) 329–31; M. McManus, "Dynamic Cournot-type Oligopoly Models: A Correction," *ibid.*, pp. 337–39; R. L. Bishop, "The Stability of the Cournot Oligopoly Solution," further comment, *ibid.*, pp. 332–36; and C. R. Frank, Jr. and R. E. Quandt, "On the Existence of Cournot Equilibrium," *International Economic Review*, Vol. IV (January, 1963), 92–96.

[2] Fellner, *Competition Among the Few.*, p. 57.

The Cournot model begins with a demand curve which shows the dependence of the market price of mineral water on the total quantity offered by the duopolists, firm A and firm B. Therefore, for a given price, an increase in either firm's output will cause a reduction in the optimum level of the other firm's output. For any level of output offered by firm A, there exists an output for firm B which will maximize firm B's profits. In Fig. 9-1 the locus of these points gives the output reaction curve R_bR_b

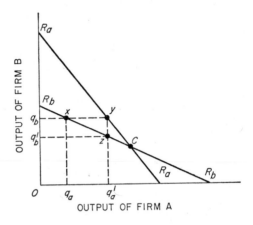

Fig. 9-1. *The Cournot Model*

for firm B. Similarly, for any level of output offered by firm B, there exists an output for firm A which will maximize firm A's profits. The locus of these points gives the output reaction curve R_aR_a in Fig. 9-1.

If firm A produces output Oq_a, firm B will move to point x on its output reaction curve where it produces output Oq_b. The output level Oq_b will maximize firm B's profits for the existing level of firm A's output. However, the change in firm B's output will leave firm A unsatisfied with its previous output level Oq_a, since its profits are no longer being maximized. The profits of firm A were reduced by the increased output of firm B. To maximize profits firm A must move on its output reaction curve to point y, or output level Oq_a'. At this new level firm A will be doing the best it can so long as firm B continues to produce output Oq_b.

After firm A changes its output to Oq_a', firm B finds that it is advantageous once again to change its output, this time to Oq_b'. The process continues with the duopolists staying on their reaction curves and stubbornly adhering to the belief that each time they move their opponent will not retaliate by also changing its output. Finally, the two firms will reach point C, where their output reaction curves intersect, their strategies coincide, and an equilibrium is achieved. Point C in Fig. 9-1, which is often referred to as the "Cournot point," gives the solution to this duopoly model.

An understanding of the derivation of output reaction curves is necessary before we proceed to more advanced duopoly models. The dashed curves in Fig. 9-2, which are concave to the horizontal axis, are profit

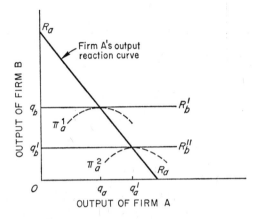

Fig. 9-2. *Construction of the Output Reaction Curve for Firm A*

indifference curves for firm A. Each curve represents various combinations of outputs of firm A and firm B which leave firm A with the same amount of profit. Initially, firm A believes erroneously that firm B has a horizontal reaction curve such as $q_b R_b'$ in Fig. 9-2, and will maintain a constant output at a level Oq_b. Firm A will produce output Oq_a, which is determined by the point of tangency of firm A's profit indifference curve Π_a^1 and $q_b R_b'$. This point of tangency marks the greatest profit which can be earned by firm A when firm B produces output Oq_b.

In the next period, firm B changes its output from Oq_b to Oq_b'. Firm A once again takes the output level of its opponent as fixed and attempts to maximize its own profits. Firm A will select output Oq_a', which is determined by the tangency of its profit indifference curve Π_a^2 and $q_b' R_b''$. The connection of these points of tangency forms the actual output reaction curve of firm A, designated $R_a R_a$. Firm A's output reaction curve shows the most profitable output level for firm A for each level of output produced by firm B.

Note that the profit indifference curves of firm A represent higher levels of profit for firm A as they approach the horizontal axis. For a given output of firm A, a lower profit indifference curve for firm A implies a lower output level for the competitor firm B, and hence, a higher profit for firm A. Thus, Π_a^2 represents a higher level of profit for firm A than Π_a^1.

As firm B produces less output, the profit indifference curves that are closer to the horizontal axis become available to firm A, and firm A can earn a higher total profit.

Output reaction curves for firm B can be similarly constructed. In Fig. 9-3, firm B erroneously believes in the first period that firm A has a

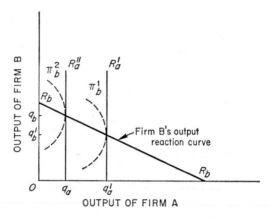

Fig. 9-3. *Construction of the Output Reaction Curve for Firm B*

vertical output reaction curve such as $q_a'R_a'$, and that firm A will maintain a constant output at a level Oq_a'. Firm B will produce that level of output which, taken in conjunction with firm A's given output Oq_a', will maximize firm B's profits. The point of tangency of the profit indifference curve Π_b' with $q_a'R_a'$ represents the greatest profit that can be earned by firm B when firm A produces output Oq_a'. In the next period, firm A changes its output level to Oq_a, and firm B selects output Oq_b, where its profit indifference curve Π_b^2 is tangent to q_aR_a''.

The connection of these vertical points of tangency gives the output reaction curve of firm B, designated R_bR_b. Note that firm B's profit indifference curves are concave to the vertical axis, and represent higher fixed levels of profit for firm B the closer they are to the vertical axis.

The Bertrand Duopoly Price Model

Each of the duopolists in the Bertrand model acts independently under the naïve belief that regardless of what price changes it makes, the price charged by its opponent will remain fixed.[3] The behavior of each duopolist

---

[3] J. Bertrand, Review of Cournot and Walras in *Journal des Savants* (Paris: September, 1883), pp. 499–508. Also see W. J. Baumol, *Business Behavior, Value and Growth* (New York: The Macmillan Company, 1959), pp. 18–20; H. G. Lewis, "Some Observations on Duopoly Theory," *American Economic Review*, Vol. XXVIII (Proceedings, 1948), 1–9; and Machlup, *The Economics of Sellers Competition*, pp. 377–80.

is described by a price reaction curve which is analogous to the output reaction curves in the Cournot model. In Fig. 9-4 firm A has a price reaction curve, R_aR_a, which shows the prices which maximize its profits at various price levels maintained by firm B. Similarly, firm B has a price reaction curve, R_bR_b, which shows the prices which maximize its profits at various price levels maintained by firm A.

The duopolists arrive at the equilibrium point C in Fig. 9-4 through successive movements along their price reaction curves. The behavior pattern followed by the duopolists in the Bertrand model is similar to that of the duopolists in the Cournot model with the modification that the competitive moves are in terms of price changes rather than output changes.

If the duopolists produce an identical product, a divergence of prices between each firm can last only temporarily. Therefore, for an equilibrium to be obtained, both firms must have the same price, and their price reaction curves must intersect on a 45-degree line from the origin. However, if some extent of product differentiation is introduced, the price reaction curves

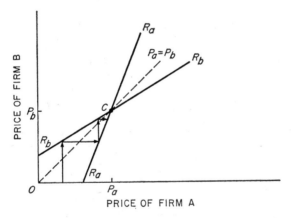

Fig. 9-4. *The Bertrand Model*

need not intersect on the 45-degree line in order for an equilibrium to occur. Bertrand argued that if a competitor assumes that his rival's price will not change, the competitor will charge a slightly lower price and thereby dispose of his entire output. His rival, making the same assumption, will also continue to undercut price until finally they both eliminate all profit and reach the competitive equilibrium.

A price reaction curve for firm A is constructed in Fig. 9-5. The axes have price rather than output, and the profit indifference curves are convex rather than concave to their respective axes. If firm B is selling its product at price OP_b, firm A will sell its product at OP_a' in order to get to the higher profit indifference curve Π_a^4, which is tangent to P_bR_b'. Similarly, when firm B is selling its product at price OP_b', firm A will sell its product at price OP_a in order to reach indifference curve Π_a^3. The connection of the respective points of tangency of firm A's profit indifference curves and the horizontal lines in Fig. 9-5, which represent given output levels for firm B, describes firm A's price reaction curve.

Note that in the duopoly price models higher profit indifference curves represent greater amounts of profit for a given firm. In Fig. 9-5, Π_a^4 rep-

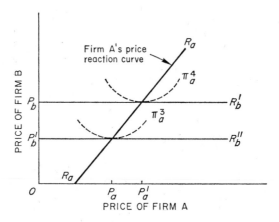

Fig. 9-5. *Construction of the Price Reaction Curve for Firm A*

resents a greater profit for firm A than Π_a^3. Firm A's price becomes relatively lower as firm B charges higher prices. Thus, for a given output P_a', firm A can reach higher profit indifference curves such as Π_a^4 only if firm B raises its price to OP_b. In this connection the convexity of the profit indifference curves can, in part, be explained. The positively sloped segments of these profit indifference curves indicate that a rise in firm A's price will reduce its profits unless firm B also increases its price.

The Edgeworth Duopoly Model

Edgeworth extended the analysis of Bertrand by considering a market divided evenly between two sellers, in which the sellers undercut each other's price until both approach the point of competitive equilibrium where price equals marginal cost.[4] At this price, one firm puts the rest of

[4] F. Y. Edgeworth, *Papers Relating to Political Economy,* Vol. I (London: Macmillan & Co., Ltd., 1925), 111–42, and *Mathematical Physics* (London: Routledge & Kegan Paul, Ltd., 1881); A. J. Nichol, "Edgeworth's Theory of Duopoly Price," *Economic Journal,* Vol. XLV (March, 1935), 51–66; and G. W. Nutter, "Duopoly, Oligopoly, and Emerging Competition," *Southern Economic Journal,* Vol. XXX (April, 1964), 342.

its supply on the market and thereby leaves the other firm in a position where it can raise its price to almost the monopoly level in serving the remaining customers.

Unlike the Bertrand and Cournot models, where each firm has practically an unlimited capacity to produce, the Edgeworth model limits the output of the duopolists so that neither can supply the whole market demand at a low price.[5] "In order for the price to descend, their individual markets are completely merged into one, each drawing customers freely from the other by a slight reduction in price. But in order for it to rise again, their markets are completely separated," with the result that each seller becomes a monopolist dealing with a portion of the buyers in isolation.[6] Thus, the Edgeworth duopoly solution consists of a fluctuating price in the approximate range of the monopoly price and the competitive equilibrium price.

Output Leadership Models

In the more complex duopoly models the duopolists recognize the interdependence of their prices and output levels. For example, the output of firm A (q_a) could be positively related to the output of firm B (q_b) in such a manner that firm A always produces some multiple k of the output produced by firm B. In mathematical notation, $q_a = kq_b$. Firm A might be prepared to match the output of firm B ($k = 1$) in order to maintain a constant market share of 50 per cent. Similarly, each firm might react to a definite rule which keeps its prices, its profits, or its advertising expenditures as a fixed proportion of the amount maintained by its rival duopolist.

A duopoly model which has one firm react according to some given multiple k times a variable of another firm almost forces a solution. In the more general duopoly case the firm is not sure of its opponent's future course of conduct. Alternatively stated, the firms may not react according to some single function once they observe that alternative courses of conduct may yield higher profits. Under these circumstances, the reaction curves are discarded and the moves and countermoves of the duopolists involve a high degree of market strategy. The following two duopoly output models illustrate the results that can be obtained when one or both of the duopolists abandon their reaction curves.[7]

[5]F. Machlup, *The Economics of Sellers Competition*, pp. 380–87.

[6]Chamberlin, *The Theory of Monopolistic Competition*, 7th ed., pp. 40–41.

[7]A discussion of these two models can be found in Weintraub, *Price Theory*, pp. 160–68. A learning curve duopoly model is given in P. Suppes and J. Carlsmith, "Experimental Learning Theory," *International Economic Review*, Vol. III (January, 1962), 60–78.

Suppose firm A finally learns the actual behavior pattern of firm B. In a Cournot model firm A would observe that its opponent is a follower, *i.e.*, firm B always follows the moves initiated by firm A. Firm A has the opportunity to become a leader and ignore its own "follower" reaction curve which it abided by in the Cournot model. The optimum strategy for firm A, now that this firm alone knows about its rival's reaction curve, is to select that output which will evoke an output reaction from firm B such that the profits for firm A will be maximized.

Assume that firm A selects output Oq'_a in Fig. 9-6. Firm B will follow with a change in output to Oq'_b, which allows firm A to attain the profit

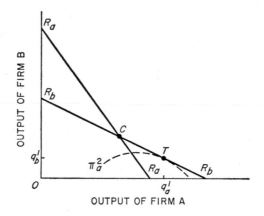

Fig. 9-6. *Output Leadership*

indifference curve Π^2_a. By ignoring its output reaction curve, firm A has moved the equilibrium point from point C (the Cournot point) to point T, where firm B has a lower output and firm A has a higher profit and output. The analysis suggests that firm A obtains an advantage of higher profits when it becomes an output leader rather than an output follower.

Suppose firm A and firm B both seek to be leaders and dispense with their output reaction curves. In Fig. 9-7 firm A selects output Oq'_a, expecting firm B to stay on reaction curve R_bR_b and produce output Oq'_b. This output combination would place the firms at point T, an advantageous profit position for firm A. Firm B, however, has other plans: It also wants to be an output leader. Firm B produces output Oq''_b, expecting firm A to stay on reaction curve R_aR_a and produce output Oq''_a. This output combination would place the firms at point S, an advantageous profit position for firm B. However, firm A and firm B will be surprised to find that their opponent has not behaved as expected, with the result that the two firms end up neither at point S (firm B's expected equilibrium point) nor at point T (firm A's expected equilibrium point). Rather, the firms end up at point M, which is off both their reaction curves.

Both firms may be worse off when each attempts to be an output leader than when one consents to be a follower. In Fig. 9-7 the profit indifference

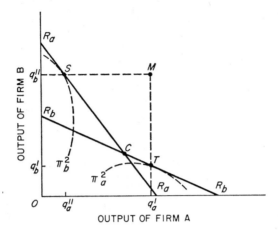

Fig. 9-7. *Contesting Output Leadership*

curves of firm A represent higher profits as they approach the horizontal axis, and the profit indifference curves of firm B represent higher profits as they approach the vertical axis. Consequently, firm A earns a higher profit at point T than at point M, and firm B earns a higher profit at point S than at point M. It is, therefore, possible that the output combinations represented by points S or T may yield a greater aggregate profit to the duopolists than the output combination represented by point M. In this event one solution to the model might be for firm B to consent to be a passive follower, provided that firm A gives it a side payment or some other form of compensation.

Conclusion

The determination of which firm will become the follower and which one the leader becomes of paramount importance once the duopolists recognize that neither their individual nor aggregate profits are maximized when both attempt to be output leaders. The German economist von Stackelberg maintained that contending output leadership results in economic warfare.[8] Both duopolists are in a worse position as contending

[8]H. Von Stackelberg, *Marktform and Gleichgewicht* (Berlin: Julius Springer, 1934); W. Leontieff, "Stackelberg on Monopolistic Competition," *Journal of Political Economy*,

output leaders than they would be if one were to give up and retire as a follower. "But they both sacrifice small profits now in the hope of eliminating the other competitor so that they will receive large profits in the future."[9] Only in special cases, Stackelberg argues, will a duopolist come to the conclusion that his follower position will secure him higher profits than his leadership position. Therefore, duopoly market structures are almost always unstable. The next chapter doubts the general validity of this conclusion, and finds that the prices of duopolists, in contrast to their outputs, tend to find stable positions.

Vol. XLIV (August, 1936), 554–59; E. J. R. Heyward, "H. von Stackelberg's Work on Duopoly," *Economic Record*, Vol. XVIII (June, 1941), 99–106; J. R. Hicks, "Review of Stackelberg, 'Marktform und Gleichgewicht,' " *Economic Journal*, Vol. XLV (June, 1935), 334–36; and Henderson and Quandt, *Microeconomics*, pp. 180–82.

[9]H. von Stackelberg, *The Theory of the Market Economy* (1934), translated from the German by A. T. Peacock (New York: Oxford University Press, 1952), p. 194.

CHAPTER TEN

Oligopoly Behavior Models

Price leadership constitutes a tacit or informal understanding among oligopolists that they will adhere to a price change initiated by a designated member. The varieties of price leadership models range from cases where the leader is acting as a market barometer for the rest of the industry, and sets a price which reflects the prevailing demand and supply conditions, to instances of outright collusion among member firms with the price leader directing a conspiracy in setting an unduly high price for the benefit of the industry.

Von Stackelberg Model

Oligopolists selling a homogeneous or identical product cannot attain an equilibrium position so long as their respective prices diverge. The existence of a degree of product differentiation permits different prices to exist simultaneously in the same market, and allows a continuation of the leadership-followership analysis applied in the preceding chapter to output determination.

Von Stackelberg defines a price leader as a firm which does not observe its reaction curve. A follower is a dependent or passive firm which remains on its reaction curve and sets its price to maximize its own profits after its rival has made a price decision. Price leadership equilibrium implies an asymmetric duopoly market structure in which one firm is content to remain as a follower and allow the other firm to act as a leader. If both firms attempt to be followers, as in the Cournot case, or if both firms attempt to be leaders, the duopoly structure is said to be symmetric. In the words of Professor Fellner: "Thus, follower's policies on the part of both firms result in an equilibrium corresponding to the intersection point of the two reaction functions, while leadership policies of one firm coupled with followership policies of the other result in leadership equilibrium, and leadership policies on the part of both firms result in Stackelberg disequilibrium."[1]

A model of contesting price leadership is presented in Fig. 10-1, which shows both firm A and firm B attempting to be price leaders, each assuming that the other will be a price follower.[2] The profit maximizing position for

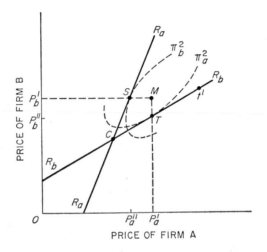

Fig. 10-1. *Contesting Price Leadership*

firm B, as a price leader, is point S, where its profit indifference curve Π_b^2 is tangent to R_aR_a, the price reaction curve of firm A. Similarly, the profit maximizing position for firm A, as a price leader, is point T, where its profit indifference curve Π_a^2 is tangent to R_bR_b, the price reaction curve of firm B. In the contesting price leadership model, each firm ignores its own price reaction curve, and forecasts erroneously that its rival will remain a follower. Consequently, the firms end up at point M, which is on neither firm's reaction curve.

Unlike the *output* leadership case in Fig. 9-7, where an error in forecasting that one's rival would be a follower rather than a leader proved to be

[1]Fellner, *Competition Among the Few*, p. 102.

[2]For a discussion of this model see Weintraub, *Price Theory*, pp. 191–93; W. J. Baumol, *Economic Theory and Operations Analysis*, p. 228, and *Business Behavior, Value and Growth* p. 20; and Fellner, *Competition Among the Few*, p. 109.

costly, an error in the contesting price leadership model can be advantageous to both firms. Since a higher profit indifference curve in a price leadership model implies a higher profit, it can be shown that point M will leave each firm better off in Fig. 10-1 than either of the price leadership positions (points S and T).

In Fig. 10-2 Π_a^4 represents the highest profit for firm A among the four profit indifference curves shown. When firm A acts as a price leader, it

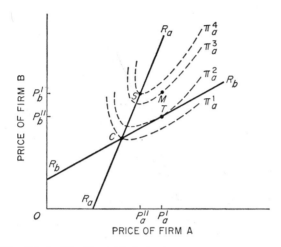

Fig. 10-2. *The Profit Indifference Curves for Firm A*

selects price P_a' in order to attain profit indifference curve Π_a^2, which is tangent at point T to firm B's price reaction curve. At point T firm A is at the highest possible point of tangency between its rival's reaction curve (R_bR_b) and its own profit indifference curve system. The decision of firm A to be a price leader has not placed it in the highest possible profit position. In terms of the model in Fig. 10-2, firm A would earn a higher profit at point S (where firm A is a follower and firm B is a leader) or point M (where firms A and B are both leaders).

An examination of Fig. 10-3, where Π_b^4 represents the highest profit for firm B among the profit indifference curves shown, will show why firm A is always in a better position when firm B is a price leader. If firm B acts as a price leader, it will raise its price from P_b'' to P_b' in order to attain point S on its profit indifference curve Π_b^2. This price increase by firm B will leave firm A's price relatively lower. Thus, once firm B acts as a price leader and raises its price, firm A will be in a relatively better position regardless of whether it continues as a price leader or changes to a price follower.

The same reasoning can lead firm B to induce its rival to be a leader.

Firm B earns higher profits in Fig. 10-3 when firm A is a leader. Firm B's highest level of profit, in terms of the indifference curves shown, is at Π_b^4 or point T, where it is a follower and firm A is a leader. A lower level of profits for firm B is at point M, where firm A is a leader and firm B is also a leader. However, both of these points (T and M), where firm A is a leader, place firm B in a better profit position than points S and C, where firm A becomes a follower.

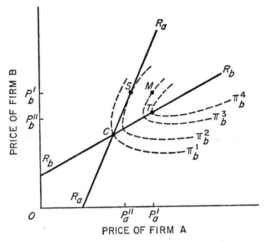

Fig. 10-3. *The Profit Indifference Curves for Firm B*

The foregoing model suggests that once a firm becomes a price leader, it is more profitable for the rival to be a follower than a leader.[3] Therefore, an incentive exists for each firm to be a follower once it expects its rival will act as a price leader. If the firm is wrong in its expectation, and its rival remains a follower, both firms will arrive at point C. The next section will explain in terms of game theory matrices why the firms will be reluctant to stay at the mutually disadvantageous point C.

---

[3]Different price leadership models can be constructed by changing the slopes of the reaction curves, the shapes of the indifference curves, and the various points of tangency. For example, in Fig. 10-1 if the point of tangency of Π_a^2 with R_bR_b was at t' instead of T, both firms acting as price leaders would no longer arrive at higher indifference curves than they had expected. Firm A will be worse off, since the final meeting place of the two leaders will be at a point (not shown) directly below t'.

A Game Theory Model

A game can be described within the previously described duopoly market structure by noting that there exist two strategies for firm A and two strategies for firm B. Firm A can attempt to be either a price leader (A_L), or a price follower (A_F); similarly, firm B can be either a price leader (B_L), or a price follower (B_F). A game matrix can be constructed which has the strategies of firm B in the columns, and the strategies of firm A

	B_L	B_F
A_L	M	T
A_F	S	C

Fig. 10-4. *A Price Leadership Game Matrix*

	B_L	B_F
A_L	3	2
A_F	4	1

Fig. 10-5. *Payoff Matrix for Firm A*

in the rows. The matrix in Fig. 10-4 describes the possible outcomes of the previously discussed Fig. 10-1. For example, if firm A and firm B each attempts to be a price leader, they will end up at point M, which is given in the matrix in Fig. 10-4 by row A_L and column B_L. If each firm attempts to be a follower (A_F, B_F), point C is reached in both the diagram and the matrix.

The profit indifference curves for firm A and firm B, which are given in Figs. 10-2 and 10-3 respectively, are numbered from 1 to 4. As the firm achieves higher levels of profits, its profit indifference curves increase in value from 1 to 4. These values can be substituted into the above matrix and will yield a *payoff matrix* for each firm. The payoff matrix describes the profit resulting to a particular firm for various outcomes within a game.

	B_L	B_F
A_L	3	4
A_F	2	1

Fig. 10-6. *Payoff Matrix for Firm B*

	B_L	B_F
A_L	(3,3)	(2,4)
A_F	(4,2)	(1,1)

Fig. 10-7. *Combined Payoff Matrix*

The payoff matrix for firm A is shown in Fig. 10-5. At point M in Fig. 10-2 firm A is on its profit indifference curve Π_a^3; its corresponding position in its payoff matrix (A_L, B_L) is therefore given the value 3. The values of the remaining profit indifference curves for firm A are placed in their appropriate matrix positions.

Firm B's payoff matrix can be constructed from Fig. 10-3, which shows the values of its profit indifference curves for the various outcomes of the game. Firm B's payoff matrix is shown in Fig. 10-6.

The two payoff matrices can be combined into one by placing in each parenthesis found in the matrix in Fig. 10-7 first, firm A's profits, and second, firm B's profits. Hence, the pair of strategies (2, 4) shows that firm A would gain 2 and firm B would gain 4.

The Cournot point (A_F, B_F) was described previously as an equilibrium point, determined by the intersection of the reaction curves of each firm. But the equilibrium point in the output model ceases to be an equilibrium point in the context of the price leadership game in Fig. 10-7. The pair of price strategies (A_F, B_F) gives the lowest possible profit to the two firms; any other pair of strategies leaves these firms better off, since either firm can gain more than one unit by choosing another strategy.

If firm B knew that firm A was going to pursue its follower strategy, firm B would select its leadership strategy. Conversely, if firm A knew that firm B was going to adhere to a leadership strategy, firm A would select its follower strategy. Thus, profit position (4, 2) is an equilibrium position under these circumstances. However, the same argument will show that profit position (2, 4) is also an equilibrium position. Since each of these equilibrium points favors a different firm, the difficulty in the game involves whether a firm can enforce the strategy most beneficial for itself. If neither firm has such power, the outcome of the game can oscillate between different profit combinations, depending upon the behavior paths followed by the firms.

Suppose the firms have tacitly agreed to follow the joint leadership strategy in order to obtain an even division of profits (3, 3), but firm B double-crosses firm A by switching to his "follower" strategy in order to receive an additional unit of profit (2, 4).

Firm A has two alternatives: (1) to allow the wayward firm B to earn its extra unit of profit at the expense of firm A, or (2) to punish firm B by also employing its own "follower" strategy. The second alternative, which leaves the firms in the (1, 1) profit position, can be rationalized by firm A as the cost of teaching firm B not to deviate from the joint leadership strategy which divides profit evenly at (3, 3). It is doubtful whether the players would stay at (1, 1) for any protracted period of time since either firm, by employing a leadership strategy, can be guaranteed a minimum security above the 1 unit of profit regardless of the strategy selected by the other. For example, firm B by playing strategy B_L is guaranteed to receive 2 units of profit, but in playing strategy B_F is assured of receiving only 1 unit. Similarly, firm A can be confident of 2 units in playing strategy A_L, but can be confident of only 1 unit of profit in playing strategy A_F. If each firm selects the strategy which gives it the maximum value of its guaranteed profits, then each is following a *maximin* strategy (maximum of the minimum security levels of profits), and the firms will settle at position (A_L, B_L).[4]

The Dominant Firm Model

One type of price leadership consists of a dominant firm which sets a price, allows minor firms to sell what they wish, and supplies the remainder of the quantity demanded.[5] In this model the minor firms have no reason for charging a lower price, since they are able to sell as much as they wish at the leader's price. The leader knows that at any price he might set the followers will sell the quantity that equates their marginal costs to that price, leaving the remainder of the market to the leader. The dominant firm will therefore select the price which is most profitable for itself.

The additional assumptions implicit in the model of dominant firm price leadership are "(a) the large producer has almost complete control of market price; (b) other firms act like pure competitors (each regarding its own demand function as perfectly elastic at the leader's price); (c) all firms, excepting the dominant firm, ignore any effects they may have on market price and output; (d) the dominant firm can estimate the market demand curve for the product (presumably, his 'subjective' feeling concerning the 'objective' demand function, both as to position and shape); and (e) the dominant firm can predict with reasonable accuracy the supplies of other sellers at each price."[6] The dominant firm, as summarized by Professor Stigler, "supplies a substantial part of total sales (probably

---

[4]See L. Hurwicz, "The Theory of Economic Behavior," *American Economic Review*, Vol. XXXV (1945), 909–25; reprinted in American Economic Association, *Readings in Price Theory* (Homewood, Ill.: Richard D. Irwin, Inc., 1952), pp. 505–26; and O. Morgenstern, "Oligopoly, Monopolistic Competition, and The Theory of Games," *American Economic Review*, Vol. XXXVIII (1948), 10-18.

[5]K. Forchheimer, "Theretisches zum unvollstaendigen Monopol," *Schmollers Jahrbuch* (Berlin: Erstes Heft, 1908). Also see A. J. Nichol, *Partial Monopoly and Price Leadership* (Philadelphia, 1930); Fellner, *Competition Among the Few*, p. 138; and G. J. Stigler, "The Kinky Oligopoly Demand Curve and Rigid Prices," *Journal of Political Economy*, Vol. LV (October, 1947), 432–49; reprinted in American Economic Association, *Readings in Price Theory* (Homewood, Ill.: Richard D. Irwin, Inc., 1952), p. 433. Also see his "Notes on the Theory of Duopoly," *Journal of Political Economy*, Vol. XLVIII (August, 1940), 521–41.

[6]Reprinted by permission of the publishers from R. F. Lanzillotti, "Competitive Price Leadership — A Critique of Price Leadership Models," *Review of Economics and Statistics*, Vol. XXXIX (February, 1957) (Cambridge, Mass.: Harvard University Press), copyright 1957 by the President and Fellows of Harvard College, pp. 55-56. Also see R. M. Cyert and R. G. March, "Organizational Factors in the Theory of Oligopoly," *Quarterly Journal of Economics*, Vol. LXX (February, 1956), 44–64.

one-fourth at a minimum). It has small, independent rivals, but the situation can be viewed as one of duopoly because all these firms behave competitively (i.e., they operate at the output where marginal cost equals price). The dominant firm behaves passively — it fixes the price and allows the minor firms to sell all they wish at this price."[7]

In Fig. 10-8 the industry demand curve (D_i) for a product is composed of the demand curve for the dominant firm (D_d) and the demand curve for the remaining firms. The profit-maximizing output of the dominant firm is at OQ, the level at which its marginal revenue curve (MR_d) intersects its marginal cost curve (MC_d). Since the industry price is set by the

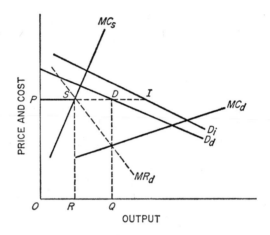

Fig. 10–8. Dominant Firm Price Leadership

dominant firm, the price for output OQ is determined by the dominant firm's demand curve rather than by the demand curve for the industry. The remaining firms, whose horizontal sum of their marginal cost curves is given by the supply curve MC_s, sell all their output, OR, at the price set by the dominant firm. The demand curve for the remaining firms is the horizontal line PS when the dominant firm sets the price at OP. Therefore, at any price OP there will be a total industry demand of PI, of which PS is supplied by the smaller firms and the remainder, $PI - PS = PD$, is demanded from the dominant firm. It follows from the geometry that $DI = PS$.

Professor Markham has observed that "the rationale of price making by the dominant or partial monopolist differs but little from that employed by the pure monopolist. They both, presumably, have complete control

[7]G. J. Stigler, *The Theory of Price* (New York: The Macmillan Company, 1947), p. 227.

over prices, but the partial monopolist, unlike the pure monopolist must take account of the quantity that the competitive sector of the industry will offer at any price he may set."[8] Therefore, the dominant firm price leader may not necessarily charge the same price that a monopolist operating in the same market would charge. For example, a dominant firm may fear that setting a price which maximizes industry profit would "fatten" the smaller firms and encourage their output expansion.[9]

One of the real tests of a dominant firm price leader is the extent to which "followership" is maintained in soft markets.[10] A model of dominant firm price leadership may disintegrate once the remaining firms in an industry cease to be obedient followers. "The erratic behavior of the competitive fringe around the oligopoly core directly contradicts the implicit assumption of the models that fringe firms will accept the leader's prices in a manner similar to the pure competitor."[11] With dissimilar cost curves between different-sized firms, the same price may not maximize short-run profits for both large and small firms. "Under some market conditions large firms may be operating beyond the range of least-cost outputs; consequently, they may be anxious for increased sales. The fringe may not be at capacity output, however, and thus may not follow the leader's prices. In periods of slack demand, the fringe and others may attempt to stimulate sales by lowering prices."[12]

Smaller firms, aware that price cutting or over-stepping market shares will probably result in retaliation by larger firms, may still take a chance on not being obedient followers. The smaller firms may believe that the larger firms will be reluctant to upset an entire market merely to punish violators of negligible size. However, as the number of fringe firms which refuse to be obedient followers increases, the pressure will mount on the dominant firm or oligopolistic core of firms to lower the existing price level.

The price leader in the above market setting will have at least two possible motives for lowering its price: (1) to protect its own market share from being nibbled away by the smaller firms that are cutting prices, and (2) to retaliate with the hope that the future will be marked by greater price discipline throughout the whole industry. If the smaller firms operate

[8]J. W. Markham, "The Nature and Significance of Price Leadership," *American Economic Review*, Vol. XLI (December, 1951), 891–905; reprinted in American Economic Association, *Readings in Industrial Organization and Public Policy* (Homewood, Ill.: Richard D. Irwin, Inc., 1958), p. 179.

[9]J. S. Bain, "A Note on Pricing in Monopoly and Oligopoly," *American Economic Review*, Vol. XXXIX (March, 1949), 448–64; reprinted in American Economic Association, *Readings in Industrial Organization and Public Policy*, pp. 220–35.

[10]Lanzillotti, "Competitive Price Leadership," p. 61.

[11]*Ibid.*, p. 63.

[12]*Ibid.*, p. 56.

at higher costs than the larger firms, they may be vulnerable to a protracted decrease in their volume as a result of the larger firms' lowering of the oligopoly price level. Thus, the fringe firms must weigh carefully the short-term transitional profits gained by not following the leader's price changes against the repercussions which may ensue if they upset the entire market and the oligopolistic core or dominant firm lowers the industry price level.

Other Price Leadership Models

Another model of price leadership consists of a firm which initiates price changes only after being prompted by alterations in market demand and cost conditions. This type of price leader is referred to as the *barometric* firm, since its price adjustments command adherence by rival firms only to the extent that they are timely reflections of changes in the market atmosphere.[13]

The fact that the barometric firm reacts to changes in market conditions raises the question of whether a market structure in which such a firm operates is competitive.[14] In a case where the price set by the barometric firm is responsive to market conditions and is equal to the price which would occur under approximately purely competitive conditions, it is probably a moot question whether the firms are actually competitive or are simulating competition. For instance, Professor Lanzillotti observes that "barometric price leadership thus appears to be essentially a special situation where the conjectures of the barometric price leader turn out to be correct, which only rarely would be the case in a dynamic economy under the assumptions postulated. In effect, the special case is very special indeed; it amounts to essentially a competitive model of price behavior."[14]

Professor Markham, on the other hand, believes that it is often possible to distinguish between types of barometric price leadership that are competitive and other types that are monopolistic. "Patently, it is not possible in every case to judge when barometric price leadership is monopolistic and when it is competitive in character without making a thorough investigation, but there are certain visible market features associated with competitive price leadership."[15] These features include occasional changes in the identity of the price leader, absence of uniformity of prices immediately following a price change, and variations in market shares. Professor Markham concludes that "barometric price leadership which follows the

---

[13]Markham, "The Nature and Significance of Price Leadership," p. 181.

[14]Lanzillotti, "Competitive Price Leadership," p. 61.

[15]Markham, "The Nature and Significance of Price Leadership," pp. 181–82.

above lines probably does not greatly circumvent the public interest," and "appears to do little more than set prices which would eventually be set by forces of competition."[16]

In their study of the pricing policies of the larger corporations in the United States, Professors Kaplan, Dirlam, and Lanzillotti observed the prevalence of an attitude toward price leadership akin to the barometric firm model. "Leadership, to the firms involved in this study, meant something more than single market dominance. All the firms considered were sufficiently large, even though in any particular market they may have ranked only second, third, or lower, to feel the inhibitions of leadership as well as its power. . . . Leadership was not regarded as a method by which a single firm could impose its own judgment on the market."[17]

For price leadership to be effective, either the price leader must be relatively large and possess sufficient economic power to discipline any competitor failing to adhere to the announced price, or the price leader must display the unusual perspicacity of the barometric firm in reflecting the consensus of the industry.[18] Whether or not the price leader will select the same price which would have been obtained by the oligopolists in the absence of price leadership is a question which cannot be readily answered. The price level selected will depend upon the objectives of the oligopolists. Thus, the price leadership procedure may be considered by the established firms as a means to instill discipline in a market where sellers would otherwise be prone to engage in cutthroat competition, to forestall the entry of new firms into the industry, or to adjust to changes in existing demand and supply conditions.

Several other types of price leadership models can be constructed through the acceptance or rejection of the various assumptions required for the dominant firm and barometric firm models. The remainder of this section will show the importance in price leadership models of economic factors such as demand, costs, entry conditions, product differentiation, and product diversity.

DIFFERENT COST CURVES. If the firms in an industry do not have similar cost curves, a price conflict can exist as to whether the industry should have either a low price and a high output level, or a high price and

[16]*Ibid.*, p. 185. Cf. J. S. Bain, "Price Leaders, Barometers, and Kinks," *Journal of Business*, Vol. XXXIII (July, 1960), 202.

[17]A. D. H. Kaplan, J. B. Dirlam, and R. F. Lanzillotti, *Pricing In Big Business* (Washington, D.C.: Brookings Institution, 1958), pp. 270–71.

[18]I. R. Barnes, "Considerations Concerning a Public Policy Toward Administered Prices," in United States, Senate Subcommittee on Antitrust and Monopoly of the Committee on the Judiciary, *Administered Prices: A Compendium on Public Policy*, 88th Cong., 1st Sess. (Washington, D.C.: Government Printing Office, 1963), p. 60.

a smaller output level. Professor Boulding presents a theoretical analysis
of an industry composed of two firms with equal market shares, but different marginal cost curves.[19] One firm, whose costs correspond to those
of a dominant firm, has low costs, or a high capacity, with a marginal cost
curve designated MC_d in Fig. 10-9. The remaining firm has high costs,
or low capacity, with a marginal cost curve represented by MC_s. Note
that the capacity of a firm is measured by the distance of its marginal cost
curve from the vertical axis. The further the firm's marginal cost curve
lies to the right, the greater the output that can be attained at any given
marginal cost.

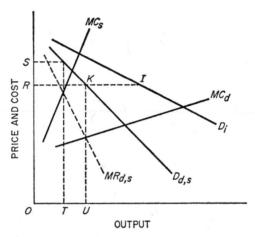

Fig. 10-9. *Price Leadership with Different Cost Curves*

The demand curves for these two firms are different from those found
in the dominant firm case where one firm was assumed to hold a relatively
large share of the market. Under the present assumption of equal market
shares, each firm has an identical demand curve. The industry demand
at price OR is therefore the summation of RK for one firm plus RK for
the other firm ($RK = KI$).

The low-cost, high-capacity firm prefers a large volume (OU) and a
lower price (OR) in order to maximize its profits at the level where its
marginal cost curve (MC_d) intersects its marginal revenue curve ($MR_{d,s}$).
On the other hand, the high-cost, low-capacity firm prefers a smaller volume
(OT) and a higher price (OS) in order to maximize its profits at the level
where its marginal costs (MC_s) intersect its marginal revenue curve ($MR_{d,s}$).
A conflict of policy must inevitably arise in this case, since no price can

[19]K. E. Boulding, *Economic Analysis*, 3rd ed. (New York: Harper & Row, Publishers,
1955), pp. 581-87.

equate marginal cost and marginal revenue for both firms. The high-capacity, low-cost firm has the advantage, since the price it prefers is lower than the price preferred by the low-capacity, high-cost firm.

The resulting conflict in price and output policies cannot be resolved by adopting a price leader so long as all firms remain in the industry. "Low-cost firms will not accept the price leadership of high-cost firms since there is a better option in the form of a lower price and a higher rate of output open to them. They can therefore force the high-cost sector of the industry to adopt the lower price but, if the differences in costs between high-cost firms and low-cost firms are significant, high-cost firms will not recover full costs and will gradually be eliminated from the industry."[20]

INEQUALITY OF MARKET SHARES. A pricing conflict can also occur in an industry of two firms having identical marginal cost curves but different market shares. Professor Boulding has observed that the firm with the smaller market share may be able to set the price for the industry, and will therefore become the price leader. In his words,

The price is set by those firms which are not getting a very large share of the market. In the first instance they may have cut their price below that of the more fortunate firms in order to try to attract new customers. The other firms also cut prices to follow suit. At this lower price the firms with the larger share of the market may still be making profits, though not maximum profits — i.e., they would prefer to have everybody charge a higher price. But the firms with the small share would be worse off if everybody raised prices, for having already a small share of the market the reduction in total sales which would follow a rise in price would hit them proportionately harder than it would hit the firms with the larger share of a market. Consequently, the firms with the small share of the market refuse to raise their price, and the firms with the larger share cannot compel them to do so. The relative permanence of cut-rate gasoline in many centers is probably an example of this phenomenon. The stations with the small share of the market, however, can set the price only as long as the capacity of all stations is approximately equal.[21]

In Fig. 10-10 the firm with the larger market share possesses the demand curve D_d, and the smaller firm in the industry has the demand curve D_s. Since identical costs are assumed, the marginal cost curve $MC_{d,s}$ serves as the cost curve for each of the firms. The industry price is set by the smaller firm, whose profit-maximizing price is the lower of the two firms. The intersection of the smaller firm's marginal revenue curve MR_s is at the output level OT, and determines the lower price OP_s. Note that $MC_{d,s}$ must be rising and intersect MR_d at a higher level than MR_s in order for the smaller firm to be the price leader.

[20]Markham, "The Nature and Significance of Price Leadership," p. 187.

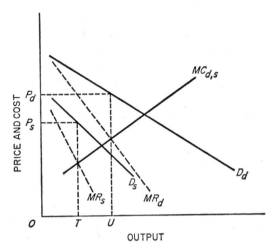

Fig. 10-10. *Price Leadership with Unequal Market Shares*

DEGREE OF ENTRY. If barriers to entry exist, such as high capital expenditures for plant and equipment or vital patents, the price leader can set the industry price at a high level. Conversely, if new firms can readily enter the industry, the price leader may be reluctant to raise the price to a level where newcomers will be attracted.

In the settings of an oligopoly with low to moderate barriers to entry, the price leader may persistently forego setting prices high enough to maximize the industry profit for the established sellers. The output of these new firms would tend to lower both the demand for the products of the established firms and their profits. Professor Bain has labelled the highest price that the established sellers believe they can charge in common without inducing at least one significant entrant, as the "limit price."[22]

In Fig. 10-11 the limit price is P_o. At any price level above P_o, such as P_m, the established sellers can expect entry and a change in the position of their long-term industry demand curve DD' and its corresponding marginal revenue curve MR. The long-term industry demand curve for the output of the established firms will become indeterminate somewhere in the range to the left of point D, once the established sellers charge more than the limit price and attract new entrants. Note that the established sellers do *not* produce output OQ_m, where industry marginal revenue equals

[22]Bain, "A Note on Pricing in Monopoly and Oligopoly," and *Barriers to New Competition*. Also see P. Sylos-Labini, *Oligopoly and Technical Progress* (Cambridge, Mass.: Harvard University Press, 1962); F. Modigliani, "New Developments on the Oligopoly Front," *Journal of Political Economy*, Vol. LXVI (June, 1958), 215–32; and O.E. Williamson, "Selling Expense as a Barrier to Entry," *Quarterly Journal of Economics*, Vol. LXXVII (February, 1963), 112–28.

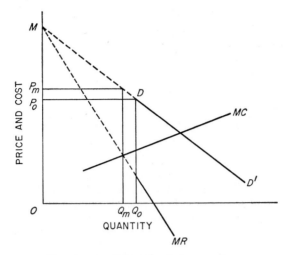

Fig. 10-11. *Effects of Potential Entry*

the aggregate marginal cost curve of the industry members (MC) and the industry profit would be maximized. Rather, the oligopolists produce output OQ_o, and charge a price P_o, which is lower than the industry profit-maximizing price P_m.

It is assumed in the limit price model that the potential entrant is primarily influenced by the price charged (and profit earned) by the established sellers — "influenced not because he expects this price to hold unchanged after entry, but because he regards it as 'proving' the industry demand at a given level and as a critical indicator of the projected state of rivalry or price policy after entry."[23] On the other hand, some potential entrants may regard the limit price as a bluff, and their entry may not be forestalled by the existing industry price. Thus, the price leader of the established sellers will have to decide whether the potential entrant will believe that the industry price does in fact reflect demand conditions. The effectiveness of the limit price, in the words of Professor Bain, "depends ultimately upon the cost functions which potential entrants expect to have, upon their estimates of the industry demand and of the share of the market which they can capture if they enter, and upon their view of the degree of competition or collusion which will obtain in the industry after their entry."[24]

DEGREE OF PRODUCT DIVERSITY AND PRODUCT DIFFERENTIATION. "Where the output of each firm is differentiated to the extent that it is

[23]Bain, "Price Leaders, Barometers, and Kinks," p. 225.
[24]*Ibid.*, p. 226.

only a moderately good substitute for the output of other firms, price leadership, of course, is meaningless."[25] Unless each producer views the output of all other firms as close substitutes to his own, a uniform price policy is highly unlikely, since each firm will view its own conduct as having no repercussions on the other firms. Similarly, if each firm carries several secondary lines of products, some of which are related to the principal product, a diversity of pricing interests may occur between firms with different output mixes. Furthermore, the marginal cost curves for the firms with regard to a particular product are not likely to be similar unless the manner of allocating common costs among various products is the same for each firm.[26] Finally, the minor firms in an industry may be insulated from the actions of the dominant firm price leader to the extent that their secondary product lines are able to furnish them with a temporary profit cushion for subsidization of the principal product.

ELASTICITY OF DEMAND. Both the elasticity of the demand curve for the firm and the demand curve for the industry are relevant in appraising the potential effectiveness of price leadership. Price leadership is more likely to be competitive rather than monopolistic if the elasticity of the industry demand curve greatly exceeds unity (highly elastic), and the demand curve for some firms is more elastic than the above industry demand curve. "If demand for the output of the industry is elastic because the oligopoly is only a segment of a larger monopolistically competitive market, the prices of closely competing products severely limit or possibly even eliminate the gains to be derived from adopting a price leader. Moreover, if demand for the output of the oligopoly is highly elastic, firms are not likely to adhere to the price leader's price if to do so would result in substantially less than capacity operations, since each firm could still stimulate its own sales considerably by lowering its price, even though all other firms met the new price."[27]

A highly elastic industry demand curve indicates the existence of near-substitutes for the given product which are able to set an upper limit beyond which price leadership cannot carry price. Although this condition is conducive to competitive rather than monopolistic price leadership, it is still possible that price leadership may be able to raise price to the point where near-substitutes prevent further price increases; yet, in the absence of price leadership, prices may be far lower.[28]

[25]Markham, "The Nature and Significance of Price Leadership," p. 186.

[26]Lanzillotti, "Competitive Price Leadership," p. 62.

[27]Markham, "The Nature and Significance of Price Leadership," pp. 186–87.

[28]A. R. Oxenfeldt, "Professor Markham on Price Leadership," *American Economic Review*, Vol. XLII (June, 1952), p. 383.

The Constrained Sales Maximization Model

Professor Baumol has suggested that oligopolists may seek to maximize sales after a minimum level of profits has been achieved.[29] A model of a firm maximizing sales subject to a minimum profit constraint is shown in Fig. 10-12. The firm's sales, or total revenue, are represented by curve TR, and its total costs by curve TC. Point S is the point of maximum sales, and is achieved when the firm sells quantity OQ_s. Point P marks the peak of the total profit curve, and is achieved when the firm sells quantity OQ_p.

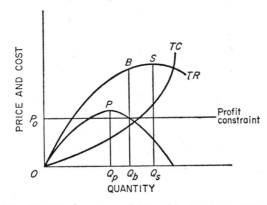

Fig. 10-12. *Constrained Sales Maximization Model*

Professor Baumol argues that an oligopolist will generally select neither the sales-maximizing output level nor the profit-maximizing output level. Rather, the oligopolist will expand sales to an intermediate point, such as OQ_b, where any further expansion of sales will decrease profits below a minimum acceptable level. The latter profit constraint is determined by the need for oligopolists to provide its shareholders with "competitively acceptable earnings," and to retain a sufficient amount of funds for future plant expansion.

In the language of organizational theory, the firm in the Baumol model "satisfices" rather than maximizes its profits.[30] Satisficing consists of

[29]W. J. Baumol, "On the Theory of Oligopoly," *Economica*, New Series, Vol. XXIV (August, 1958), 187–98, and *Business Behavior, Value and Growth.*

[30]The concept of "satisficing" is discussed in H. A. Simon, *Models of Man* (New York: John Wiley & Sons, Inc. 1957) and *Adminsitrative Behavior*, 2nd ed. (New York: The Macmillan Company, 1957). Also see J. Margolis, "The Analysis of the Firm: Rationalism, Conventionalism, and Behaviorism," *Journal of Business*, Vol. XXXI (July, 1958), 187–99; N. W. Chamberlain, *A General Theory of Economic Progress* (New York: Harper & Row, Publishers, 1955); and F. Machlup, "Theories of the Firm: Marginalist, Behavioral, Managerial," *American Economic Review*, Vol. LVII (March, 1967), 1-33.

settling for a course of conduct that is "good enough," *i.e.*, satisfactory although not optimal. Thus, a firm may satisfice for a "fair price," or a "normal profit," or a "competitively acceptable level of earnings."[31]

The rejection of the profit-maximizing goal of the firm raises one of the most important questions in oligopoly theory: What is the goal, or complex of goals, which gives direction to oligopolistic behavior? If the firm is considered a bureaucratic organization with communication problems within its own framework, its actions may be as difficult to predict as the myriad of executive personalities affecting its administration. For example, fear of either a labor strike if men are laid off, or the loss of important distributors may place the expansion of sales over profits as the goal of the firm. On the other hand, the fear of a dissident stockholders' suit may encourage top management to improve its earnings per share through the elimination of unprofitable products.

Some firms may recognize a dependence of future profits on present sales and may seek to maximize long-term profits by extending present sales beyond the maximum level of short-term profits.[32] Other companies, sensitive to their market share positions, may seek to maximize short-term profit subject to the constraint to maintain a minimum percentage of industry sales.[33]

Another interesting question raised in the Baumol model concerns the degree of interdependence in an oligopoly market structure. In contrast to the previous von Stackelberg duopoly models, the oligopolist in the constrained sales maximization model does not fear retaliation by rivals; the firm is free to choose between lower sales at higher prices or higher sales at lower prices.[34] In other words, the oligopolist seeks to exploit his own market by extending his sales subject only to a profit constraint. The interdependence found in most of the earlier duopoly and oligopoly models is therefore rejected.

Professor Baumol maintains that the decision-making apparatus is too clumsy and slow-moving in most large departmentalized organizations for

[31]J. W. McGuire, *Theories of Business Behavior* (Englewood Cliffs, N. J.: Prentice-Hall, Inc., 1964), p. 182.

[32]D. K. Osborne, "The Goals of the Firm," *Quarterly Journal of Economics*, Vol. LXXVIII (November, 1964), 592–603. Cf. F. M. Fisher, Comment on "The Goals of the Firm," *Quarterly Journal of Economics*, Vol. LXXIX (August, 1965), 500–503; and Reply by Osborne, *ibid.*, p. 504.

[33]This situation, labeled as one of "constrained profit maximization," should be contrasted to the model of "constrained sales maximization." See F. M. Fisher, "Review of Professor Baumol's *Business Behavior, Value and Growth*," *Journal of Political Economy*, Vol. LXVIII (June, 1960), 314–15 and Comment on "The Goals of the Firm," as cited in the preceding footnote; and J. Williamson, "Profit Growth and Sales Maximization," *Economica*, Vol. XXXIII (February, 1966), 1-16.

[34]P. W. S. Andrews, *On Competition in Economic Theory* (London: Macmillan & Co. Ltd., 1964), p. 50.

the effective interplay of strategy and counter-strategy among oligopolists.[35] However, where communication has been highly developed in companies and market structures, such as in a number of basic industries with administered price structures, the competitive reactions of firms to price changes may be swift — often a matter of one or two days. The important point is that the degree of interdependence as well as the extent of independent rivalry depends upon the organization within firms as well as among firms.[36]

The Kinky Demand Curve Model

The kinky demand curve model is not directly concerned with the determination of output and price under conditions of price leadership; rather, the model is utilized by those who seek to justify the apparent rigidity of oligopoly prices. In other words, the model may reveal why oligopoly prices remain where they are, but it does not explain how the prices got to their present level.

Professor Sweezy describes the kinky oligopoly demand curve model as follows:

If producer A raises his price, his rival producer B will acquire new customers. If, on the other hand, A lowers his price, B will lose customers. Ordinarily the reaction to a gain in business is a pleasurable feeling calling for no particular action; the reaction to a loss in business, however, is likely to be some viewing with alarm accompanied by measures designed to recoup the loss. If the cause of the loss is obviously a rival's price cut, the natural retaliation is a similar cut. From the point of any particular producer this means simply that if he raises his price he must expect to lose business to his rivals (his demand curve tends to be elastic going up), while if he cuts his price he has no reason to believe he will succeed in taking business away from his rivals (his demand curve tends to be inelastic going down). In other words, the imagined demand curve has a "corner" at the current price.[37]

[35]*Business Behavior, Value and Growth*, p. 28. For a discussion of managerial models of the firm, see R. Marris, "A Model of the 'Managerial' Enterprise," *Quarterly Journal of Economics*, Vol. LXXVII (May, 1963), 185–209; and O. E. Williamson, *The Economics of Discretionary Behavior* (Englewood Cliffs, N.J.: Prentice-Hall, Inc., 1964), Chap. 1–4.

[36]See A. Phillips, *Market Structure, Organization and Performance* (Cambridge, Mass.: Harvard University Press, 1962); O. E. Williamson, "A Dynamic Theory of Interfirm Behavior," *Quarterly Journal of Economics*, Vol. LXXIX (November, 1965), 579–607; R. M. Cyert and R. G. March, *A Behavioral Theory of the Firm* (Englewood Cliffs, N.J.: Prentice-Hall, Inc., 1963); and G. J. Stigler, "A Theory of Oligopoly," *Journal of Political Economy*, Vol. LXXII (February, 1964), 44–61.

[37]P. M. Sweezy, "Demand Under Conditions of Oligopoly," *Journal of Political Economy*, Vol. XLVII (August, 1939), 568–73; reprinted in American Economic Association, *Readings in Price Theory*, pp. 404–9. Also see R. L. Hall and C. J. Hitch, "Price Theory and Business Behavior," *Oxford Economic Papers*, No. 2 (May, 1939), pp. 12–46; J. J. Spengler, "Kinked Demand Curves: By Whom First Used?," *Southern Journal of Economics*, Vol. XXXII (July, 1965), 81–84; and F. Machlup, "Marginal Analysis and Empirical Research," *American Economic Review*, Vol. XXXVI (1946), 519–54.

Professor Sweezy concludes that there is little incentive for a firm in this market setting to change its price from the level at which the kink or "corner" in its demand curve exists. In Fig. 10-13 an oligopolist has a demand curve dKD' with a kink at point K.

The derivation of the kinky demand curve is related to the construction of the Rothschild monopoly index (Fig. 8-2 in Chapter 8). In the discussion of the Rothschild index it was observed that a firm in an oligopoly market structure can be treated as facing two types of demand curves. The first is the "genus" demand curve (DD'), which describes the demand facing the firm if all other firms in an industry match its price changes. The second, called the "species" demand curve (dd'), describes the demand facing a firm under the assumption that its rivals hold their prices constant after the firm changes its price. In Fig. 10-13 the "genus" demand curve

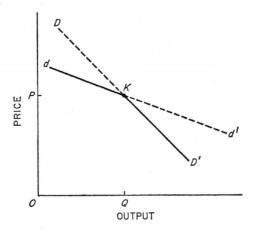

Fig. 10-13. *The Kinky Demand Curve*

(DD') is applicable to downward price changes from price OP, *i.e.*, line segment KD'. But the "species" demand curve (dd'), where the prices of competitors are assumed to be constant, is applicable to price increases from price OP, *i.e.*, line segment Kd. Under these assumptions, there is little incentive for the firm to change its price.

The marginal revenue curve has a discontinuity directly beneath the point where the demand curve in Fig. 10-14 has a kink. If the marginal cost curve passes through this gap in the marginal revenue curve, several interesting theoretical results can occur. First of all, the conditions for short-run equilibrium become ambiguous. The condition that marginal revenue equal marginal cost cannot be applied, since marginal revenue is not determinate at output OQ. All one can know at this output level is that marginal cost is not greater than marginal revenue; it can be the same

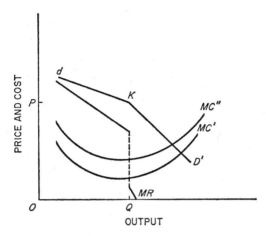

Fig. 10-14. *The Kinky Demand Curve and Changes in Marginal Costs*

or less. Second, any change in the marginal cost curve, such as a shift from MC' to MC'' in Fig. 10-14, will have no effect on either the profit-maximizing price or output so long as this curve passes through the gap in the marginal revenue curve.

THE KINKY DEMAND CURVE AND THE BUSINESS CYCLE. It is possible that the Sweezy proposition, that rivals of an oligopolist will not follow a price rise but will follow a price reduction, is limited to periods of slack demand and excess capacity. A firm in this situation will have decreasing short-run average costs and will be eager for sales. Consequently, the firm can be expected to prefer increased volume to higher prices. "The belief that rivals are operating at less than optimum scale and are therefore so hungry for orders that they will not raise prices, even when costs rise or demand increases, is the very signum of depression."[38] Rivals operating at excess capacity also tend to be highly fearful of reduced sales from a competitor's price cut, and can reasonably be expected to follow any downward price cut by a fellow oligopolist.

In a period of inflationary demand, however, the cost position of the firm reverses itself. As the firm approaches its capacity point, each addition in the level of output increases the firm's short-run average costs. Therefore, a firm facing an abundance of orders, many of which it may be unable to fulfill, is likely to follow a price rise made by a rival firm, but will be reluctant to follow a price reduction which would simply induce further

[38]C. W. Efroymson, "A Note on Kinked Demand Curves," *American Economic Review* Vol. XXXIII (March, 1943), 103.

volume. In short, in periods of inflationary demand the firm prefers a higher price to increased volume, and can generally be expected to follow a price rise.

Professor Lange states: "An increase in the demand for the products of the firms as a rule strengthens the 'discipline' of the oligopolistic group and leads to higher markups. For, when the market is expanding, firms need have little fear that they will get out of step with the rest of the group by increasing their prices. Each such action is likely to be followed by similar actions of other members of the group."[39] Professor Cyert, in contrast, departs from the belief in greater price discipline during periods of prosperity and rising demand. In an empirical study of three oligopolistic industries (cigarettes, automobiles, and potash), Cyert concludes that oligopoly price behavior is independent of the business cycle; the behavior patterns of the oligopolists were found to be no different in the upswing than they were in the downswing.[40]

The geometric implications of the above inflationary kinky demand curve, where the oligopolists are willing to follow a price rise but are reluctant to go along with a price reduction, are unusual.[41] First, the wings or line segments of the kinky demand curve in Fig. 10-14 change from an obtuse angle to a reflex angle, as shown in Fig. 10-15. The dashed line segments from the two types of demand curves facing the oligopolist in Fig. 10-13, which were ignored in the kinky demand curve, are now utilized to form the inflationary kinky demand curve. A marginal cost curve which passes through the gap in the marginal revenue curve intersects the marginal revenue curve both to the left and right of the discontinuity. Finally, the profit-maximizing output of the firm will not be directly below the kink in the demand curve. In Fig. 10-15 area A represents the loss in total revenue involved in moving from output OQ' to OQ (a range in which MC exceeds MR). Area B represents the gain in total revenue in moving from output OQ to OQ'' (a range in which MR exceeds MC). The firm will not produce at output OQ, since it has assumed a loss equivalent to area A and has denied itself a much larger gain, as drawn in Fig. 10-15, equivalent to area B.[42] If it is assumed that a condition of inflation exists, there will be an upward pressure on marginal costs. If this cost push is greater than the increase in demand for the firm's

[39]O. Lange, *Price Flexibility and Employment* (Bloomington, Ind.: Principia Press, 1944), p. 41.

[40]R. M. Cyert, "Oligopoly Behavior and the Business Cycle," *Journal of Political Economy*, Vol. LXIII (1955), 41–51.

[41]C. W. Efroymson, "The Kinked Demand Curve Reconsidered," *Quarterly Journal of Economics*, Vol. LXIX (February, 1955), 119–36. Also see M. Bronfenbrenner, "Applications of the Discontinuous Oligopoly Demand Curve," *Journal of Political Economy*, Vol. XLVIII (June, 1940), 420–27.

[42]Efroymson, "A Note on Kinked Demand Curves," p. 106.

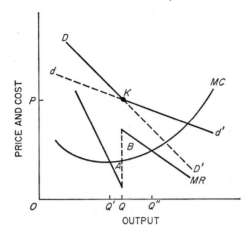

Fig. 10-15. *The Inflationary Kinky Demand Curve*

product, the marginal cost curve will tend to shift upwards more than the marginal revenue curve. Consequently, area *B* will become smaller than area *A*, and the profit-maximizing output of the firm will be reduced from *OQ″* to *OQ′*.

EMPIRICAL VERIFICATION OF THE KINK. Professor Stigler, after an analysis of seven oligopolies (cigarettes, automobiles, anthracite coal, steel, potash, dynamite, and gasoline) in the period 1929-37, concluded that "the empirical evidence reveals neither price experiences that would lead oligopolists to believe in the existence of a kink nor the pattern of changes of price quotations that the theory leads us to expect."[43] He finds for the seven oligopolies, "that price increases are more nearly simultaneous than price decreases — the opposite of the kinky demand curve assumption."

The Stigler test for verifying empirically the kink in the oligopoly demand curve was criticized by Professor Efroymson: "Stigler here seems to imply that 'belief' in the kinked demand curve, and even its existence (as a basis of entrepreneurial decision) depend on continuing or repeated corroboration by (unhappy) experiences of the conjectures which it describes. . . . But the fact that in these cases, oligopolistic demand curves were proven, as it were by the events, to be unkinked does not mean that they are never or only infrequently kinked. It appears, merely, that the oligopolists raised prices when they had reason to believe that rivals would follow."[45]

[43]"A Theory of Oligopoly," p. 435.

[44]*Ibid.*, p. 427.

[45]"The Kinked Demand Curve Reconsidered," pp. 122–24. The subsequent two paragraphs summarize a number of points made in this article.

During periods of prosperity or inflation the oligopolists in an industry may be eager to increase price. A price leader in such an industry may know with confidence that if it increases its price, the other firms will follow, if not simultaneously, at least promptly thereafter. The price leader is unlikely to encounter a kink in its demand curve where the prices of its competitors move together with its own. Under entirely different market conditions, such as a period of slack demand, the price leader is apt to encounter a kink in its demand curve if it initiates a price rise. Any upward price revision would leave the leader in the disadvantageous position of being the firm with the highest price in its field. Under these conditions the leader would be forced to retreat and return to the going market price being maintained by the remaining firms.

A leader which is forced to withdraw a recently attempted price increase has made an error in initiating a price move. The leader believed erroneously that its price increase would stick for the industry. If the leader correctly knew that there was a kink in its demand curve, and no one would follow, it would not have attempted a price rise. Only when the leader does *not* believe there is a kink in its demand curve, but is wrong, and must make a price retreat, will evidence of a kinky demand curve occur.

Price Leadership and Administered Prices

A price leader may maintain a stable price for an industry during a period of time in which short run changes in demand and supply conditions are occurring. The price leader and other oligopolists in this setting adjust to the changes in market conditions not by lowering or raising prices but by altering their level of output and employment. The term "administered prices" has been used to characterize these prices, as well as other price structures where sellers have a range of discretion in setting prices.[46]

[46]The more recent literature on administered prices includes United States, Senate Subcommittee on Antitrust and Monopoly of the Committee on the Judiciary, *Administered Prices: A Compendium on Public Policy*, 88th Cong., 1st Sess.; R. Ruggles, "The Nature of Price Flexibility and the Determinants of Relative Price Changes in the Economy," *Business Concentration and Price Policy*, Universities-National Bureau Committee for Economic Research (Princeton, N.J.: Princeton University Press, 1955), pp. 441–95; Kaplan, Dirlam, and Lanzillotti, *Pricing in Big Business*; J. K. Galbraith, "Market Structure and Stabilization Policy," *Review of Economics and Statistics*, Vol. XXXIX (May, 1957), 124–33; M. A. Adelman, "Steel, Administered Prices and Inflation," *Quarterly Journal of Economics*, Vol. LXXV (February, 1961), 16–40; H. J. Depodwin and R. T. Selden, "Business Pricing Policies and Inflation," *Journal of Political Economy*, Vol. LXXI (April, 1963), 477–88; R. B. Heflebower, "Do Administered Prices Involve an Antitrust Problem?," *Northwestern University Law Review*, Vol. LVII (May-June, 1962), 189–94, and "Parallelism and Administered Prices," in *Perspectives*

Since a high proportion of manufacturing industries, and virtually all trade and service industries, offer a seller an opportunity to choose among alternative price policies, the term "administered prices" can be broadly interpreted. However, a number of economists have employed the term to focus on the price policies of large enterprises in concentrated industries. They have asked: Do industries with high concentration have greater or less price flexibility than industries with low concentration? Do administered prices contribute to inflation in the economy? Do administered prices amplify fluctuations in production and employment during periods of recession and inflation?

Underlying these questions has been a concern by economists with the basic process of price formation. A price leader may not know the precise location of either his own or the industry's demand curve. Consequently, a price leader may have to grope and move in discrete steps in terms of price changes, over a period of years, searching for a profit-maximizing

on *Antitrust Policy*, A. Phillips, ed. pp. 88–116; G. J. Stigler, "Administered Prices and Oligopolistic Inflation," *The Journal of Business*, Vol. XXXV (January, 1962), 1–13.

The extensive Congressional hearings beginning in the late 1950's on administered prices can be found in United States, Senate Subcommittee on Antitrust and Monopoly of the Committee on the Judiciary, *Administered Prices: Steel*, Senate Report No. 1387, 85th Cong., 2nd Sess. (Washington, D.C.: Government Printing Office, 1958); *Administered Prices: Automobiles*, Committee Print, 85th Cong., 2nd Sess. (Washington, D.C.: Government Printing Office, 1958); *Administered Prices: Bread*, Senate Report No. 1923, 86th Cong., 2nd Sess. (Washington, D.C.: Government Printing Office, 1959); and *Administered Prices: Drugs*, Senate Report No. 448, 87th Cong., 1st Sess. (Washington, D.C.: Government Printing Office, 1961).

For the older literature on administered prices see G. C. Means, "Industrial Prices and Their Relative Inflexibility," Sen. Doc. No. 13, 74th Cong., 1st Sess. (Washington, D.C.: Government Printing Office, 1935) and *The Structure of the American Economy*, Part I, "Basic Characteristics," National Resources Committee (Washington, D.C.: Government Printing Office, 1939); S. Nelson and W. G. Keim, *Price Behavior and Price Policy*, Temporary National Economic Committee Monograph No. 1, 76th Cong., 3rd Sess. (Washington, D.C.: Government Printing Office, 1940); W. L. Thorp and W. F. Crowder, "The Structure of Industry," Temporary National Economic Committee Monograph No. 27, *ibid.* (Washington, D.C.: Government Printing Office, 1941); and "Concentration and Product Characteristics as Factors in Price-Quantity Behavior," *American Economic Review*, Vol. XXX (February, 1941), 390–408; A. C. Neal, *Industrial Concentration and Price Inflexibility*, American Council of Public Affairs (Washington, D.C., 1942); J. M. Blair, "Economic Concentration and Depression Price Rigidity," *American Economic Review*, Vol. XLV (May Proceedings, 1955), 566–82; and "Means, Thorp, and Neal on Price Inflexibility," *Review of Economics and Statistics*, Vol. XXXVIII (November, 1956), 427–35; J. Backman, "Economic Concentration and Price Inflexibility," *Review of Economics and Statistics*, Vol. XL (November, 1958), 399–404, "Price Inflexibility — War and Postwar," *Journal of Political Economy*, Vol. LVI (October, 1948), 428–37, and "The Causes of Price Inflexibility," *Quarterly Journal of Economics*, Vol. LIV (May, 1940), 474–89; and E. S. Mason, "Price Inflexibility," *Review of Economics and Statistics*, Vol. XX (May, 1938), 53–64.

position which, in turn, is continually moving. Or the price leader may seek to develop a wider market for the industry's basic product: the less erratic the prices for the products of the industry, the easier it may be for potential customers to plan ahead and compute probable cost economies for new uses of the product. A price leader with these long-run objectives, lasting over periods of economic fluctuations, may also take into account the threat of potential entry, protection and development of the capacity of present members of the industry, the threat of foreign competition, cost changes such as the wage demands of unions, the attainment of a target rate of return on stockholders' equity, the threat of antitrust action, public relations, and the need to build reserves for new products and technical change.

The term "administered prices" cannot explain the reason for a price leader selecting a particular price. Neither can the term, in and of itself, lend insight into whether oligopoly structures have pricing patterns which are consistent with the competitive goals of a free enterprise system. The terminology of administered prices is limited in its usefulness to emphasizing the fact that the formation of most prices does not conform to a theoretical market model of pure competition; that few prices are readily predicted from a particular set of demand and cost conditions; and, finally, that the process of price formation is related to, but not identical with, the process of competing.

CHAPTER ELEVEN

Parallel Business Behavior

The economic models of oligopoly postulated a mutual awareness of each firm to the actions of its rivals. The market and profit position of one oligopolist was dependent upon the price and output policies of its competitors. But the oligopolists in the model were still considered completely *independent* of each other in the sense that there was no actual or tacit agreement among them. The same distinction was made in the early 1930's by Professor Chamberlin: "Each is forced by the situation itself to take into account the policy of his rival in determining his own, and this cannot be construed as a 'tacit agreement' between the two."[1]

Introduction on Proof of Conspiracy

The mutual awareness and often identical movement by oligopolists has not been treated by the courts as a contract or conspiracy in restraint of trade under Sec. 1 of the Sherman Act. For example, in *Theater Enterprises, Inc.* v. *Paramount Film Distributing Corp.*[2] the Supreme Court refused relief in an action for treble damages brought by a suburban theater owner against motion picture producers and distributors for violating the antitrust laws by conspiring to restrict "first run" pictures to downtown Baltimore theaters. Suburban theaters could therefore only exhibit subsequent runs. The Court found that the conduct of the defendants, despite its uniformity, could be adequately explained by *independent*

[1]*The Theory of Monopolistic Competition*, 7th ed., p. 31.
[2]346 U. S. 537 (1954).

111

business justification. The suburban theater owned by the party bringing the action was located in a small shopping center with an audience drawing ability of less then one-tenth of a downtown area. The downtown theaters were found to "offer far greater opportunities for the widespread advertisement and exploitation of newly released features, which is thought necessary to maximize the overall return from subsequent runs as well as first-runs." The *Theater Enterprises* case established that uniform business conduct is not sufficient in and of itself to establish a conspiracy. In the words of the Court,

> But this Court has never held that proof of parallel business behavior conclusively establishes agreement or, phrased differently, that such behavior itself constitutes a Sherman Act offense. Circumstantial evidence of consciously parallel behavior may have made heavy inroads into the traditional judicial attitude toward conspiracy; but "conscious parallelism" has not yet read conspiracy out of the Sherman Act entirely.[3]

Business behavior is admissible as circumstantial evidence from which an agreement may be inferred or a conspiracy implied. For instance, in *Eastern States Retail Lumber Dealers Association* v. *United States*[4] the Supreme Court found a conspiracy in restraint of trade by the concerted actions of a trade association which systematically circulated among its members reports naming wholesalers that sold directly to consumers. Upon receipt of these notices from the trade association, retailers generally refused to do business with the offending wholesalers. The Court noted that "It is elementary . . . that conspiracies are seldom capable of proof by direct testimony and may be inferred from the things actually done. . . ."[5] Similarly, in *Interstate Circuit, Inc.* v. *United States*[6] the Supreme Court found, absent direct testimony of an agreement among eight film distribu-

[3]346 U.S. 573, p. 541. For selected views on consious parallelism, see Heflebower, "Parallelism and Administered Prices," pp. 88–116; United States, *Report of the Attorney General's National Committee to Study the Antitrust Laws*, pp. 36–42, A. Phillips, "Policy Implications of the Theory of Interfirm Organization," *American Economic Review*, Vol. LI (May, 1961), 245–52; R. A. Givens, "Parallel Business Conduct Under the Sherman Act," *Antitrust Bulletin*, Vol. V (May–June, 1960), 273; A. Phillips and G. R. Hall, "The Salk Vaccine Case: Parallelism, Conspiracy and Other Hypotheses," *Virginia Law Review*, Vol. XLVI (1960), 717; M. Conant, "Consciously Parallel Action in Restraint of Trade," *Minnesota Law Review*, Vol. XXXVIII (1954), 794; L. Schwartz, "New Approaches to the Control of Oligopoly," *University of Pennsylvania Law Review*, Vol. CIX (1960), 31; W. H. Nicholls, "The Tobacco Case of 1946," *American Economic Review*, Vol. XXXIX (1949), 284–96; and Markham, "The Nature and Significance of Price Leadership," pp. 891–905.

[4]234 U.S. 600 (1914).

[5]*Ibid.*, p. 612.

[6]306 U.S. 208 (1939).

tors, a conspiracy might be implied by their signing similar contracts with the same theater chain operator. The contracts fixed the admission charges and provided that the movies could not be subsequently run on a double bill. Although there was no evidence that the film distributors spoke or communicated among themselves, each knew that the other distributors were asked to participate. Therefore, the Court concluded:

> Acceptance by competitors, without previous agreement, of an invitation to participate in a plan, the necessary consequence of which, if carried out, is restraint of interstate commerce, is sufficient to establish an unlawful conspiracy under the Sherman Act.[7]

The cases involving implied conspiracy and conscious parallelism demonstrate that in antitrust the means adopted for a course of action are as important as the ends accomplished. Identity of price may be encouraged by the statistical reporting activities of trade associations, by the historic conduct of a price leader initially recognizing changes in market conditions, by direct price fixing schemes or by a resale price maintenance program. From a legal viewpoint, the means by which one arrives at the identity of prices are most important. Mere uniformity of competitors' prices in the sale of a product is not in itself evidence of a violation of the Sherman Act.[8] Proof of an agreement, express or implied, must be shown for the establishment of a conspiracy under the antitrust laws.[9]

Direct Price-fixing Agreements

One of the classic antitrust cases condemning direct price fixing as an unreasonable *per se* restraint of trade under Sec. 1 of the Sherman Act is *United States* v. *Trenton Potteries Co.*[10] The defendants were 23 corporations

---

[7]*Ibid.*, p. 227. Also see *United States* v. *Masonite Corp.*, 316 U.S. 265, 275 (1942); *American Tobacco Co.* v. *United States*, 328 U.S. 781 (1946); *United States* v. *Paramount Pictures, Inc.* 334 U.S. 131 (1948); *Federal Trade Commission* v. *Cement Institute*, 333 U.S. 683 (1948); *National Lead Co.* v. *Federal Trade Commission* 227 F. 2nd 825, 832–34 (7th Cir., 1955), reversed on other ground 352 U.S. 419 (1957).

[8]*Pevely Dairy Co.* v. *United States*, 178 F. 2nd 363 (8th Cir., 1949), *certiorari denied* 339 U.S. 942 (1950). Cf. *C-O-Two Fire Equipment Co.* v. *United States*, 197 F. 2nd 489 (9th Cir., 1952), *certiorari denied* 344 U.S. 892 (1952).

[9]United States, *Report of the Attorney General's National Committee to Study the Antitrust Laws*, p. 39.

[10]273 U.S. 392 (1927). For a discussion of direct price-fixing agreements see G. W. Stocking and M. W. Watkins, *Monopoly and Free Enterprise* (New York: Twentieth Century Fund, 1951), *Cartels or Competition?* (New York: Twentieth Century Fund, 1948), and *Cartels in Action* (New York: Twentieth Century Fund, 1946). Also see Phillips, *Market Structure, Organization and Performance*; and J. Rahl, "Conspiracy and the Antitrust Laws," *Illinois Law Review*, Vol. XLIV (1950), 743.

which manufactured and distributed 82 per cent of the vitreous pottery bathroom fixtures produced in the United States. All the defendants were members of a trade association known as the Sanitary Potters' Association. The defendant did not object to the allegation that they fixed prices, limited sales, and possessed both the economic power to fix prices and to control the market. The only defense raised was that the trial court should have submitted to the jury the question of whether the price-fixing agreements were unreasonable restraints of trade. The Supreme Court held that whether the prices actually agreed upon were reasonable or unreasonable was immaterial; the price-fixing agreements were *per se* unreasonable. In the words of the Court,

> Agreements which create such potential power may well be held to be in themselves unreasonable or unlawful restraints, without the necessity of minute inquiry whether a particular price is reasonable or unreasonable as fixed and without placing on the government in enforcing the Sherman Law the burden of ascertaining from day to day whether it has become unreasonable through the mere variation of economic conditions.[11]

In February 1961, General Electric, Westinghouse, Allis Chalmers, and a number of other electrical equipment producers pleaded guilty to collusive price fixing in violation of Sec. 1 of the Sherman Act.[12] As a result of this illegal price-fixing conspiracy, approximately 2000 treble damage suits were brought against the defendants by companies which had purchased electrical equipment at allegedly higher price levels than would have existed had there been no price-fixing agreements.

In *Ohio Valley Electric Corp.* v. *General Electric Co.*[13] two electric utility companies sued General Electric and Westinghouse under Sec. 4 of the Clayton Act for treble damages amounting to $16 million. The defendants were alleged to have conspired to establish uniform book prices and to keep order prices as close as possible to their published list or "book prices." The utility companies sought to establish the price they would have paid for 11 steam turbines purchased in 1952 if there had not existed a price-fixing conspiracy between the defendants.

---

[11]273 U.S. 392, 398 (1927).

[12]*City of Philadelphia* v. *Westinghouse Electric Corp.*, 210 F. Supp. 483 (E. D. Penn., 1962). See P. Neal and P. Goldberg, "The Electrical Equipment Cases: Novel Judicial Administration," *American Bar Association Journal*, Vol. L (1964), 621–28; and R. A. Smith, "The Incredible Electrical Conspiracy," *Fortune* (April, 1961), p. 132 and (May, 1961), p. 161.

[13]244 F. Supp. 914 (S.D.N.Y., 1965). Also see W. M. Sayre, "Developments in Multiple Treble Damage Act Litigation — Introduction," *N.Y. State Bar Association Antitrust Law Symposium* (New York: Commerce Clearing House, 1966), pp. 46–54; and W. L. Kaapcke, "Proof and Measure of Damages in Antitrust Cases," *ibid.*, pp. 143–68.

The theory of damages advanced by Ohio Valley was a comparison of the actual discount off-book prices received in 1952, amounting to 11 percent, with the substantially larger discounts, amounting to 25 per cent, given by the defendant companies after 1959 when the conspiracy was exposed. The District Court found that the 1952 and postconspiracy discounts off-book prices were comparable, since in both periods defendants considered the book prices as realistic anticipated sales prices.

The equipment manufacturers argued that even if there was a price-fixing conspiracy in 1952 it had no effect on the prices paid by Ohio Valley. The defense introduced in evidence the testimony of two economists to show that a "reconstructed competitive unit price," which was based on extensive calculations of average costs and rates of utilized capacity, was higher at the time of purchase than the price actually paid by Ohio Valley for the steam turbines. The District Court judge noted that an acceptance of the economic testimony as to the "reconstructed competitive unit price" would be tantamount to a finding that "the conspirators were completely wasting their time at these meetings."

The District Court refused to conclude that the conspiracy in the *Ohio Valley* case was ineffective. However, the changes in discount from book prices after 1959 were found to be not entirely a result of the termination of the conspiracy. The District Court found that the postconspiracy period included the presence of foreign competition for the first time, an increase in the manufacturers' capacity to produce steam turbine generators which caused an over-supply, a lessening of ordinary growth in demand, and a drop in manufacturing cost which allowed defendants to offer their products at lower prices. Accordingly, the District Court reduced the claim for damages of Ohio Valley by 30 per cent to take account of changes in the estimated price level that would have prevailed in the absence of the price conspiracy.

Trade Association Price Reporting Plans

Trade associations generally provide their members with industry data or information concerning at least one of the following subjects: sales, production, planned or actual capacity, credit worthiness of individual members, cost accounting, quality standards, innovation, and research developments. Trade association activities which serve to encourage better products, to avoid waste and inefficiency, and to promote better relations with labor, the public, or government are not inimical to the antitrust laws. Such activities do not hamper the independent decision-making functions of members with respect to price policies and levels of production. However, activities of trade associations which tend to fix or raise prices, restrict output, allocate territories or markets, or standardize products with the aim of achieving uniform prices have been found illegal.

In *The Sugar Institute, Inc.* v. *United States*[14] the Supreme Court held illegal under the Sherman Act a trade association price-filing plan which required members to announce their prices publicly in advance of sales, and to adhere to these prices until they publicly announced changes. The fifteen defendant companies, all members of the Sugar Institute, refined practically all imported raw sugar processed in the United States, and supplied approximately 80 per cent of the sugar consumed here. The Institute was formed primarily to stop secret concessions and price discriminations granted by ten so-called "unethical" sugar refiners to principally large buyers. It was estimated that at least 30 per cent of the sugar sold before the Sugar Institute was formed carried secret concessions of some kind. Other secondary purposes for forming the Institute included (1) the supplying exclusively to the fifteen members accurate trade statistics regarding production, deliveries, and stocks on hand, (2) the elimination of wasteful practices, (3) the creation of a credit bureau, and (4) the institution of an advertising program to increase consumption, lagging in part because of a public "slimness campaign."

The Supreme Court found that the sugar industry, before the Institute was organized, was in a "demoralized state which called for remedial measures;" but the steps taken by the sugar refiners were held to have gone too far. Since the formation of the Sugar Institute there were fewer price changes for refined as compared to raw sugar, and the price level for refined sugar remained relatively higher as compared to the price for raw sugar. The Institute brought a "friendly cooperative spirit" to the sugar industry, since each refiner was given the assurance that "he need meet only the prices, terms, and conditions announced by his competitors in advance of sales." The trial court found, and the Supreme Court agreed, that any unfair method of competition caused by the secret concession system could have been prevented by immediate publicity given to the prices and conditions in all closed transactions. The basis of illegality was in the requirement that the defendant trade association members adhere to the publicly announced prices:

> For the question, as we have seen, is not really with respect to the practice of making price announcements in advance of sales, but as to defendants' requirement of adherence to such announcements without the deviations which open and fair competition might require or justify.[15]

The Supreme Court found of paramount importance two facts: (1) the relative industry position of the fifteen defendants, *i.e.*, they refined prac-

[14]297 U.S. 553 (1936).
[15]*Ibid.*, p. 582.

tically all the imported raw sugar processed in the United States, and (2) the standardized product of the defendant. Even though domestic refined sugar competes with beet sugar and imported refined sugar (called "off-shore refined"), the Court found that "the maintenance of fair competition between the defendants themselves in the sale of domestic refined sugar is manifestly of serious public concern." Furthermore, because sugar is a standardized commodity, sold largely on price, there is a "strong tendency to uniformity of price," which, in the words of the Court, "makes it the more important that such opportunities as may exist for fair competition should not be impaired."

In *Tag Manufacturers Institute* v. *Federal Trade Commission*,[16] an action was brought under Sec. 5 of the Federal Trade Commission Act to enjoin as an "unfair method of competition" the publication and filing of price lists and off-list prices made by members of the Tag Manufacturers Institute. The members of the trade association sold approximately 95 per cent of the tag products purchased in the United States. The members agreed to report to the Institute by the close of the next business day any changes in their price lists, as well as the prices, terms, and conditions of each sale of any tag products. The trade association mailed to the members daily bulletins or "pink sheets" recording all off-list transactions. The "pink sheets" showed the name of the seller, description of the tag product, quantity, list price, actual price of the particular off-list transaction, and the state where the customer was located. The name of the buyer was not disclosed.

The Court of Appeals found that (1) approximately 80 per cent of the business was custom made-to-order tags, with an almost unlimited variety of features; (2) only past prices were submitted to the Institute; (3) the published reports of the Institute could be subscribed to by interested purchasers of tag products and were also available for public inspection in the New York City office of the Institute; (4) no actual or implied agreement existed among members to adhere to the prices submitted to the Institute, and most importantly, (5) approximately 25 per cent of the dollar volume of the aggregate total sales of all subscribing manufacturers had been at off-list prices. Upon these findings, the Court of Appeals held that the reporting activities of the Institute did not constitute an "unfair method of competition."[17]

---

[16]174 F. 2nd 452 (1st Cir., 1949).

[17]For further discussion of the antitrust implications of trade association activities, see Symposium on Trade Associations, "Codes of Ethics and the Antitrust Laws," *American Bar Association Antitrust Section*, Vol. XXVII (April, 1965), 163–79; G. P. Lamb and S. S. Kittelle, *Trade Association Law and Practice*, Trade Regulation Series, S. Chesterfield Oppenheim, ed.; C. A. Pearce, *Trade Association Survey*, Temporary National Economic Committee Monograph No. 18 (Washington, D.C.: Government

Resale Price Maintenance

Resale price maintenance describes a contractual arrangement between manufacturers, wholesalers, or other suppliers, and retailers whereby the latter agree to resell a product at not less than a minimum or at a fixed price.[18] The general purpose of these contracts is to prevent retailers from price-cutting a branded product.

Without the sanction of special legislation, "fair trade" laws, a manufacturer or other supplier could not legally approach his customers and contract with each of them to maintain a fixed or minimum price. Each retailer in this situation could be expected to know that his participation in the agreement was dependent on the participation of other competing retailers selling the manufacturer's product. This type of action would be condemned as an implied conspiracy to fix prices.[19]

STATE FAIR TRADE LEGISLATION. In 1931 California passed the first state fair trade law which exempted from the *state* antitrust statutes resale price maintenance agreements. The California fair trade law required both

Printing Office, 1941); Oppenheim, *Federal Antitrust Laws* pp. 131–80; G. W. Stocking, "The Rule of Reason, Workable Competition, and The Legality of Trade Association Activities," *University of Chicago Law Review*, Vol. XXI (1954), 527–619; and Stocking and Watkins, *Monopoly and Free Enterprise*, pp. 231–55.

[18]See generally, United States, Federal Trade Commission, *Resale Price Maintenance* (Washington, D.C.: Government Printing Office, 1945); United States, Select Committee on Small Business of the House of Representatives, *Fair Trade: The Problem and the Issues* (82nd Cong., 2nd Sess., House Report No. 1292, 1952); United States, *Report of the Attorney General's National Committee to Study the Antitrust Laws*, pp. 149–55; E. T. Grether, *Price Control under Fair Trade Legislation* (New York: Oxford University Press, 1939); C. Wilcox, *Public Policies Toward Business*, rev. ed. (Homewood, Ill.: Richard D. Irwin, Inc., 1960), pp. 378–90; R. S. Alexander and R. M. Hill, "What to Do about the Discount House," *Harvard Business Review*, Vol. XXXIII (1955), 53–65; G. E. Weston, "Fair Trade, Alias Quality Stabilization: Status, Problems and Prospects," *American Bar Association Antitrust Section*, Vol. XXII (April, 1963), 76–105; S. C. Oppenheim, *Unfair Trade Practices*, 2nd ed. (St. Paul, Minn.: West Publishing Company, 1965), Chap. 7, pp. 405–43; C. H. Fulda, "Resale Price Maintenance in the United States,"*University of Chicago Law Review*, Vol. XXI (1954), 175–211; W. Bowman, "The Prerequisites and Effects of Resale Price Maintenance," *ibid.*, Vol. XXII (1955), 825, and "Resale Price Maintenance — A Monopoly Problem" *University of Chicago Journal of Business*, Vol. XXV (1952) 141–55; W. Adams, "Resale Price Maintenance: Fact and Fancy," *Yale Law Journal*, Vol. LXIV (1955), 967–90, and "Fair Trade and the Art of Prestidigitation," *ibid.*, Vol. LXV (1955), 199–207; J. Rahl, "The Case Against Fair Trade," *Illinois Bar Journal, Vol.* XLIV (1956), 754; and B. S. Yamey, "The Origins of Resale Price Maintenance," *Economic Journal*, Vol. LXII (1952), 522–45; and P. W. S. Andrews and F. A. Friday, *Fair Trade: Resale Price Maintenance Re-examined* (London: Macmillan & Co. Ltd., 1964).

[19]See the discussion of the *Interstate Circuit* case, pp. 112-13.

parties to the contract to be located within the state boundaries. Since the vast majority of branded goods have manufacturers and retailers located in different states, the breadth of coverage of the law was not extensive. Furthermore, retailers not signing resale price maintenance contracts with their suppliers were able to engage in price cutting to the detriment of those retailers who did sign contracts.

In 1933 California adopted a "nonsigners" clause, which provided that once a supplier or manufacturer makes a resale price contract with *one* retailer, it is illegal for any other retailer knowingly to undercut the price specified in the contract. Thus, the nonsigners clause permits a manufacturer to introduce a resale price maintenance system in his state by making a contract with one retailer and serving notice on all other retailers carrying his product in the state. The California fair trade law, including the nonsigners clause, became a model which was followed by most other states.[20]

Federal sanction of fair trade contracts for branded goods in *interstate* commerce was provided by the Miller-Tydings Act of 1937. The act exempted interstate resale price maintenance contracts from Sec. 1 of the Sherman Act. Two conditions had to be met to qualify under the terms of the Miller-Tydings Act: (1) the products covered by the resale price contract had to be branded and in free and open competition with goods of the same general class produced or distributed by others, and (2) the laws of the state or states concerned had to sanction resale price maintenance.

The Miller-Tydings Act is enabling legislation which permits states to follow or reject a policy of resale price maintenance. After the passage of this Act, all but a few states promptly adopted fair trade laws. The only states which did not have fair trade laws in 1966 were Alaska, Kansas, Missouri, Nebraska, Nevada, Texas, and Vermont. The District of Columbia also did not have a fair trade law.[21]

In 1951 the Supreme Court ruled in the *Schwegmann* case[22] that the nonsigners clause had not been legalized by the Miller-Tydings Act and, therefore, interstate resale price maintenance contracts could not be enforced against nonsigners. To remedy this situation Congress passed in 1952 the McGuire Act, amending Sec. 5 of the Federal Trade Commission Act. The McGuire Act provides that nonsigner clauses authorized by state laws are

---

[20]In *Old Dearborn Distributing Co.* v. *Seagram Distillers Corp.*, 299 U.S. 183 (1936), the Supreme Court held the nonsigners clause in the fair trade law of Illinois, which had been copied after the California nonsigners clause, was constitutional.

[21]The nonsigner provision has been repealed in Hawaii, Virgina and Ohio. For recent developments in fair trade laws, see *Trade Regulation Reporter*, Vol. 2 (Chicago: Commerce Clearing House).

[22]*Schwegmann Brothers* v. *Calvert Distillers Corp. and Seagram Distillers Corp.*, 341 U.S. 384.

not in violation of federal antitrust statutes where the resale price maintenance contracts cover branded goods in interstate commerce.

In 1957 the Supreme Court in *General Electric Co.* v. *Masters Mail Order
Co.*[23] denied review of a lower court holding that mail order sales from the
District of Columbia, which does not have a fair trade law, to customers in
New York State at prices below those fixed by resale price agreements did
not violate the New York State fair trade laws. The lower court reasoned
that the sales were made, or title passed, in the District of Columbia and
not in New York. As a consequence of this decision, General Electric and
a number of other manufacturers had to abandon resale price maintenance
on smaller household appliances which had low freight costs and could be
shipped economically from non-fair trade states.

RIGHT OF REFUSAL TO DEAL. Both before and after the enactment of
federal and state legislation permitting resale price maintenance, the
courts recognized the right of a supplier to select his own customers. Furthermore, a supplier or manufacturer has always been permitted individually to refuse to supply those of his customers who cut suggested resale prices.
But this right has been closely scrutinized by the courts.

In *United States* v. *Colgate & Co.*[24] a manufacturer specified resale prices
for its products and followed a policy of refusing to sell to any dealer who
failed to maintain them. The Supreme Court found that the Colgate
policy was permissible and did not violate Sec. 1 of the Sherman Act. In
the words of the Court,

> In the absence of any purpose to create or maintain a monopoly, the act does not
> restrict the long recognized right of trader or manufacturer engaged in an entirely
> private business, freely to exercise his own independent discretion as to parties with
> whom he will deal; and of course, he may announce in advance the circumstances
> under which he will refuse to sell.[25]

The narrowness of the Colgate doctrine was more clearly defined in
Federal Trade Commission v. *Beech Nut Packing Co.*[26] Beech-Nut had
adopted a policy of refusing to deal with wholesalers or retailers who would
not adhere to a schedule of resale prices; it also refused to deal with wholesalers who in turn sold to retailers not adhering to the suggested resale
prices. Beech-Nut utilized a system of key numbers or symbols stamped on
cases containing the "Beech-Nut" brand products, which enabled its salesmen and special agents to ascertain the identity of distributors from whom

[23]244 F. 2nd 681 (2nd Cir., 1957), *cert. denied* 355 U.S. 824.
[24]250 U.S. 300 (1919).
[25]*Ibid.*, p. 307.
[26]257 U.S. 441 (1921).

the price cutters received their products. Beech-Nut also circulated a blacklist of distributors who were found to have sold below the suggested resale prices. These cards bore the following headings: "Undesirable — Price Cutters," and "Do Not Sell." When an offender was cut off, he would be reinstated as a customer by giving assurances to Beech-Nut that he would maintain prices in the future. The Court found that the *cooperative* enforcement policy, such as the blacklists for reporting price cutters, went beyond the unilateral policy found in the *Colgate* case, and constituted an "implied agreement." The Supreme Court held that the Beech-Nut resale price maintenance system was contrary to Sec. 1 of the Sherman Act and, therefore, constituted an "unfair method of competition" under Sec. 5 of the Federal Trade Commission Act which was the basis of the action.

In 1960 the Colgate doctrine was again brought under the scrutiny of the Supreme Court. In *United States* v. *Parke, Davis and Co.*[27] a resale price maintenance system was held illegal on the grounds that the company policy of cutting off wholesalers who sold to price-cutting retailers was an attempt to use wholesalers as a lever to gain the acquiescence of retailers in the price program. In the words of the Court,

Although Parke Davis' originally announced wholesalers' policy would not under Colgate have violated the Sherman Act if its action thereunder was the simple refusal to deal with wholesalers who did not observe the wholesalers' Net Price Selling Schedule, that entire policy was tainted . . . when Parke Davis used it as the vehicle to gain the wholesalers' participation in the program to effectuate the retailers' adherence to the suggested retail prices.[28]

There was also evidence that Parke, Davis had individual discussions with a number of larger retailers in Washington, D.C. and Virginia who had been cutting prices of the products of Parke, Davis. In other words, Parke, Davis was able to gain adherence to a resale price policy only by actively bringing about substantial unanimity and assurances from the companies primarily responsible for the price wars. In a strongly written dissent, Justice Harlan found no evidence of an agreement or understanding of any kind between Parke, Davis and its distributors, nor any evidence of coercion. Furthermore, Justice Harlan was of the opinion that the majority had "done no less than send to its demise the *Colgate* doctrine."

*   *   *

A common theme which runs throughout the literature on price fixing, trade associations, and resale price maintenance is the protection of firms from ruinous price competition. In the early *Trans-Missouri Freight Assn.*

[27]362 U.S. 29.
[28]*Ibid.*, p. 46.

(1896) case,[29] the railroad companies argued that the purpose of their association was to maintain reasonable rates and without some such agreement "the competition between them for traffic would be so severe as to cause great losses to each defendant and possibly ruin the companies in the agreement." More recently, in the *General Electric-Westinghouse* case,[30] the defendants stated that a major purpose of their price conspiracy was to keep the smaller electrical equipment manufacturers in business. Their belief was not unfounded; after the conspiracy was revealed to the public several of the lesser-sized companies withdrew from the heavy electrical equipment industry. For example, in the *Ohio Valley* case,[31] it was noted that Allis-Chalmers ceased manufacturing electrical steam turbines after the price conspiracy was exposed. One of the ironic aspects of the General Electric-Westinghouse price-fixing cases was "that men in the larger companies believed they had to protect the position of the smaller companies or run the risk of antitrust prosecution."[32] The executives may have been in error in their belief, but their viewpoint exemplifies the strong theme of protectionism in the price-fixing cases.

The leading proponents for fair trade laws have been independent retailer associations such as the National Association of Retail Druggists. Smaller retailers have maintained that their businesses cannot survive if they have to match the loss-leader and other lower prices of large discount houses and chain stores, which have cost advantages in mass purchasing and distribution. The public is benefited, argue the retail associations, by having many neighboring stores with personal service. Price competition is ended, but it is replaced by more energetic sales efforts and service. However, it is unclear why the public should not be allowed to make the choice between buying in stores with low prices, modest decor, self-service, and a minimum of assistance by salesmen, or in stores with higher prices and superior services.

A related argument raised in the discussion of resale price maintenance is that price cutting and the use of loss leaders by retailers will undermine a premium price image of a product. Discount stores will fail to provide the necessary service and maintenance to appliances sold in their stores and, thereby, will injure the goodwill and confidence which consumers formerly had in the manufacturers' products.

Both of these arguments will be explored in the discussion of tying arrangements, where the loss leader will be seen not in isolation, but as part of

---

[29]*United States* v. *Trans-Missouri Freight Assn.*, 166 U.S. 290.

[30]See footnote 12.

[31]See footnote 13.

[32]*Wall Street Journal*, January 10, 12, 1962. Reprinted in *Monopoly Power and Economic Performance*, p. 81.

the over-all multiple product competition engaged in by retailers. If a product was always sold as a loss leader, or did not have a brand name, it would be ineffective in attracting customers into a store. In general, the temporary nature of a particular loss leader used by a retail store results in different products being selected continually as the promotional attraction of a store. The prices and volume of branded goods used sporadically as loss leaders are in flux. This instability in retailing is removed, or at least dampened, when all stores in a state charge the same fair trade price for a branded good.

If competition among retailers is viewed in terms of multiple product dimensions, a retailer using a loss leader can be seen as following a policy whereby a loss or unduly low profit margin on one item is expected to be more than compensated by additional sales of other goods which are purchased by customers attracted into a store. The need for service in a store or for the repair of a product can also be seen in terms of multiple product analysis. A consumer may choose either a tying arrangement of an appliance with guaranteed prompt service and repair, or a less costly appliance with the burden of finding a reliable independent repair shop for service.

Finally, the interests of the general public in having strong price competition should be contrasted to the interests of manufacturers and retailers in being secure from the ravages of ruinous price competition. In avoiding the latter catastrophic forms of competition, resale price maintenance and collusive arrangements such as price fixing prevent "injury to competitors" but, in the opinion of many observers of antitrust policy, at the high cost of "injury to competition."[33]

[33]See footnote 18.

SECTION D

Concentration

CHAPTER TWELVE

Relative Concentration
In Antitrust Law

Economic concentration of business firms within various industries can be measured by different types of indexes.[1] Absolute measures of concentration refer to the percentages of assets, employees, or value of shipments accounted for by a given number of leading firms in an industry. Relative measures of concentration, which are less frequently employed, consider the size of competitors in relationship to each other. An industry with sales fairly evenly divided among a few firms may simultaneously possess a high degree of absolute concentration but a low degree of relative concentration. For example, an industry including four firms each with 25 per cent of total sales has a high degree of absolute concentration since the top three firms account for 75 per cent of sales, but the relative concentration in this industry is nil since each competitor is equal in size as measured by their respective sales.

The use of the concept of relative concentration is increasingly being resorted to as a judicial economic tool for appraising market structures in antitrust settings. Relative concentration, which requires a focus on the inequality of sizes of firms in an industry, can be related to concepts of competition which emphasize the potential power struggle between different sized firms. As an analytical tool, relative concentration measures can be applied as usefully as the more conventional measures of absolute concentration.

---

[1]This chapter is taken primarily from my article entitled, "The Concept of Relative Concentration in Antitrust Law," *American Bar Association Journal*, Vol. LII (March, 1966), 246–50.

The Manufacturers Hanover Case (1965)

The District Court decision in *United States* v. *Manufacturers Hanover Trust Co.*[2] marked a high point in the development of the concept of relative concentration. The case involved the merger of two New York City banks, Manufacturers Trust and the Hanover Bank, into the Manufacturers Hanover Trust Company. Before the merger, Hanover was primarily a wholesale bank, generating most of its business from the deposits and loans of large corporate customers. Manufacturers, on the other hand, had a tradition of retail banking, emphasizing service to smaller individual customers. At the time of the merger, eight of the New York City banks held over $1 billion in assets, five others over a half billion, and eleven others over $100 million.

Measured by deposits before the merger, Manufacturers was fourth largest among 72 commercial banks in the metropolitan area, and sixth largest among the over 13,000 commercial banks in the nation. Hanover ranked eighth in the metropolitan area and fourteenth in the nation. See Table 12–1. The Government claimed this merger eliminated substantial competition between the parties and constituted an unreasonable restraint of trade, in violation of Sec. 1 of the Sherman Act, as well as a reasonable probability of a substantial lessening of competition, in violation of Sec. 7 of the Clayton Act. In March 1965 the District Court ruled in favor of the Government. A year later, Congress passed the 1966 Bank Merger Act, which included a provision terminating the legal proceedings against the merger.[3]

The relative concentration of the local market in the *Manufacturers Hanover* case can be seen in the last two columns of Table 12-1. Before the merger, Chase Manhattan, the largest New York City bank, was more than twice the size of Manufacturers Trust, the fourth ranking bank. However, after the merger, Chase Manhattan was only one and a half times as large as Manufacturers Hanover Trust, which now ranked third. The 9 per cent of Manufacturers Trust combined with the 5 per cent of Hanover gave the new bank 14 per cent of the deposits in the New York metropolitan area, and placed it in the size category of the top two banks, Chase Manhattan and First National City. In terms of relative concentration, the

[2]240 F. Supp. 867 (S.D.N.Y., 1965).

[3]The Bank Merger Act of 1966, enacted as Public Law 89-356, 80 Stat. 7, was an amendment to Sec. 18(c) of the Federal Deposit Insurance Act, 12 U.S.C.A., Sec. 1828(c). Section 2(c) of the Amendment terminated pending antitrust actions involving bank mergers consummated after June 16, 1963. The *Manufacturers Hanover* case was covered by this section.

market structure for the three leading firms changed from (100-88-51) before the merger to (100-88-70) after the merger.

In comparing the relative concentration existing in the metropolitan area before and after the merger, the District Court found that "there can be no question that the merger created a firm with an increased share, but the increment resulted in a bank over one-third to one-half smaller than its two larger local competitors, and only slightly larger than the next three."[4] Therefore, the District Court concluded, the gap previously existing in the market structure between the second and third largest bank was narrowed, and the "merger thereby improved the competitive structure and intensified competition for the three leaders."[5] Nevertheless, the District Court found the merger to be a violation of Section 7 of the Clayton Act.

TABLE 12-1

MARKET STRUCTURE IN THE MANUFACTURERS HANOVER BANK CASE

Pre-Merger Rank	Name of Bank	% N.Y. Deposits	Pre-Merger Absolute Concentration	Pre-Merger Relative Size*	Post-Merger Relative Size*
1	Chase Manhattan	20.0	20.0%	100	100
2	First National City	17.6	37.6	88	88
	(Manufacturers Hanover)	(13.8)	—	—	70
3	Chemical Bank	10.2	47.8	51	51
4	Manufacturers Trust	9.2	57.0	46	—
5	Morgan Guaranty	9.1	66.1	46	46
6	Bankers Trust	7.8	73.9	39	39
7	Irving Trust	5.3	79.2	27	27
8	Hanover	4.6	83.8	23	—
9	Franklin National	1.9	85.7	10	10
10–72	Other banks	14.3			
	Total	100.0			

*Chase Manhattan's 20.0 per cent of deposits in the New York metropolitan area in 1960 is equal to 100.

The Philadelphia Bank Case (1963)

The most immediate comparison with the *Manufacturers Hanover* case is the Supreme Court decision in *United States* v. *Philadelphia National Bank*,[6] which involved the proposed merger of Philadelphia National Bank, hereafter abbreviated PNB, with Girard Trust. As shown in Table 12-2, the

[4]240 F. Supp. 867, 932.

[5]*Ibid.*, p. 933.

[6]374 U.S. 321 (1963).

proposed merger would have combined PNB with 21 per cent of the market and Girard with 15 per cent into a single bank, which would have 36 per cent of the market. The proposed merger would have created a bank considerably larger than even First Pennsylvania, the largest bank in the market before the merger. The new bank, PNB-Girard, would enjoy "better than a 50 per cent advantage in market share over its nearest rival. Moreover, if the merger was consummated significant disparities would separate each bank except two from its closer smaller competitor thereby upsetting the competitive balance of the market structure."[7] In terms of relative concentration, as shown in Table 12-2, the market structure in the Philadelphia case would change for the three leading firms from (100-96-66) before the merger to (100-62-28) after the merger.

TABLE 12-2

MARKET STRUCTURE IN THE PHILADELPHIA BANK CASE

Pre-merger Rank	Name of Bank	Per Cent Phila. Deposits	Pre-merger Absolute Concentration	Pre-merger Relative Size*	Post-merger Relative Size†
	(PNB-Girard)	(35.8)	—	—	100
1	First Pa.	22.1	22.1%	100	62
2	PNB	21.3	43.4	96	—
3	Girard	14.5	57.9	66	—
4	Provident	9.9	67.8	45	28
5	Fidelity	9.3	77.1	42	26
6–42	37 other banks	22.9			
	Total	100.0			

*First Pa.'s 22.1 per cent of deposits in metropolitan Philadelphia area in 1959 is equal to 100.
†PNB-Girard's combined share of 35.8 per cent is equal to 100.

In the *Manufacturers Hanover* case the defendant could have argued that the proposed merger of the fourth and eighth largest ranking banks would intensify competition against the disproportionately larger top two banks, namely, Chase Manhattan and First National City. However, in the *Philadelphia Bank* case the proposed merger would place the newly formed bank not only first in its market but also in a position one and a half times larger than the next largest bank, First Pennsylvania. Before the merger, the top two banks in Philadelphia were approximately equal in size, but after the merger the top two banks became substantially unequal in size. Thus, the proposed merger could offer no favorable attributes to the competitive balance existing in the Philadelphia area. However, the defense argued that competition would be intensified with the larger New York City banks. The argument was rejected by the Supreme Court:

[7]240 F. Supp. 867, 931 (S.D.N.Y., 1965).

. . . it is suggested that the increased lending limit of the resulting bank will enable it to compete with the large out-of-state bank, particularly, the New York banks, for very large loans. We reject this application of the concept of 'countervailing power.'[8]

A related argument was made that Philadelphia needed a larger bank in order to bring business into the city and stimulate its economic development. The Court rejected also this argument, and stated:

> We are clear, however, that a merger the effect of which "may be substantially to lessen competition" is not saved because, on some ultimate reckoning of social or economic debits and credits, it may be deemed beneficial. A value choice of such magnitude is beyond the ordinary limits of judicial competence . . . .[9]

Finally, the Supreme Court was of the opinion that the merger between the two banks would trigger further mergers among the remaining smaller banks:

> If anticompetitive effects in one market could be justified by procompetitive consequences in another, the logical upshot would be that every firm in an industry could, without violating §7, embark on a series of mergers that would make it in the end as large as the industry leader.[10]

The Bethlehem-Youngstown Case (1958)

A similar position was taken by the District Court in the earlier case of *United States* v. *Bethlehem Steel* Corp.[11] The District Court held that the proposed merger between Bethlehem (No. 2 in the industry) with Youngstown (No. 6 in the industry) "offers an incipient threat of setting into motion a chain reaction of further mergers by the other less powerful companies in the steel industry."[12] See Table 12-3 . If there were logic in the argument that the merger of Bethlehem and Youngstown was justified to offer challenging competition to U.S. Steel (No. 1 in the industry), then, concluded the District Court, "the remaining large producers in the 'Big 12'

---

[8]374 U.S. 321, 370 (1963).

[9]*Ibid.*, p. 371. In contrast, the 1966 Bank Merger Act, Sec. 5(B), provides that the responsible agency shall not approve any proposed merger transaction which shall violate the specified antitrust standards "unless it finds that the anticompetitive effects of the proposed transaction are clearly outweighed in the public interest by the probable effect of the transaction in meeting the convenience and needs of the community to be served."

[10]In December, 1965 the Central-Penn National Bank of Philadelphia and the Provident National Bank of Philadelphia applied to the Comptroller of the Currency for permission to merge. In April, 1966 the Department of Justice filed an action to enjoin the proposed merger. The injunction was upheld by the Supreme Court, 386 U.S. 361 (1967).

[11]168 F. Supp. 576 (S.D.N.Y., 1958).

[12]*Ibid.*, p. 618.

TABLE 12-3
MARKET STRUCTURE IN THE BETHLEHEM YOUNGSTOWN CASE

Pre-Merger Rank	Name of Company	% Ingot Capacity	Pre-Merger Absolute Concentration	Pre-Merger Relative Size*	Post-Merger Relative Size*
1	U.S. Steel	29.7	29.7%	100	100
2	Bethlehem	15.4	45.1	52	—
	(Beth.-Youngstown)	(20.1)	—	—	68
3	Republic	8.3	53.4	28	28
4	Jones & Laughlin	4.9	58.3	17	17
5	Youngstown	4.7	63.0	16	—
6	National	4.6	67.6	15	15
7	Armco	4.5	72.1	15	15
8	Inland	4.1	76.2	14	14
9–24	16 other integrated producers	13.8			
	Total	90.0			

*U.S. Steel's ingot capacity in 1957 of 29.7 per cent of the steel industry equals 100.

could with equal logic urge that they, too, be permitted to join forces and to concentrate their economic resources in order to give more effective competition to the enhanced 'Big 2' ... "[13] The Court in this statement is focusing only upon the upward potential competition resulting from the newly merged larger companies. If the procompetitive effects among the larger companies with respect to the newly merged company were weighed against the potential anticompetitive effects of the large companies vis à vis the lesser-sized companies, all the remaining companies would not necessarily have as a matter of "equal logic" the right to merge.

The Upward Competition Defense

As the structure of an industry moves away from one dominant industry leader with no competitors in its size category, the need for upward competition diminishes and the need for protecting the competitive balance between the larger- and lesser-sized firms is correspondingly enhanced. For example, in the Bethlehem-Youngstown case there was a dominant price leader with 30 per cent of the market and its largest competitor was half its size. In the Manufacturers Hanover case there were two large, leading firms on the top, which were approximately equal in size. Therefore, the need for upward competition was not as great in the Manufacturers Hanover case as it may have been in the Bethlehem-Youngstown case.

[13]Ibid.

The upward competition defense, by its very nature, is double-edged: if two smaller- or medium-sized companies can combine to challenge the power of the larger leading firms, it follows that the new combination will be able to challenge more forcefully any remaining smaller firms in an industry. A second reason why courts have traditionally rejected the upward competition defense is that in most of its applicable structural settings a trend toward oligopoly will be enhanced. Two judicial rules have been enunciated by the Supreme Court in this connection: (1) where concentration is already great, even slight increases must be prevented, and (2) where there is a strong trend toward oligopoly, further tendencies in that direction are to be curbed in their incipiency, whatever the number, or vigor, of remaining competitors.[14]

The Choice Between Oligopolies

The contrast between the polar market conditions of pure competition and pure monopoly has given rise to the proposition, or at least an inference, that as the number of independent firms in a market is reduced competition is lessened. The use of numbers of firms as an index of competition cannot be justified by the fact that as the number of independent sellers reach unity, the market obviously reaches monopoly. Within the spectrum of market structures existing between monopoly and pure competition, the intensity of competition is not always lessened as the number of firms is reduced. A market with six firms may not necessarily be less competitive than a market with seven firms, nor more competitive than a market with five firms.

The Supreme Court has stated that it is common ground among economists that competition is likely to be greatest when there are many sellers, none of which has any significant market share. For support of this thesis in the *Philadelphia Bank* case the Court footnoted references to the discussions by two economists of the model of pure competition.[15] But the Court was not called upon to decide whether a market structure of a large number of small sellers was likely to be more competitive than a market with only a few firms. Rather, the choice involved two oligopoly-type market structures with a difference between them of only one firm, namely, the acquired firm.

The Supreme Court could not stop a "trend toward oligopoly" or a "rising tide of economic concentration." The market structure had reached these advanced stages even before the merger in question occurred. The

[14]*United States* v. *Philadelphia National Bank*, 374 U.S. 321, 365, fn. 42 (1962); and *Brown Shoe Co.* v. *United States*, 370 U.S. 294, 346 (1963).

[15]374 U.S. 321, 363, fn. 39 (1962).

choice was therefore not between unconcentrated or concentrated market structures, nor oligopoly or pure competition, but between two highly concentrated market structures.

In considering the proposed merger between Bethlehem and Youngstown, the District Court had to accept as an unalterable, pre-existing power structure the presence of U.S. Steel as the acknowledged price leader and holder of 30 per cent of the steel industry's ingot capacity. Since U.S. Steel was not a party to the case, the District Court could not directly affect the position of this company. The Court was limited in its choice between the following two market structures: (1) a market in which the largest company was twice the size of the second largest company, and (2) a market in which the largest company was one and a half times the size of the second largest. In either of these market structures the two leading firms accounted for over 45 per cent of the industry capacity.

Merger Versus Internal Growth

The proposed merger in the *Bethlehem-Youngstown* case clearly did not involve two smaller companies, as evidenced by the fact that Bethlehem at the end of 1957 had total assets of $2260 million and Youngstown had total assets of $636 million. Bethlehem, which was located primarily in the East, argued that it needed the ingot facilities of the Youngstown Chicago plant as a prerequisite to building a new plate mill and new structural shape mill in the Chicago area. The District Court recognized that "it is undoubtedly easier and cheaper to acquire and develop existing plant capacity than to build entirely anew." However, each defendant, in urging the merger, took a "dim view of its ability to undertake, on its own, a program to meet the existing and anticipated demand for heavy structural shapes and plates in the Chicago area." The District Court was not convinced that without the merger the companies would not enter the Chicago plate and structural shape market. The following quotation by the District Court showed remarkable foresight: "The defendants' apprehensions, which, of course, involve matters of business judgment and, in a sense, matters of preference, are not persuasive in the light of their prior activities and history, their financial resources, their growth and demonstrated capacity through the years to meet the challenge of a constantly growing economy."[16] Six years after this decision, in 1964, Bethlehem's first of three ingot mills in the Chicago area began operation. On its Burns Harbor site along the Indiana shore of Lake Michigan, Bethlehem undertook at the time the largest private construction project in the world.

[16]168 F. Supp. 576, 616 (S.D.N.Y., 1958).

The competitive implications of Burns Harbor are noteworthy. Bethlehem, by not being able to buy the older and partially outmoded Chicago facilities of Youngstown, built in the late 1960's one of the most efficient steel mills in the country. Bethlehem may have accomplished, even more effectively than by merger, both the potential for vigorous upward competition against U.S. Steel, as well as the ability for strong downward competition against the smaller, less efficient steel producers. The District Court, by finding illegal the proposed merger between Bethlehem and Youngstown, encouraged the independent entry of new capacity in the Chicago area by Bethlehem.

The Balance of Power in Antitrust

The logical development of relative concentration, which considers inequality of firm size in an industry, is a concept of balance of power, which takes the further step of translating disparity in firm size into disparity in market power. By increasing market power among weaker firms, such as by allowing them to merge, a closer balance in the market structure is achieved and competition with the formerly larger rival firms may be intensified.[17] Since the merger of these firms generally results in a higher degree of absolute concentration in an industry, the concept of balance of power in antitrust carries with it the specter of the growth of larger economic power groups.

One aspect of the concept of balance of power in antitrust, which achieved wide publicity over a decade ago, involved the power relationship between suppliers and their respective customers. Professor Galbraith, in *American Capitalism*, maintained that in markets of few sellers, the active restraint in terms of price levels is provided not by competitors, but from the other side of the market by strong buyers. This balance of power between buyers and sellers is referred to as "countervailing power." In situations where the bargaining power between buyers and sellers is substantially unequal it should be incumbent upon the government, he argues, to give countervailing power freedom to develop even though absolute economic concentration will thereby increase. Although Professor Galbraith

[17]In November, 1966 the Justice Department moved for dismissal of a Government antitrust suit against the acquisition by General Telephone & Electronics Corporation of three independent telephone companies. In a Department of Justice *News Release* (November 14, 1966), it was stated that "in view of the unique conditions of this industry, where similar vertical relationships exist among other companies — including a company of vastly greater size — the department determined it would be inappropriate to prosecute its suit against a single company at this time." In 1966 General Telephone had sales and revenues of approximately $2 billion in contrast to American Telephone & Telegraph Co., which had total sales and revenues of approximately $12 billion.

limits his analysis to the power relationship between buyers and sellers, his observation, that the economic power of a group in a market should not be viewed in isolation but in terms of its effect on other related power structures, has a much broader application. The following passage by Galbraith is noteworthy in this respect:

... the mere possession and exercise of market power is not a useful criterion for antitrust action. The further and very practical question must be asked: Against whom and for what purposes is the power being exercised? Unless this question is asked and the answer makes clear that the public is the victim, the antitrust laws . . . can as well enhance as reduce monopoly power.[18]

The seeming paradox of the enforcement of the antitrust laws sometimes increasing, or at least preserving, monopoly power instead of reducing it can be readily understood when market groups are analyzed in terms of interwoven market structures whose balance can be either favorably or unfavorably upset. Leading firms in an industry may have achieved their present positions largely as a result of mergers and a weakly enforced set of antitrust laws. The market positions of these companies are often perpetuated and permanently insulated by an active set of antitrust laws which prevents lesser-sized companies from merging on the grounds that undue concentration already exists. The antitrust laws can therefore be used to reach the anomalous result that protection is afforded to the larger, leading companies, which need it the least, and their market power is preserved, whereas stronger competition from the merger of smaller and middle-sized companies is correspondingly stifled.[19]

The creation of medium-sized economic power groups through the merger of lesser-sized companies may challenge the market power of a dominant firm in the same market and intensify competitive rivalry; or the merger may permit greater equalization of bargaining power between suppliers and

[18]*American Capitalism* (Boston: Houghton Mifflin Company, 1952), p. 149.

[19]A. Fortas, Remarks during a symposium on "Re-evaluation of the Impact of Present-Day Antitrust Policy on the Economy," *American Bar Association Section of Antitrust Law*, Vol. XXIII (August, 1963), 328–29: "Actually, I think that unless government is very careful in what they are doing with respect to mergers, their action is going to be the most important thing that has happened to this country to promote and encourage and insure the domination of the number one companies. . . . It is idle in most of our situations where there is a dominant number one company to talk about growth of the lesser sized companies by a so-called natural process to the point where they can be a real threat to the dominance of the number one company. Because of the dominance of number one, the other companies cannot use price or advertising — or in many cases, even research, to break the position of the top company. The only process by which they can compete with the number one company effectively is the process of merger. I do not say that all such mergers ought to be approved. Some should and some should not, depending upon the specific economic situation."

customers. But the same merger may create a greater hazard to the survival of smaller sized companies; it may trigger more mergers and significantly increase absolute concentration. Antitrust enforcement is therefore presented with a multitude of conflicting power structures between smaller-, medium-, and larger-sized firms on the sellers' side of the market, on the buyers' side of the market, and between buyers and sellers. The courts of law are given the task not only of unraveling these various market structures and identifying the interests of the relatively different-sized members, but of reconciling the aversion of our antitrust lawmakers toward huge economic power groups and their aspiration for the development of a strong productive competitive economy.

CHAPTER THIRTEEN

Concentration Indexes

The most commonly used business concentration indexes consider the percentage of assets, employees, value of shipments, or value added accounted for by a given number of leading firms in an industry.[1] A second type of concentration index, called a "summary measure," covers the distribution of all firms in an industry and is normally related to various

[1]This chapter is taken from my article, "The Structure of Industrial Concentration Indexes," *Antitrust Bulletin*, Vol. X (January–April, 1965), 75–104. See National Resource Committee, *The Structure of the American Economy* (Washington, D.C.: Government Printing Office, 1939); W. L. Thorp and W. F. Crowder, " The Structure of Industry," Part I, Temporary National Economic Committee Monograph No. 27; United States, Federal Trade Commission, *Report on Changes in Concentration in Manufacturing*, 1935–1947 and 1950 (Washington, D.C.: Government Printing Office, 1954); *ibid., The Divergence Between Plant and Company Concentration, 1947* (Washington, D.C.: Government Printing Office, 1950); United States, Senate Subcommittee on Antitrust and Monopoly of the Committee of the Judiciary, *Concentration in American Industry*, 85th Cong., 1st Sess. (Washington, D.C.: Government Printing Office, 1957), and *Concentration Ratios in Manufacturing Industry, 1958*, Parts I and II, 87th Cong., 2nd Sess. (Washington, D.C.: Government Printing Office, 1962); Nelson, *Concentration in the Manufacturing Industries of the United States*; N. R. Collins and L. E. Preston, "The Size Structure of the Largest Industrial Firms, 1909–1958," *American Economic Review*, Vol. LI (December, 1961), 968–1011; W. G. Shepherd, "Trends of Concentration in American Manufacturing Industries, 1947–1958," *Review of Economics and Statistics*, Vol. XLVI (May, 1964), 200–212; C. Kaysen and D. Turner *Antitrust Policy* (Cambridge, Mass.: Harvard University Press, 1959), pp. 275–80, and 297–98; L. W. Weiss, "Factors in Changing Concentration," *Review of Economics and Statistics*, Vol. XLV (February, 1963), 70–77, and "Average Concentration Ratios and Industrial Performance," *Journal of Industrial Economics*, Vol. XI (July, 1963), 237–54. Also see G. Rosenbluth, *Concentration in Canadian Manufacturing Industries* (Princeton, N. J.: Princeton University Press, 1957); R. Evely and I. M. D. Little, *Concentration in British Industry* (London: Cambridge University Press, 1960); and H. Leak and A. Maizels, "The Structure of British Industry," *Journal of the Royal Statistical Society*, Vol. CVIII (1945), 142–99.

statistical concepts of dispersion. An ordinary percentage measure may be sufficient for the analytic needs of those interested in the "phenomena of big business," where the problem is defined as follows: "What we are really trying to describe are the very small numbers of very large firms, and their place in the economy."[2] But the study of the structure of industries need not be confined to the top few firms. Changes in the disparity of firm sizes can have significant repercussions on competition in an industry even though the effects upon the leading firms or top asset class are minimal. To rule out these areas of study as not being an essential part of industrial concentration is tantamount to restricting an antitrust policy to the surveillance of only the leading firms in industries.

The earlier studies of concentration indexes by Gini and Lorenz were concerned primarily with the relative distribution of income and wealth among individuals in the upper, middle, and lower classes.[3] These studies employed statistical summary measures of dispersion to analyze the inequality existing among the various income classes. It was therefore natural for Gibrat in his studies of the wealth of French business firms to use these same measures of dispersion.[4] Hart and Prais, in a recent study of British industry, also use the term concentration as synonymous with dispersion of firm sizes within an industry: "the greater the dispersion, that is the greater the disparity between the sizes of the largest and the smallest firms, the greater the degree of business concentration."[5] Butters, Lintner,

[2]Reprinted by permission of the publishers from M. A. Adelman, "The Measurement of Industrial Concentration," *Review of Economics and Statistics*, Vol. XXXIII (November, 1951) (Cambridge, Mass.: Harvard University Press), copyright 1951 by the President and Fellow of Harvard College, pp. 269–296. Cf. G. Means, "Thoughts on Concentration," *1962 Proceedings of the Business and Economic Statistics Section of the American Association*, pp. 118–26.

[3]C. Gini, *Variabilita e Mutabilita* (Bologna, 1912); M. O. Lorenz, "Methods of Measuring the Concentration of Wealth," *American Statistical Association Journal* Vol. IX, N. S. (June, 1905), 209–19; D. Yntema, "Measures of the Inequality in Personal Distribution of Wealth or Income," *ibid.*, Vol. XXVIII (December, 1933), 423–33.

[4]R. Gibrat, *Les Inequalities Economiques* (Paris: Sirey, 1931); M. Kalecki, "On the Gibrat Distribution," *Econometrica*, Vol. XIII (April, 1945), 161–70. Gibrat argued that the change in sizes of firms could be described by a lognormal distribution. Gibrat's name is associated with the law of poportionate effect which states that a lognormal distribution is generated if the probability for a given proportional growth is the same for all firms, irrespective of their absolute size. Cf. J. Aitchison and J. A. C. Brown, *The Lognormal Distribution* (London: Cambridge University Press, 1957); H. A. Simon and C. P. Bonini, "The Size Distribution of Firms," *American Economic Review*, Vol. XLVIII (September, 1958), 607–17; and R. E. Quandt, "On the Size Distribution of Firms," *American Economic Review*, Vol. LVI (June, 1966), 416–32.

[5]J. S. Prais, "The Statistical Conditions for a Change in Business Concentration," *Review of Economics and Statistics*, Vol. XL (August, 1958), 268. Also see P. E. Hart and J. S. Prais, "The Analysis of Business Concentration: A Statistical Approach," *Journal of the Royal Statistical Society*, Series A, Vol. CIXX, Part II (1956), 150–81; and P. E. Hart, "On Measuring Concentration," *Bulletin of Oxford Institute of Statistics*, Vol. XIX (August, 1957), 225.

and Cary, in their study of the effects of taxes on corporate mergers in the United States, followed a statistical measure proposed by Gini "because it summarizes changes in concentration occurring throughout all asset classes rather than solely within the top size classes."[6]

Professor Adelman, however, maintains that defining concentration as a measure of dispersion is improper, and that the ordinary percentage measure is superior for studies of business concentration. Adelman states, ". . . the proper object of study is fewness of sellers or buyers. Dispersion has no economic consequences; fewness is an essential part of the theory and study of competition and monopoly."[7] A similar position is taken by Dr. John Blair, who maintains that "it is the dominance of the few, quite apart from the number of sellers, which tend to influence the market."[8]

A related problem arises over the proper selection of a *unit* of measurement, *e.g.*, sales, assets, or employees. One unit of measurement may not necessarily be better or worse than another, since each has a limited usefulness in portraying a particular aspect of a group of firms. For example, the use of sales for measuring the size of firms in a concentration index is often criticized for ignoring the underlying assets behind firms which are vertically integrated: "Sales provide the most easily available measure of size, but the weakest, in that they disregard the extent of vertical integration. Thus, two firms may each make ten percent of an industry's sales; but if one merely purchases all the components, adds 'a lick and a promise,' and resells, it is obviously much smaller than the other, which undertakes all or much of the whole productive process."[9] This standard criticism is an implicit acceptance of another unit of measurement, since the two firms are exactly equal in size when the unit of measurement is sales; the nonintegrated firm is "obviously much smaller" only when another unit of measurement, such as assets, is used. The converse argument would claim that assets are an inadequate measure of size, since the sales or market shares of firms are neglected. Thus, a concentration index does not "measure" industrial concentration in the sense that a ruler measures length, but only offers a partial description of an economic group.

[6]J. K. Butters, J. Lintner, and W. L. Cary, *Effects of Taxation on Corporate Mergers* (Cambridge, Mass.: Harvard University Press, 1951), p. 277. Also see Sylos-Labini, *Oligopoly and Technical Progress*, pp. 5–8.

[7]M. A. Adelman, "Differential Rates and Changes in Concentration," *Review of Economics and Statistics*, Vol. XLI (February, 1959), 68–69.

[8]J. M. Blair, "Statistical Measures of Concentration in Business: Problems of Compiling and Interpretation," *Bulletin of the Oxford University Institute of Statistics*, Vol. XVIII (November, 1956), 355–56 (reprint of paper delivered to the annual convention of the American Statistical Association on December 29, 1950).

[9]Adelman, "The Measurement of Industrial Concentration."

The basic question in the selection of either a percentage or summary concentration index is not which one is the best measure of concentration, but which one describes the aspect of the distribution in which the investigator is concerned. Both the summary indexes, which consider concentration changes with respect to all classes of firm sizes, and the ordinary percentage indexes, which consider concentration in terms of the top asset classes, are presented in order to illustrate the fundamentally different methodological approaches to industrial concentration. A percentage index is discussed in terms of the "concentration curve." The summary indexes are analyzed with reference to the Lorenz curve, the Gini Coefficient, the Pietra Ratio, the relative mean deviation intercept, and the Herfindahl Summary Index.

The Concentration Curve

A concentration curve depicts the cumulative percentages of total industry assets, employees, or related economic variables that are held by the leading firms in an industry.[10] A concentration curve for hypothetical industry A, composed of four firms with assets $70, $15, $10 and $5 million, respectively, is drawn in Fig. 13-1. Note that the horizontal axis presents

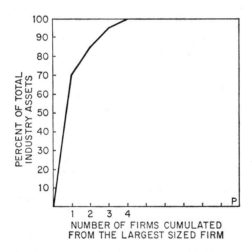

Fig. 13-1. *The Concentration Curve*

[10]United States, Federal Trade Commission, *Concentration of Productive Facilities, 1947* (Washington, D.C.: Government Printing Office, 1949). The area under a concentration curve is used as an index of concentration in Federal Trade Commission, *The Divergence Between Plant and Company Concentration, 1947*, and Nelson, *Concentration in the Manufacturing Industries of the United States*, pp. 20–21 and Table 5:A.

the number of firms cumulated from the largest-sized firm, and the vertical axis lists the percentage of industry assets accounted for by these firms. The data plotted in Fig. 13-1 are presented in column (2), Table 13-1. A steeply rising concentration curve indicates a higher degree of absolute concentration than a gradually rising concentration curve. A concentration curve for one industry which lies completely above the concentration curve of another industry indicates that the former industry has a higher degree of absolute concentration than the latter industry. In the case where two concentration curves cross, an ambiguity exists as to which curve represents the higher degree of absolute concentration.

TABLE 13-1
CUMULATED ASSET PERCENTAGES FOR INDUSTRY A

Assets of Each Firm ($000,000)	Per cent of Industry Assets Cumulated From the Largest Sized Firm	Per cent of Industry Assets Cumulated From the Smallest Sized Firm	Cumulated Per cent of the Number of Firms
(1)	(2)	(3)	(4)
70	70	5	25
15	85	15	50
10	95	30	75
5	100	100	100

The use of percentage of total assets, rather than dollar value of assets, on the vertical axis of a concentration curve permits comparisons to be made between different industries, or between different points of time for the same industry. With absolute quantities of assets on the vertical axis, comparisons of different industries could be made meaningfully only in the rare case where the assets of industries were approximately equal. The use of percentages of assets also has limitations. A concentration curve fails to indicate the relative economic importance of the industries being compared.

Concentration indexes that consider the percentage of assets or the amount of some other economic variable accounted for by the leading four or eight firms in an industry constitute a selection of one or two points along the concentration curve. By using only a few of the points on the curve, one conceals the full structure of the industry. For example, two industries may appear identical in terms of the percentage of assets held by the four leading firms, yet one of the industries might include a hundred more firms than the other.

The Lorenz Curve

The Lorenz curve, a measure of concentration which takes account of the total number of firms in an industry, requires a change in the labeling of the horizontal axis from the *"number* of firms cumulated from the largest sized firm" to the *"percent* of firms cumulated from the smallest sized firm."[11] Note that both of the axes of the Lorenz curve have values expressed in terms of percentages. The Lorenz curve for industry A is depicted by the broken line *RWVUS* in Fig. 13-2. The data for Fig. 13-2 are presented in column (3), Table 13-1.

An industry composed of firms identical in size has a Lorenz curve which coincides with a diagonal passing through the coordinates (0, 0) and (100, 100), such as line *RS* in Fig. 13-2. This line will be referred to as the *diagonal of equal distribution.* An industry with assets equally distributed among member firms does not possess any concentration under this method, even though there are only a few firms in the industry and the physical

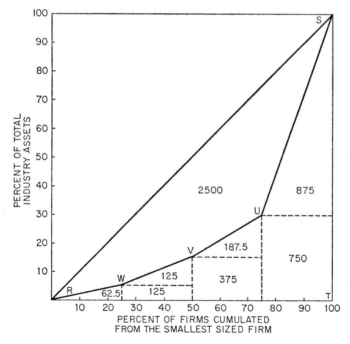

Fig. 13-2. *The Lorenz Curve and the Gini Ratio of Concentration*

[11]Lorenz, "Methods of Measuring the Concentration of Wealth." Only the discontinuous Lorenz curve will be discussed.

asset size of each firm is economically large relative to firms outside the industry. To avoid this type of ambiguity in the concept of concentration, the Lorenz curve, which indicates the *percentage* of the cumulated number of firms in the industry, is referred to as a measure of *inequality* or *relative* concentration; and the concentration curve, which indicates actual *numbers* of cumulated firms, is referred to as a measure of *absolute* concentration.

The steepness of a concentration curve (from the origin) depends upon the scale selected for the horizontal axis. In the event that all firms in an industry are accommodated by the horizontal axis of a concentration curve, a Lorenz curve is formed. For example, by magnifying the units on the horizontal scale in Fig. 13-1, so that the fourth unit is moved over to point P, a broken line is created which is identical in appearance to $RABCS$ in Fig. 13-4 (page 150). The latter is a reverse reflection of the Lorenz curve $RWVUS$ in Fig. 13-4; it is achieved when the firms are cumulated from the largest-sized firm rather than the smallest-sized firm.

Indexes of inequality have not been employed as frequently as absolute measures in studies of specific industries. The lack of application of relative concentration measures may be accounted for in part by the greater statistical and mathematical complexities of these measures, the lack of data for individual medium- and smaller-sized companies, as well as the preoccupation with the limited number of leading companies in an industry. For the purpose of studying the full structure of the distribution of assets within an industry, the measures of inequality offer considerable analytical content. Not only will a greater quantity of information be summarized, but changes in concentration occurring throughout all asset classes will be accounted for rather than changes solely with respect to the largest asset class. Thus, there may occur instances where relative concentration, as seen from the point of view of the whole distribution, has decreased, at the same time that absolute concentration, as seen in terms of the uppermost partition of the cumulative distribution, has increased.

The pitfalls in not distinguishing between the different meanings of the term "concentration" emerge in the following quotation: "The economist teaches us that a decline in the number of sellers is a datum indicating the growth of monopoly and concentration. But the statistician, by using the *legerdemain* of the Lorenz curve, can demonstrate that the decline in the number of sellers brings about a decrease in concentration."[12] The reference to the economist is in terms of absolute concentration. A decline in the number of sellers in an industry will increase the market shares held by the remaining firms. Absolute concentration will therefore tend to increase with a decline in the number of sellers. The reference to the statistician, however, is in terms of relative concentration. A decline in the number of

[12] Blair, "Statistical Measures of Concentration in Business," p. 356.

firms in an industry which leaves the remaining firms closer in size has reduced the relative concentration or inequality.

If emphasis were placed on how to *describe* the distribution of firm sizes in an industry, rather than on the selection of a "proper" definition of concentration, both relative and absolute concentration measures could be jointly employed with logical consistency. Each type of concentration measure would describe one aspect of the distribution of firm sizes, but in so doing would neglect other important aspects. The use of several measures, therefore, limits the conclusions that would otherwise tend to be drawn on the basis of only one of the measures.

The direct relationship between the number of firms and the position of the Lorenz curve has been advanced as a reason for invalidating the use of this curve for measuring business concentration. For instance, Dr. Blair maintains that "there exists in most industries a considerable number of very small enterprises which exert little, if any, influence on the industry's behavior with respect to price, production, etc. Any measure of concentration which fluctuates with changes in the number of these tiny enterprises is not meaningful from an economic point of view."[13] Similarly, Professor Adelman argues that methods of dispersion are "inapplicable to the study of business concentration" because "in any industry or meaningful group, the number of firms, an essential magnitude . . . is usually unknowable with any precision."[14]

Proponents of measures of dispersion, on the other hand, have answered these criticisms as follows: ". . . that these difficulties invalidate the use of Lorenz curves and associated measures is hardly tenable in its extreme form, for an increase in the number of firms may be accompanied by a rise or by a fall in the Lorenz curve depending on how the dispersion is affected. What has happened is a question of fact, and the fact may have to be assessed by reference to the change in both the number of firms and in their dispersion."[15] Furthermore, "it is difficult to see how any satisfactory judgment on changes in monopolistic tendencies in an industry can be made without a knowledge of the number of firms engaged in that industry . . ."[16]

The influence on concentration measures by marginal firms in an industry can be avoided partially by employing *truncated* indexes. Nelson employs as an additional measure of absolute concentration "the number of largest companies required to produce 80 per cent of an industry's output. The measure describes the breadth of the population of largely nonmarginal firms producing the preponderance of industry output and for

---

[13] *Ibid.*, p. 352.

[14] Adelman, "Differential Rates and Changes in Concentration," p. 68.

[15] Hart and Prais, "The Analysis of Business Concentration," p. 153.

[16] *Ibid.*, p. 152.

many purposes may be more meaningful than the count of all firms. By excluding the often marginal and transient part of the population, capricious industry-to-industry variations in firm numbers are minimized. These variations are in part augmented by the not infrequent and necessary Census Bureau practice of making rather arbitrary assignments of industry codes to wholesale lots of very small establishments. The practice has little effect on the Census' estimates of industry totals but of course can radically affect the counts of establishments and firms."[17] Nelson also employs a truncated Herfindahl Index, *infra*, for measuring the dispersion of the 50 largest units in an industry, and concludes, "it can be shown, however, that the difference between the truncated and the true index is negligible. The contribution to the total index of units ranking below 50th in size is so small as to have virtually no effect on its absolute value."[18]

The Gini Coefficient

The extent to which the Lorenz curve deviates from the diagonal of equal distribution is another indicator of relative concentration, and is customarily designated the *area of concentration*. For industry A the area of concentration is given by the polygon $RSUVW$ in Fig. 13-2.

In his studies of the inequality of income distribution, Gini labeled the proportion given by the area of concentration over the area below the diagonal of equal distribution as the coefficient of concentration.[19] The Gini coefficient for industry A is given by the area of polygon $RSUVW$ in Fig. 13-2 over the area of triangle RST. If all firms in an industry were of equal size, the Gini coefficient would equal zero; the Lorenz curve would coincide with the diagonal of equal distribution, and there would be no area of concentration. At the other extreme, where one firm is a monopoly and accounts for all the assets in an industry, the area of concentration coincides

[17]Nelson, *Concentration in the Manufacturing Industries of the United States*, p. 20. A truncated concentration index based on the number of firms required to account for 80 per cent of the industry's employment is used in G. Rosenbluth, "Measures of Concentration," in *Business Concentration and Price Policy*, p. 85, Table 10.

[18]Nelson, *Concentration in the Manufacturing Industries of the United States*, p. 19, fn. 7.

[19] C. Gini, "Sulla misure della concentrazione e della variabilita dei carattere," *Atti del Reale Istituto Veneto di Scienze, Lettere ed Arti*, Tome LXXIII, Parte Seconda, pp. 1207 ff. (1913-1914). Only the discountinous case will be discussed. A general formula for the Gini coefficient which utilizes the Stieltjes integral for expressing sums and integrals in one formula, and can thus be applied to both discontinuous and continuous distributions is given in H. Wold, "A Study on the Mean Difference, Concentration Curves and Concentration Ratio," *Metron*, Vol. XII (1935), 47.

with the area under the diagonal of equal distribution and the Gini coefficient is equal to unity.[20]

The Gini coefficient can be computed by the following steps: (1) Find the sum of the areas of the dashed lined triangles and rectangles in Fig. 13-2 beneath the Lorenz curve. (2) Subtract this sum from the area under the diagonal of equal distribution, which is always equal to 5000. (3) Divide the result of (2) by 5000.

Computation of the Gini Coefficient for Industry A

(1) Sum of the areas below the Lorenz curve:

$$62.5 + 125 + 125 + 375 + 187.5 + 750 + 875 = 2500$$

(2) Area of concentration: $5000 - 2500 = 2500$

(3) Gini coefficient: $\dfrac{2500}{5000} = 0.50$

An alternative method for computing the Gini coefficient is through a technique called "mean differences." A discussion of this measure is rarely found in modern statistics textbooks,[21] but the breadth of its application was appreciated by Professor Bowley, who noted:

Professor Gini has introduced a new measure of variation (Variabilita e Mutabilita: Fascicolo I: Bologna, 1912, pp. 19 et seq.). He contends that the problem that arises in the study of variability of demographic, anthropological, biological or economic characters is: How much do the different magnitudes differ between themselves? and not How much do diverse measurements differ from their arithmetic mean? The second question is appropriate in physical science, but not in the description of groups. Accordingly, he proposes as a measurement the arithmetic mean of the $\frac{1}{2}n(n-1)$ differences that are to be found between n quantities. This we may call the *mean difference* and denote it by the letter g. It has not yet come into general use, possibly because (except in the simplest cases) the arithmetic involved in its calculation is indirect and rather arduous; but it cannot be denied that the conception is simple and logical.[22]

[20]The Gini coefficient is applied in W. S. Woytinsky, *Earnings and Social Security in the United States*, Social Security Research Council (Washington, D.C.: 1943); H. Mendershausen, *Changes in Income Distribution During the Great Depression* (New York: National Bureau of Economic Research, 1946), Appendix C-2; A. Horowitz and I. Horowitz, "Firms in a Declining Market: the Brewing Case," *Journal of Industrial Organization*, Vol. XIII (March, 1965), 129–53; B. A. Kemp, "More on Measures of Market Structure," *Systems Evaluation Group Research Contribution No. 6*, Center for Naval Analyses (Washington, D.C.: The Franklin Institute, 1966).

[21] An exception is M. G. Kendall, *The Advanced Theory of Statistics* (London: Charles Griffin, 1943), Vol. I, 42–45.

[22]A. Bowley, *Elements of Statistics*, 4th ed., (London: P. S. King & Son, 1920), p. 114.

The above mean difference will be described subsequently as the "mean difference without repetition." The purpose of the nomenclature is to distinguish the different methods of taking differences between the sizes of firms. For instance, Fig. 13-3(A) shows the absolute values of the differ-

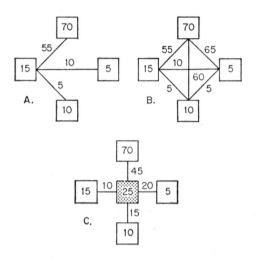

Fig. 13–3 (A, B, C). *The Mean Difference*

ences taken between a firm with assets of \$15 million and the remaining firms in industry A. But these differences are only from the vantage point of one firm. Another set of differences arises if one begins with the top firm with assets of \$70 million. Figure 13-3(B) shows the absolute values of *all* the differences without regard to any firm in particular.

The *mean difference without repetition* is computed by finding the absolute values of the differences between firm sizes, as performed in Fig. 13-3(B), and dividing their sum by the number of the above differences.[23] The *relative* mean difference without repetition is obtained by dividing the mean difference without repetition by the mean of the total assets of all the firms in the industry. The results are as follows for industry A.

[23]In mathematical notation, we have

$$\frac{\frac{1}{2} \sum\limits_{i} \sum\limits_{j} |x_i - x_j|}{\frac{1}{2} n (n - 1)} \qquad (i \neq j)$$

Cancelling out each $\frac{1}{2}$ in the fraction leaves the sum of the absolute differences in both directions over the number of differences in both directions. Thus, the arithmetic mean is the same for differences in one or both directions.

Computation of the Mean Difference Without Repetition

$$\text{Mean difference without repetition} = \frac{\text{Sum of the absolute differences in one direction}}{\text{Number of differences}}$$

$$= \frac{5 + 10 + 65 + 5 + 60 + 55}{6} = \frac{200}{6} = 33.3$$

$$\text{Relative mean difference without repetition} = \frac{\text{Mean difference without repetition}}{\text{Mean}} = \frac{33.3}{25} = 1.21$$

The *mean difference with repetition* includes differences between firms taken in both directions. For example, one could maintain that in Fig. 13-3(B) there are not six differences but twelve differences. There exists one difference of $55 million between the firm with $15 million in assets and the firm $70 million in assets, if one looks at the industry in terms of the firm with $15 million in assets (Fig. 13-3A). But from the point of view of the firm with $70 million in assets there is also a difference of $55 million between itself and the firm with $15 million. More technically, there exist $\frac{1}{2}n(n-1)$ differences in one direction between various pairs of n firms in an industry. There are exactly twice this number, or $n(n-1)$ differences, if the differences are taken in both directions.

The mean difference with repetition also includes an esoteric difference which is an *auto-difference:* the assets of each firm are subtracted from themselves, leaving a difference of zero. Auto-differences have no effect on the summation of the absolute values of differences; however, they do affect the computation of the number of possible differences existing within a set of data. Since the number of auto-differences for n firms is equal to n, and the differences in both directions are equal to $n(n-1)$, the total number of mean differences with repetition is equal to $n(n-1) + n = n^2$. The inclusion of the n auto-differences becomes less important as the number of firms in an industry becomes large.[24]

Each of the differences required in the computation of the mean difference with repetition can be observed in the matrix below, which lists the

[24]In mathematical notation, we have

$$\frac{\sum\limits_{i} \sum\limits_{j} |x_i - x_j|}{n^2}$$

The mean difference with repetition has no restriction that i is not equal to j, and therefore its denominator has n additional differences. The mean difference without repetition can be converted into the mean difference with repetition by multiplying the former by $(n-1)/n$.

assets of each firm in industry A on the top row and first column. Note that the matrix is symmetrical, with each of the absolute values of the differences listed twice, and therefore includes differences taken in both directions. The diagonal of n zeroes represents the n auto-differences.

The Matrix of "Mean Differences with Repetition"
for Industry A

Asset Size	5	10	15	70	Row Sum
5	0	5	10	65 =	80
10	5	0	5	60 =	70
15	10	5	0	55 =	70
70	65	60	55	0 =	180
					400

The mean difference with repetition is determined by dividing the summation of all the elements in the matrix above, by the number of these differences. It is therefore equal to the average of all the differences which are recorded in the matrix. The *relative* mean difference with repetition is found by dividing the above mean difference by the mean. For industry A the computation of both these measures is as follows:

Computation of the Mean Difference With Repetition

$$\text{Mean difference with repetition} = \frac{\text{Sum of the matrix elements}}{\text{Number of these elements}} = \frac{400}{16} = 25$$

$$\text{Relative mean difference with repetition} = \frac{\text{Mean difference with repetition}}{\text{Mean}} = \frac{25}{25} = 1.00$$

The relative mean difference with repetition is equal to twice the value of the Gini coefficient for the discontinuous case.[25] Or alternatively,

Gini coefficient = $\frac{1}{2}$ relative mean difference with repetition

The above relationship has been cited as the justification for using the Gini coefficient as a measure of inequality.[26] Furthermore, the method of

[25] A geometric proof of this proposition is given in Woytinsky, *Earnings and Social Security in the United States*, p. 251. A mathematical proof for the continuous case is given in Kendall, *The Advanced Theory of Statistics*, p. 43. In the continuous case the Gini coefficent is equal to one-half the relative mean deviation without repetition. Wold, *"A Study on the Mean Difference,"* p. 48.

[26] Woytinsky, *Earnings and Social Security in the United States*, p. 251.

mean differences, in providing another procedure for computing the Gini coefficient, demonstrates the freedom of the Gini coefficient from the arbitrary choice of a central position from which deviations are computed.[27]

The Relative Mean Deviation Intercept

The distribution of industry assets can be observed as a statistical dispersion which measures the extent to which the assets of each member firm differ from the assets of the average-sized firm in the industry or the mean value of the total industry assets. Since the sum of the differences from the mean is always equal to zero, one must average the *absolute* values of these differences in order to get a measure of dispersion. The latter measure is the *mean deviation*. The *relative mean deviation* is obtained by dividing the mean deviation by the mean.

Computation of the Relative Mean Deviation for Industry A

$$\text{Mean} = \frac{\text{Total industry assets}}{\text{Number of firms}} = \frac{100}{4} = 25$$

$$\text{Mean deviation} = \frac{\text{Sum of the absolute differences from the mean}}{\text{Number of these differences}} = \frac{90}{4} = 22.5$$

$$\begin{array}{l}\text{Relative mean} \\ \text{deviation}\end{array} = \frac{\text{Mean deviation}}{\text{Mean}} = \frac{22.5}{25} = .90$$

A comparison of the foundations of the statistical measures of mean difference and mean deviation can be observed in Fig. 13-3(C), which depicts the basis of the mean deviation method of measuring dispersion of economic size. A hypothetical average-sized firm (the mean) is found by averaging the industry's assets. The average-sized firm is shaded in the center of the diagram and possesses $25 million in assets. The absolute values of the differences in the sizes between the hypothetical firm and each of the remaining firms is indicated along the connecting lines between the squares. Thus, in computation this procedure is similar in some respects to the method followed in Fig. 13-3(A), where the firm with $15 million was the focal point. In contrast, Fig. 13-3(B) did not focus on any particular firm. Figure 13-3(C) neglects differences such as those which exist between the firm with $15 million in assets and the firm with $70 million in assets.

[27]The presence of the arithmetic mean in the formula of the relative mean difference can be defended on the grounds that it represents the condition that would result under equal distribution. See Yntema, "Measures of the Inequality in Personal Distribution of Wealth or Income," p. 425.

Consequently, more information concerning the asset structures of firms is employed in the mean difference method than in the mean deviation method.

The relative mean deviation *intercept* is shown graphically for industry A in Fig. 13-4. The vertical axis, which is labeled "percent of total industry assets," was employed for the concentration curve and the Lorenz curve.

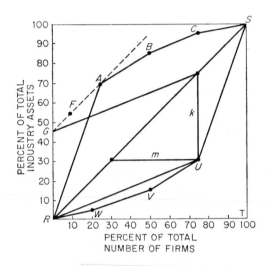

Fig. 13-4. *The Relative Mean Deviation Intercept*

The horizontal axis, however, shows the percentage of the total number of firms in the industry. The relative mean deviation intercept is found by drawing a positively sloped line parallel to the diagonal of equal distribution and tangent to the broken line showing the percentage of firms cumulated from the largest-sized firms (*RABCS*). The dashed line passing through points *G*, *F*, and *A* in Fig. 13-4 fulfill these requirements, and the point of intersection of this line with the vertical axis marks the relative mean deviation intercept. Gini observed that the relative mean deviation intercept is equal to one-half the value of the relative mean deviation. For industry A the value of the relative mean deviation intercept, given at point *G* in Fig. 13-4, is equal to 0.45 or one-half the relative mean deviation, which was found earlier to be 0.90.

Any distribution of firms, cumulated from the largest-sized firm, which is tangent to the dashed line in Fig. 13-4, will have the same relative deviation.[28] This proposition can offer some surprising results. For instance, another industry, whose distribution of firm sizes is tangent to the dashed line at point *F*, may appear to be more highly concentrated than industry A,

---

[28]U. Ricci, *L'Indici di Variabilita* (Rome, 1916), p. 2.

which is tangent at point A. At point F a distribution of firms has the largest 10 per cent of its firms holding 55 per cent of its industry's assets. In contrast, industry A, on a prorated basis, has the top 10 per cent of its firms holding merely 28 per cent of its assets. Therefore, at the 10 per cent mark on the horizontal axis, the distribution of firms which is tangent at point F would appear, in terms of absolute concentration, to be twice as concentrated as industry A. However, in terms of relative concentration, which encompasses *all* the levels of percentages on the horizontal axis, both industries are equally concentrated, since they possess the same relative mean deviation.

Basically the problem of having differently shaped distributions possessing the same relative mean deviation lies in the aggregation of data. Just as two different columns of numbers can yield the same average value, so can two different asset distributions give the same concentration measurement. The relative mean deviation intercept summarizes at point G in Fig. 13-4 the information contained in points R, A, B, C, and S. This concentration index employs one point on the graph (point G) rather than five points (the full distribution: R, A, B, C and S). Similarly, the Gini coefficient uses a single number to summarize the information contained in the configurations of two areas.

Another index of inequality, designated the Pietra ratio, is the ratio of the maximum triangle (RUS) inscribed in the area of concentration, over the area under the diagonal of equal distribution (RST).[29] The Pietra triangle is the largest of all triangles which can be constructed on the diagonal RS as a base and a vertex on the Lorenz curve. Since the denominators of the Gini coefficient and Pietra ratio are identical, and the numerators are different only to the extent that there exists a gap $(RUVW)$ between the Gini polygon and the Pietra triangle, the Pietra ratio must be less than or equal to the Gini coefficient.[30] The Pietra ratio has the unusual property of being equal to the relative mean deviation intercept. For industry A in Fig. 13-4,

$$\text{Pietra ratio} = \frac{\text{Area } RUS}{\text{Area } RST} = \frac{2250}{5000} = 0.45$$

Also,

$$\text{Pietra ratio} = \text{relative mean deviation intercept}$$

[29]G. Pietra, "Delle Relazioni tra gli Indici di Variabilita," *Atti del Reale Istituto Veneto di Scienze, Lettere ed Arti* (1914-1915), Tome LXXIV, Parte Seconda, 780–86.

[30]C. Gini, "On the Measure of Concentration with Special Reference to Income and Wealth," *Colorado College Publications*, abstracts of papers presented at the Research Conference on Economics and Statistics, held by the Cowles Commission, July 6 to August 8, 1936, p. 77.

The relationship between the Pietra ratio and the mean deviation intercept can be explained through a geometric construction in Fig. 13-4. From the vertex of the Pietra triangle (point U), draw a vertical and also a horizontal line segment to the diagonal of equal distribution. It can be proved that these two line segments (m and k) must be equal.[31] Line segment k is equal to RG, which is its opposite side of a parallelogram. Since RG is the relative mean deviation intercept, line segment k is equal to the value of the relative mean deviation intercept. It can now be shown that the Pietra ratio is equal to the value of the relative mean deviation intercept. The height of the Pietra triangle is $(k\sqrt{2})/2$, the base is $100\sqrt{2}$, and the area is $\frac{1}{2}[k\sqrt{2}/2 \times 100\sqrt{2}]$ or, simplified, $50k$. The area under the diagonal of equal distribution is 5000. Therefore, the Pietra ratio is equal to $50k/5000$ or $k/100$. For industry A, k equals 45 and the Pietra ratio is .45, which, as previously shown, is the value of the relative mean deviation intercept.

The Herfindahl Summary Index

Instead of averaging the absolute values of differences from the mean, one can study dispersion by averaging the *squares* of the differences from the mean. The average of these squared differences is known as the *variance*, denoted by s^2. The square root of the variance is known as the *standard deviation*, and is denoted by the letter s. Finally, the standard deviation divided by the mean is called the *coefficient of variation*, and is denoted by the letter c. The mean is represented by $\bar{x}$.

Computation of the Variance, Standard Deviation and Coefficient of Variation for Industry A

$$\text{Variance} = s^2 = \frac{\Sigma\,(x_i - \bar{x})^2}{n} = \frac{2750}{4} = 687.5$$

$$\text{Standard deviation} = s = \sqrt{\frac{\Sigma\,(x_i - \bar{x})^2}{n}} = \sqrt{687.5} = 26.2$$

$$\text{Coefficient of variation} = c = \frac{s}{\bar{x}} = \frac{26.2}{25} = 1.05$$

The Herfindahl summary index is defined as the sum of the squares of the sizes of firms in an industry.[32] The sizes of firms are expressed as percentages of the total industry assets. In mathematical notation, where x_i

[31]The base angles of the triangle formed by m, k, and a section of the diagonal of equal distribution are equal to 45 degrees Therefore, the opposite sides (m and k) are equal.

[32]O. C. Herfindahl, *Concentration in the Steel Industry*, Ph.D. dissertation (New York: Columbia University, 1950).

represents the assets of the n individual firms and X represents the total assets of the industry, the formula for the index is as follows:

$$\text{Herfindahl index} = \Sigma\left(\frac{x_i}{X}\right)^2 \quad (i = 1, 2, 3, \ldots, n)$$

$$\begin{array}{l}\text{Herfindahl index}\\ \text{for industry A}\end{array} = (0.05)^2 + (0.10)^2 + (0.15)^2 + (0.70)^2 = 0.5250$$

The Herfindahl index can be viewed as a measure of dispersion. For example, it can be shown that the index is equal to $(c^2 + 1)/n$, where c is the coefficient of variation.[33] This form of the Herfindahl index also permits the recognition of the outer limits of the index. When all firms are of equal size, the standard deviation equals zero, and the Herfindahl index equals $1/n$. In the case where there is only one firm in the industry, the coefficient of variation is zero, and the value of the index is one.

A more interesting relationship exists between the variance and the mean difference. It can be proved that the variance is equal to one-half the mean of the squares of each of the mean differences with repetition.[34] For example, the sum of the squares of all the elements in the matrix of mean differences with repetition for industry A equals 22,000. Dividing this amount by 16, the number of the differences, gives 1375, the mean of these squares. One-half this mean is 687.5, which is exactly equal to the value of the variance computed by squaring the deviations from the mean.

A remaining question is whether indexes employing second powers are suitable for measuring relative concentration. On this point, Professor Woytinsky states:

> In spite of the generally recognized merits of the standard deviation as a measure of dispersion, it may be questioned whether it gives a correct idea of inequality … From a mathematical point of view, the adding of deviations or differences without regard to their signs is illogical and this fallacy is avoided by squaring the deviations.

[33]Rosenbluth, *Measures of Concentration*, p. 62.

Proof:

Substituting $s^2/\bar{x}^2$ for c^2 in $(c^2 + 1)/n$ gives

$$\frac{s^2 + \bar{x}^2}{n\bar{x}^2} = \frac{\dfrac{\Sigma x_i^2}{n} - \bar{x}^2 + \bar{x}^2}{n\bar{x}^2} = \frac{\Sigma x_i^2}{n^2\bar{x}^2}.$$

Since $n\bar{x} = X$ by definition, we have

$$\frac{\Sigma x_i^2}{X^2} = \Sigma\left(\frac{x_i}{X}\right)^2$$

[34]Kendall, *The Advanced Theory of Statistics*, Vol. I.

But the simple deviations are in alignment with what most people would regard as inequality, while the squaring of differences results in overweighting the items which deviate most from the mean and are the least typical for the group.[35]

*   *   *

The ultimate purpose of measures of industry concentration is the comparative analysis of concentration between different industries, or the same industries between different points of time. In the event that two concentration curves or two Lorenz curves cross, an ambiguity exists as to which curve represents the higher degree of concentration. In the case where the Lorenz curves do not intersect, it is important to ascertain whether disparities in concentration are a result of different numbers of firms or differences in size among the same number of firms. For it is possible that an increase in the number of firms in an industry may simultaneously increase relative concentration, but decrease absolute concentration.[36]

Neither a single concentration index nor a combination of concentration indexes can be used as a direct measure of the degree of competition.[37] Except in extreme cases where a few firms produce almost all of the output

[35]Woytinsky, *Earnings and Social Security in the United States*, p. 15.

[36]Another problem concerns the comparative growth of different-sized firms in an industry. Prais has pointed out that if the dispersion of firm sizes is to remain constant over time, it is essential that the larger firms grow by a less than average amount, *and* the smaller firms grow by a more than average amount. Thus, a less than average growth rate of the larger firms is statistically an insufficient condition to prove that relative concentration has decreased. See Prais, "The Statistical Conditions for a Change in Business Concentration," pp. 268–72; reply by Adelman, "Differential Rates and Changes in Concentration," pp. 68-69. Also see Simon and Bonini, "The Size Distribution of Business Firms," pp. 607–17; I. Adelman, "A Stochastic Analysis of the Size Distribution of Firms," *Journal of the American Statistical Association*, Vol. LIII (December, 1958), 893–904; E. Mansfield, "Entry, Gibrat's Law, Innovation, and the Growth of Firms," *American Economic Review*, Vol. LII (December, 1962), 1023–51; S. Hymer and P. Pashigian, "Firm Size and Rate of Growth," *Journal of Political Economy*, Vol. LXX (December, 1962), 556–69; Comment by Simon with Reply by Hymer and Pashigian, *ibid.*, Vol. LXXII (February, 1964), 81–84.

[37]Yet the possibility seems to be suggested in the writings of Hart and Prais, "The Analysis of Business Concentration," p. 153: "Suppose the difference in sizes of two firms provides a measure of the degree of 'dominance' that the one may exert over the other's price or output; of course, there are many factors that affect dominance in any real sense, but they must be ignored for this interpretation. Then a measure of dominance for an industry as a whole may be found by taking the mean difference, irrespective of sign, between all possible pairs of firms." And see comment by Orris Herfindahl in *Business Concentration and Price Policy*, p. 96: "If we think of the measurement problem in terms of the concentration, numbers, and inequality framework . . . the various combinations of numbers and inequality produce a concentration surface for a given measure. It is not necessary that the levels of this surface be in a one-to-one correspondence with the competitive behavior of the industry . . ."

of an industry, the knowledge of the distribution of firms is insufficient, in and of itself, for the making of even a cursory judgment as to the nature of competition.[38] Additional information is required, such as whether the industry is expanding or contracting, the extent of mergers,[39] the rates of entry and exit of firms, the turnover in rank of the leading firms,[40] research and development expenditures, the importance of substitute products, imports, exports, secondary markets, and price flexibility. The calculation of concentration ratios must therefore be perceived as the beginning and not the end of an antitrust analysis of market power.

[38]E. S. Mason, *Economic Concentration and the Monopoly Problem* (Cambridge, Mass.: Harvard University Press, 1957), p. 27. Also see Chamber of Commerce of the United States, *The Significance of Concentration Ratios and The Statistical Bases of Concentration Ratios* (Washington, D.C., 1957).

[39]J. Lintner and J. K. Butters, "Effects of Mergers on Industrial Concentration," *Review of Economics and Statistics*, Vol. XXXII (February, 1950), 30–48; Reply by J. M. Blair and H. F. Houghton, *ibid.* (February, 1915), pp. 63–67; Rejoinder by Lintner and Butters, *ibid.*, pp. 68–70. Also see G. W. Nutter, *The Extent of Enterprise Monopoly in the United States, 1899–1939* (Chicago: University of Chicago Press, 1951); R. L. Nelson, *Merger Movements in American Industry, 1895–1956*, National Bureau of Economic Research (Princeton, N. J.: Princeton University Press, 1959); and J. F. Weston, *The Role of Mergers in the Growth of Large Firms* (Berkeley, Calif.: University of California Press, 1953); Federal Trade Commission, *The Present Trend of Corporate Mergers and Acquisitions, 1947* (Washington, D.C.: Government Printing Office, 1949); and United States, *Mergers and Superconcentration*, Staff Report of the Select Committee on Small Business, House of Representatives, 87th Congress (Washington, D.C.: Government Printing Office, 1962).

[40]W. L. Crum, *The Age Structure of the Corporate System* (Berkeley, Calif.: University of California Press, 1953); S. Friedland, "Turnover and Growth of the Largest Industrial Firms, 1906–1950," *Review of Economics and Statistics*, Vol. XXXIX (February, 1957), 79–84; S. Hymer and P. Pashigian, "Turnover of Firms as a Measure of Market Behavior," *ibid.*, Vol. XLIV (February, 1962), 82–87; J. Joskow, "Structural Indicia: Rank-Shift Analysis as a Supplement to Concentration Ratios," *ibid.*, Vol. XLII (February, 1960), 113–16, reprinted in *Antitrust Bulletin*, Vol. VI (January–February, 1961), 9–18; and M. Gort, "Analysis of Stability and Change in Market Shares," *Journal of Political Economy*, Vol. LXXI (February, 1963), 51–63.

CHAPTER FOURTEEN

The Compilation of Census Concentration Data

The Bureau of the Census has compiled for the Senate Subcommittee on Antitrust and Monopoly concentration ratios of manufacturing industries for the years 1947, 1954, 1958, and 1963.[1] This chapter explains the methods followed by the Census in calculating the share of total shipments accounted for by a given number of leading companies. Problems encountered in the compilation of the data are considered, and an appraisal is made of the accuracy of concentration ratios.

The Industry and Product Classification Methods

A plant, or in Census terminology, an "establishment," is classified in a particular industry if its shipments of primary products of that industry exceed in value its shipments of any other product. The *primary product* of a plant is defined as that product which accounts for the greatest portion of the total dollar value of shipments from a plant. The *secondary products* of a plant are its remaining products.

[1]This chapter is taken from my article, "Census Concentration Data: A Critical Analysis," *Antitrust Bulletin*, Vol. X (September–December, 1965), 851–78. See United States, Senate Subcommittee on Antitrust and Monopoly of the Committee of the Judiciary, *Concentration in American Industry*, 85th Cong., 1st Sess., *Concentration Ratios in Manufacturing Industry, 1958*, Parts I and II, 87th Cong., 2nd Sess., and *Concentration Ratios in Manufacturing Industry, 1963*, Parts I and II, 89th Cong., 2nd Sess. (Washington, D.C.: Government Printing Office, 1966).

The Census Bureau publishes manufacturing data on the basis of two overlapping classification concepts, the industry and the product. The *industry concept* combines the primary and secondary shipments of a plant and assigns them to the industry in which the plant is primarily engaged. Therefore, all the shipments allocated to an industry may not be primary to the industry. In Table 14-1 company K has two plants, k-1 and k-2, each of which manufactures products X and Y. Plant k-1 is assigned to industry Y, since its largest value of shipments is accounted for by product Y. Plant k-2 is assigned to industry X. Note that all the products (primary and secondary) from plant k-1, which include $5 of product X and $10 of product Y, are allocated to industry Y. Similarly, all the shipments from plant k-2 are allocated to industry X, since product X accounts for the largest value of shipments from this plant. Industry X therefore covers some shipments of product Y; and industry Y, in turn, includes some shipments of product X.

TABLE 14-1

ALLOCATION OF PLANT SHIPMENTS BY INDUSTRY

	Actual Shipments of Product X	Actual Shipments of Product Y	Allocated Shipments of Product X	Allocated Shipments of Product Y
Company K				
Plant k-1	$ 5	$10	$··	$15
Plant k-2	20	2	22	··
Total	$25	$12	$22	$15

The industry concept includes in value of shipments for all manufacturing plants classified in an industry (a) their value of products "primary" to the industry, (b) their value of "secondary" products, and (c) their "miscellaneous receipts" for repair work, sales of scrap or refuse, etc. Not only are items other than product X included in the total value of shipments for industry X, but, in certain cases, actual shipments of product X are excluded from this figure. For instance, the total value of shipments of industry X does not include (a) imports of product X and (b) secondary shipments of product X made by plants whose primary product was not product X. Shipments of product X made by plants which did not expend labor or materials, but simply resold product X in its original form were included after 1958.

The Bureau of the Census also follows a *product concept* in which the shipments of each product are classified in the industry to which that product primarily belongs. In terms of Table 14-1 the $25 of actual shipments of product X would be allocated to product class X, and the $12 of product Y would be allocated to product class Y. Product class X would therefore include only shipments of product X, and product class Y would include only shipments of product Y. Value of shipments under the product approach includes secondary shipments of product X made by plants whose primary product was not product X. Also included are shipments made by plants which did not expend labor or materials, but simply resold product X in its original form. However, shipments of product X which were imported are excluded.

The Primary Product Specialization Ratio and the Coverage Ratio

In order to measure the extent to which industry and product statistics may be compared, two measures have been developed by the Bureau of the Census to be used in conjunction with industry shipment figures: the primary product specialization ratio and the coverage ratio. In general, the higher the specialization and coverage ratios, the greater the confidence which can be placed in comparisons between product and industry statistics. In approximately half of the industries covered by the Bureau of the Census in 1958 both of these ratios were over 90 per cent, and the industry and product approaches yielded virtually identical results.[2]

The *primary product specialization ratio* measures the extent to which plants classified in a particular industry specialize in making the primary product. The ratio consists of the primary product shipments of an industry over the total (primary and secondary) shipments of the industry. Miscellaneous receipts are excluded from the ratio. For example, in the cutlery industry in 1954 there were $148 million of primary product shipments (mainly mechanics' hand-service tools), $21 million of secondary shipments, and miscellaneous receipts of $1 million. The primary product specialization ratio for the cutlery industry is 0.88, which is found by dividing the primary shipments of plants assigned to the cutlery industry ($148) by the sum of the primary and secondary shipments ($148 + $21) of these same plants.

The value 0.88 indicates that 88 per cent of the approximately $169 million listed as the total shipments made by plants classified in the cutlery industry was accounted for by cutlery products. Alternatively, 12 per

$$\begin{matrix} \text{Primary product} \\ \text{specialization} \\ \text{ratio for cutlery} \end{matrix} = \frac{\$148}{\$148 + \$21} = 0.88$$

[2] *Concentration Ratios in Manufacturing Industry, 1958*, p. 6. A discussion of these two measures is given in J. Mckie, *Industry Classification and Sector Measures of Industrial Production*, Bureau of the Census Working Paper No. 20 (Washington, D.C.: Government Printing Office, 1965).

cent of the total cutlery industry shipments were accounted for by products other than cutlery.

The *coverage ratio* measures the portion of primary shipments included in the total shipments of a given product. The ratio consists of the total value of primary shipments of plants classified in an industry over the total shipments of this product made by all plants, both in and out of the specified industry. Miscellaneous receipts are excluded from this ratio. The coverage of the industry, therefore, refers to the extent to which shipments of a given product are accounted for by plants classified in the industry. For example, in the cutlery industry the coverage ratio in 1954 was 0.96, which is found by dividing the primary shipments of plants assigned to the cutlery industry ($148) by these same primary shipments plus the shipments of cutlery made by plants which had a different primary product than cutlery ($6) and were therefore classified in other industries.

$$\text{Coverage ratio} \atop \text{for cutlery} = \frac{\$148}{\$148 + \$6} = 0.96$$

The value 0.96 indicates that 96 per cent of the approximately $154 million listed as the total shipments of cutlery was made by plants classified in the cutlery industry. In other words, shipments from plants which manufacture cutlery as a secondary product are a relatively small part of the total cutlery shipments. By subtracting the coverage ratio for cutlery from 1.00, the value 0.04 is obtained, which indicates that 4 per cent of the total value of shipments of cutlery was accounted for by plants not primarily engaged in the manufacture of cutlery.

To summarize, the primary product specialization ratio is based upon the total shipments of different types of products produced by plants which have the same major product. It asks to what extent these producers specialize in manufacturing their primary product. In contrast, the coverage ratio is based upon the total shipments of only one specific product. It asks to what extent the total shipments of a given product are accounted for by shipments from primary producers. The two ratios can be expressed in terms of the following formulas:

$$\text{Primary product} \atop \text{specialization} \atop \text{ratio} = \frac{X^*}{X^* + Y^{**}} \qquad \text{Coverage} \atop \text{ratio} = \frac{X^*}{X^* + X^{**}}$$

where

$X^* = $ value of shipments of product X from plants whose primary product is X.

$X^{**} = $ value of shipments of product X from plants whose primary product is *not* X.

$Y^{**} = $ value of shipments of secondary products from plants whose primary product is X.

Note that the numerators of the specialization and coverage ratios are the same, and the formulas are distinguished by a different term in their respective denominators. Where X^{**} is small or negligible, the value of the coverage ratio approaches unity, and signifies that all the shipments of product X are made by plants for which X is the primary product. Primary shipments would then constitute the total shipments of this product. Finally, if X was only manufactured by single product plants, X^{**} and Y^{**} would equal zero, the primary product specialization ratio would equal the coverage ratio, and the value of both ratios would be unity.

The Standard Industrial Classification Code (SIC)

Comprehensive tabulations on concentration generally follow the definitions of products and industries set forth in the Standard Industrial Classification Code, abbreviated SIC.[3] The definitions in the classification

TABLE 14-2

SIC 2-DIGIT MANUFACTURING INDUSTRY GROUPS

SIC Code	
20	Food and kindred products
21	Tobacco manufactures
22	Textile mill products
23	Apparel and other fabricated textile products
24	Lumber and wood products
25	Furniture and fixtures
26	Pulp, paper, and products
27	Printing and publishing
28	Chemicals and allied products
29	Petroleum and coal products
30	Rubber products
31	Leather and leather products
32	Stone, clay, and glass products
33	Primary metal industries
34	Fabricated metal products
35	Machinery except electrical
36	Electrical machinery
37	Transportation equipment
38	Instruments and related products
39	Miscellaneous manufactures

[3]United States, Bureau of the Budget, *Standard Industrial Classification Manual*, Vol. I (Washington, D.C.: Government Printing Office, 1945); United States, Bureau of the Census, *1954 Census of Manufactures Industry and Commodity Classification Manual* (Washington, D.C.: Government Printing Office, 1955); and F. A. Hanna, *The Compilation of Manufacturing Statistics*, U.S. Bureau of the Census (Washington, D.C.: Government Printing Office, 1959).

system become progressively narrower or more particular with successive additions of numerical digits. Starting with the broadest definitions, there are twenty 2-digit major manufacturing industry groups, which are shown in Table 14-2.

These major industry groups are subdivided into approximately 200 3-digit industry groups, which are further divided into approximately 450 4-digit industry and product groups, 1000 5-digit product classes, and finally 7500 7-digit individual products. The SIC system of product and industry subdivision can be observed in the illustration from the food industry in Table 14-3.

TABLE 14-3

SIC Code	Number of Digits	Designation	Name
20	2	Major industry group	Food and kindred products
203	3	Industry group	Canning, preserving
2033	4	Product group or industry	Canned fruits and vegetables
20332	5	Product class	Canned seasonal vegetables
2033211	7	Product	Canned asparagus

The standard industrial classification was designed for the placement of data concerning products and industries into a meaningful system which will be relatively constant over a period of time, and permit a means of comparing current data with information from earlier years. The definitions are not a result of mechanical classificatory rules but rather are generally the work-product of conferences between industry representatives and government agencies. Sometimes the definitions reflect the expediency of using existing data where the reporting activities are deeply ingrained. The standard industrial classification system was not organized for the particular task of studying industrial concentration, but rather "to serve the general purposes of the census and other governmental statistics."[4]

A concentration measure has relevance only in terms of a specific market. "Where classifications are too broadly defined and thus include a number of dissimilar products or processes or where they are too narrowly defined and thus exclude a number of closely substitute products or processes, they impart a bias to concentration measures which may render them inap-

4*Concentration in American Industry*, p. 5.

propriate for use in the analysis of market behavior."[5] The introduction
to the Senate Subcommittee Report on *Concentration in American Industry*
states:

> No attempt is made in this report to fit the census classifications to the actual
> competitive structure of industrial markets. The result is in some cases a fairly ac-
> curate reflection of the degree of market concentration, in others an overstatement,
> and in others an understatement of such concentration. . . . In view of the above
> reservations, the data on concentration in this report are not of equal significance.
> For some categories, the measure of concentration may be extremely significant in
> indicating relative market powers; for some it may not be significant at all for this
> purpose.[6]

Industry and product definitions do not necessarily coincide with market
definitions. A physically identical product may be assigned to more than
one industry. For example, process cheese from an integrated firm is
assigned to Industry 2022, Natural Cheese, but when it is produced by a
nonintegrated firm, which purchases the cheese before processing it, the
product is assigned to Industry 2025, Special Dairy Products. Other
products that are divided according to the extent of vertical integration
include sausages, rubber garments, fertilizers, shampoos, laminated glass,
and ferrous wire.[7]

The assignment of the same product to different industries may depend
upon the technologies employed or the process of manufacture. Coke made
from beehive coke ovens is classified in Industry 2931, Beehive Coke Ovens;
but coke derived as a byproduct from plants manufacturing products such
as liquor or naphthalene is classified in Industry 2932, Byproduct Coke
Ovens. Finally, the classification could depend upon the source of raw
materials from which the product is derived. Refined sugar is listed in
Industry 2062 when it is derived from sugar cane, but in Industry 2063
when it is derived from sugar beets.

The above examples suggest that "primary emphasis in defining and
describing the industry is on the supply side of the economic picture.
Physical or technological structure and homogeneity of production are more
important considerations in the classification system than close substi-
tutability of demand for products."[8] It is doubtful whether a classification

---

[5]Nelson, *Concentration in the Manufacturing Industries of the United States*, p. 38.

[6]At p. 5.

[7]M. R. Conklin and H. T. Goldstein, "Census Principles of Industry and Product
Classification, Manufacturing Industries," in *Business Concentration and Price Policy*,
pp. 34–35.

[8]*Ibid.*, p. 21.

system based on demand factors could be developed.[9] "The satisfactory grouping on a comprehensive scale, of products into markets presupposes knowledge of the behavior of prices, production, and other market responses that presently does not exist. Without such objective data (and even with the data) the grouping becomes a matter of judgment based on one's accumulated understanding of the operations of individual markets. . . ."[10]

Furthermore, the existence of overlapping product markets would require multiple combinations of product groups. For example, tin cans would have to be included with steel plates in a study of the steel industry; but steel plates would have to be excluded in a study of the container industry, which in turn would include glass and plastic products.

The Construction of Plant and Company Concentration Ratios

Concentration ratios can be constructed on either a company or plant basis. Company concentration ratios are determined by the Bureau of the Census by dividing the value of shipments of the 4, 8, and 20 largest *companies*, respectively, by the total value of shipments in an industry or product grouping. Plant concentration ratios are calculated by dividing the value of shipments of the 4, 8, and 20 largest *plants*, respectively, by the total value of shipments.

The four largest companies in Table 14-4 are marked by a dagger and the four largest plants are marked by a single asterisk in their respective product class group or industry. Note that the product X shipments of plants a-1, a-2, and a-3 (all under the common ownership of company A) are added together in column (1) in order to determine that company A is one of the largest companies in product class group X.

Table 14-4 illustrates the construction of company and plant concentration ratios for an industry and product class group. The shipments of product X made by companies A, B, C, D, E, F, G, H, and I are listed in column (1); their shipments of product Y are listed in column (2). If it is assumed that only these companies manufacture products X and Y, and the *product concept* is followed, product class group X will include all the shipments of product X, and product class group Y will include all the shipments of product Y. However, if the *industry concept* is followed,

[9]United States, Bureau of the Census, *The Role of the 1954 Census of Manufacturers in Overcoming Problems of Industry Data*, Working Paper No. 2 (Washington, D.C.: Government Printing Office, 1956).

[10]Nelson, *Concentration in the Manufacturing Industries of the United States*, p. 39.

TABLE 14-4

CONSTRUCTION OF COMPANY AND PLANT CONCENTRATION RATIOS FOR AN INDUSTRY AND PRODUCT CLASS GROUP[11]

Company and Plants	Actual Shipments of Product X (Product Class Group X) (1)	Actual Shipments of Product Y (Product Class Group Y) (2)	Allocated Shipments to Industry X (3)	Allocated Shipments to Industry Y (4)
Company A	$35†	$24†	$30†	$29†
Plant a-1	$ 0	$ 4	$—	$ 4
Plant a-2	* 25	5	* 30	—
Plant a-3	10	15	—	* 25
Company B	5	10	—	15
Plant b-1	5	10	—	15
Company C	15	20†	—	35†
Plant c-1	15	* 20	—	* 35
Company D	25†	50†	—	75
Plant d-1	* 25	* 50	—	* 75
Company E	35†	5	40†	—
Plant e-1	* 35	5	* 40	—
Company F	50†	35†	85†	—
Plant f-1	20	10	* 30	—
Plant f-2	* 30	* 25	* 55	—
Company G	2	3	—	5
Plant g-1	2	3	—	5
Company H	8	17	—	25†
Plant h-1	8	* 17	—	* 25
Company I	7	1	8†	—
Plant i-1	7	1	8	—
Value of shipments				
4 largest companies	145	129	163	164
4 largest plants	115	112	155	160
Total, all companies	182	165	163	184
Concentration ratios				
4 largest companies	80%	78%	100%	89%
4 largest plants	63%	68%	95%	87%

*One of the four largest plants.
†One of the four largest companies.

the shipments of a plant producing product X or Y must be reallocated to that industry which accounts for the largest portion of the plant's value of shipments. See columns (3) and (4) in Table 14-4.

[11]The data are hypothetical. The format of the table is adapted from B. Bock, *Concentration Patterns in Manufacturing*, Studies in Business Economics No. 65 (New York: National Industrial Conference Board, 1959), Table 1, p. 26.

As a result of the product and industry concepts, there exist four concentration ratios for the four largest *companies;* and another four ratios for the four largest *plants,* manufacturing product X or Y, or both. In Table 14-4 the *company* concentration ratios are as follows: 80 per cent for product class group X, 78 per cent for product class group Y, 100 per cent for industry X and 89 per cent for industry Y. The *plant* concentration ratios include 63 per cent for product class group X, 68 per cent for product class group Y, 95 per cent for industry X and 87 per cent for industry Y.[12]

The four leading companies in an industry are not necessarily the largest companies in terms of over-all total assets or even in terms of the actual shipments of the product which is primary to the industry. For example, the shipments of company D, one of the four largest companies in product class group X, are not included in either the plant or company concentration ratio of industry X in column (3), Table 14-4, since the plants of this company produce X as a secondary product.

In an industry in which the leading companies included in a concentration ratio operate only one plant, there is no difference between concentration measured on a plant or company basis. However, where leading companies in an industry operate more than one plant, company concentration is higher than plant concentration.[18] A final question that should be considered is whether the value of a concentration ratio is predominantly a result of the operation by the leading companies of larger than average-sized plants or to their holding of a more than proportionate number of plants. In product class group X in Table 14-4 the leading four companies (A, D, E, and F) held not only larger than average sized plants ($20.7 versus $15), but also a proportionately greater number of plants (1.75 versus 1.23). A concentration ratio is wholly explained by the multiple operation of plants where the average size of the plants of the four leading companies is the same as the average size of all plants in the industry or product class group. On the other hand, a concentration ratio is wholly explained by a larger plant size where the four leading companies each has only one plant.[14]

The Economic Accuracy of Concentration Ratios

The accuracy of concentration ratios is directly affected by differences between the economic characteristics of leading companies and their in-

[12]The Bureau of the Census does not publish plant concentration ratios. But cf. Federal Trade Commission, *The Divergence Between Plant and Company Concentration, 1947;* and Nelson, *Concentration in the Manufacturing Industries of the United States,* p. 62.

[18]The multiple operation of identical plants by companies is highest in industries, such as bread, where transportation costs are high relative to the product unit value. See Nelson, *Concentration in the Manufacturing Industries of the United States,* p. 62.

[14]*Ibid.,* p. 68.

dustries as a whole.[15] Where the leading companies export more than the industry average, the industry concentration ratio will be overvalued; it will be undervalued where the leaders import more than the industry average. The existence of different prices between the leading companies in an industry and the smaller companies will affect the value of shipments of the former even if their level of physical shipments remains unchanged. The policies of different companies in an industry in acknowledging ownership of its various subsidiaries and affiliates will influence the results of collecting the shipments of plants belonging to the companies in the numerator of an industry concentration ratio. Finally, the practice of "swaps" or transfers from one plant to another in the same industry may be followed more frequently by larger companies which own a number of plants than by smaller companies which possess only a single plant. In the latter case, the value of shipments of the leading companies will possess a greater amount of duplication, and will appear to have a larger share of the industry, because a double counting occurs in the numerator and denominator of the industry concentration ratio.

Since separate coverage and specialization ratios are not published for sets of leading companies in industries, it is difficult to determine whether the shipments of these companies are representative of their actual shipments of products classified in an industry. If the primary product specialization ratio for the leading companies is in fact lower than for the industry as a whole, the numerator of the industry concentration ratio will show the leading companies accounting for a larger share of the industry shipments than is actually the case. Similarly, if the coverage ratio for the leading companies is higher than for the industry as a whole, the numerator of the concentration ratio will be overvalued.

The problems analyzed in this section emerge from the lack of homogeneity between the set of companies classified in an industry and the component subsets of the leading 4, 8, or 20 companies. Differences in the economic characteristics existing between the two sets limit the use and reliability of concentration ratios as measuring devices. When concentration ratios are aggregated into broader classifications, the complexity of the problem increases, since another dimension is added: the characteristics of a set of leaders must be compared not only to the remaining companies in a single industry, but to sets of leaders in related industrial classifications.

---

[15]Most of the analysis in this section is covered in Bock, *Concentration Patterns in Manufacturing*, Chap. 3. Also see *Concentration in American Industry*, pp. 3–6; and M. A. Adelman, "A Current Appraisal of Concentration Statistics," American Statistical Association, *Business and Economics Statistics Section* (Proceedings, 1957), pp. 227–31.

Changes in Company Leadership in the Aggregation of Concentration Ratios

The value of shipments for a number of leading companies in industries and product groupings, published by the Bureau of the Census, cannot as a general rule be added to obtain the aggregate value of shipments for the same number of leading companies in a broader classification.[16] The sum of the shipments of the four leading companies in a 4-digit product class group does not necessarily equal the total shipments of the four leading companies in each of the component 5-digit product classes. For example, in the cutlery product group (SIC 3421) the leading four companies in product class 34211 had shipments amounting to $20,516,000, and the leading four companies in product class 34212 had total shipments amounting to $65,795,000. However, the leading four companies in the broader cutlery product class group (SIC 3421) did not account for the sum of the above two shipment figures ($20,516,000 + $65,795,000 = $86,311,000), but the lesser sum of $73,591,000. See Table 14-5.

TABLE 14-5

SIC Code	Product Class and Product Class Group	Shipments ($000) in 1954	
		All Companies	Four Leading Companies
34211	Cutlery, scissors, shears, trimmers, and snips	$ 85,485	$20,516
34212	Razor blades and razors, except electrical	67,830	65,795
3421	Cutlery	$153,315	73,591

Source: Concentration in American Industry, p. 84.

The above aggregation problem stems from the change in leadership of companies as the product classes are combined.[17] The four leading com-

[16]The problem is noted in Kaysen and Turner, *Antitrust Policy*, p. 297, and G. J. Stigler, *Capital and Rates of Return in Manufacturing Industries*, National Bureau of Economic Research (Princeton, N. J.: Princeton University Press, 1963), p. 207.

[17]Another problem in aggregation involves the duplication of shipments for manufacturing industries where the products of some industries are used as materials for others. The duplication is most pronounced in the addition of successive production stages of a product, such as the addition of flour mills to bakeries in the food group. Estimates of the over-all extent of duplication indicate that the value of shipments of finished manufactures, exclusive of such duplication, tends to approximate two-thirds of the total value of products reported in the Census. See United States, *1963 Census of Manufactures,* Vol. II, (Washington, D.C.: Government Printing Office, 1966), p. 20.

panies in one product class may not be the leaders in another product class within the same product class group; in fact, the leaders in one product class sometimes produce no items in the remaining product classes within a given product class group.

When concentration ratios are aggregated into broader classifications, the value of shipments of a set of leading companies must be considered not only with respect to the remaining companies in a product class, but also with respect to leaders in related product classes. A proof is presented, in the appendix which follows, that in the case where the four leading companies in a product class group are the same as the four leading companies in each of the component product classes, the sum of the value of shipments of the four leading companies in the product classes *equals* the sum of the value of shipments of the four leading companies in the product class group. If the leaders are different, the sum of the value of shipments of the four leaders in each of the product classes will *exceed* the value of shipments of the four leaders in the product class group. A similar relationship exists for a greater number of leaders, such as the top eight or top twenty companies in a product class group.

*   *   *

As a result of the industry and product classification methods followed by the Bureau of the Census, and the distinction between company and plant measures of concentration, there is a minimum of eight concentration ratios associated with a company manufacturing more than one product. However, only the four ratios based on company concentration are published by the Census. The accuracy of these concentration ratios is affected by divergences between the economic characteristics of leading companies and their industries as a whole. Different product mixes, price policies, degrees of vertical integration, levels of imports and exports, and inter-plant transfers, which exist between the leading companies and the remaining companies in an industry, can cause the statistical investigator to undervalue or overvalue a concentration ratio, depending upon the particular case.

Appendix on Aggregation Problems with Census Concentration Data

TWO HYPOTHETICAL AGGREGATION PROBLEMS. The Bureau of the Census, as a result of its rules against the disclosure of information pertaining to individual companies, does not identify the names or shipments of each of the leading companies in a product class group or industry. In the two cases examined below hypothetical data are employed in order to illustrate the effects of leadership changes on the total shipments and concentration ratios for a product class group and its component product classes.

Case I. The four leading companies A, B, C, and D in product group X are also the four leading companies in each of the component product classes, x_1, x_2, and x_3.

TABLE 14-6

SHIPMENTS ($000,000)

	Product Classes			Product Class Group
	x_1 +	x_2 +	x_3 =	X
Company A	100*	60*	40*	200*
Company B	80*	55*	30*	165*
Company C	70*	50*	25*	145*
Company D	60*	40*	20*	120*
Company E	10	15	10	35
Company F	5	10	5	20
4 Leading Companies	310	205	115	630
Total, All Companies	325	230	130	685
Concentration Ratios	0.954	0.891	0.885	0.92

*Asterisk indicates one of the four leading companies in a product class or product class group.

1. *Value of Shipments*

The four leading companies in product classes x_1, x_2, and x_3 made $630 million of shipments.

$$\$310 + \$205 + \$115 = \$630$$

The four leading companies in product class group X also made $630 million of shipments.

$$\$200 + \$165 + \$145 + \$120 = \$630$$

2. *Weighted Average of Concentration Ratios*

The weighted average of the product class concentration ratio is computed as follows:

$$\frac{(325 \times 0.954) + (230 \times 0.891) + (130 \times 0.885)}{325 + 230 + 130} = \frac{630}{685} = 0.92$$

The concentration ratio for the product class group is also equal to the above value.

$$\frac{630}{685} = 0.92$$

Conclusion: Where the four leading companies in a product class group are the same as the four leading companies in each of the component product classes, the sum of the value of shipments of the four leading companies in the product classes *equals* the sum of the value of shipments of the four leading companies in the product class group. Also, the weighted average of the product class concentration ratios is *equal* to the value of the concentration ratio of the product class group.

Case II. The four leading companies A, B, C, and D in product class group X are *not* the same four leading companies in the component product classes x_1, x_2, and x_3.

TABLE 14-7

SHIPMENTS ($000,000)

	Product Classes			Product Class Group
	x_1 +	x_2 +	x_3 =	X
Company A	100*	85*	95*	280*
Company B	95*	80*	90*	265*
Company C	80*	75*	85*	240*
Company D	75*	10	50*	135*
Company E	10	15	5	30
Company F	10	20	10	40
Company G	5	60*	20	85
Company H	5	10	15	30
Company I	5	10	10	25
4 Leading Companies	350	300	320	920 (970)
Total, All Companies	385	365	380	1130
Concentration Ratios	0.909	0.822	0.842	0.81

*Asterisk indicates one of the four leading companies in a product class or product class group.

1. *Value of Shipments*
   The four leading companies in product classes x_1, x_2, and x_3 made $970 million of shipments.

$$\$350 + \$300 + \$320 = \$970$$

The four leading companies in product class group X made a lesser amount of shipments, $920 million.

$$\$280 + \$265 + \$240 + \$135 = \$920$$

2. *Weighted Average of Concentration Ratios*
   The weighted average of the product class concentration ratios is computed as follows:

$$\frac{(385 \times 0.909) + (365 \times 0.822) + (380 \times 0.842)}{385 + 365 + 380} = \frac{970}{1130} = 0.86$$

The concentration ratio of the product class group is less than the above value.

$$\frac{920}{1130} = 0.81$$

Conclusion: In Case II the leadership of firms changes in moving from the product classes to the product class group. Consequently, the sum of the value of shipments of the four leading companies in the product classes exceeds in value the sum of shipments of the four leading companies in the product class group. Also, the weighted average of the product class concentration ratios exceeds in value the concentration ratio for the product class group.

In Case II the four leading companies in one product class did not make the same amount of shipments as the identical four leading companies in the product class group. Company G is one of the four leading firms in product class x_2, but is not one of the four leaders in product class group X. Company D, which is *not* one of the four leaders in product class x_2, becomes a leader under the broader classification of product class group X. Leadership changes such as these are the explanation why the value of shipments for a given number of leading companies in an industry or product class cannot be added always to obtain the value of shipments for the same number of companies in a broader classification.

*   *   *

An algebraic generalization of combining product class concentration ratios into a broader product class group concentration ratio is given in Table 14-8. For a given product class, such as x_1, the value of shipments accounted for by the leading four companies is designated V_1^*, the total value of shipments as V_1, and the concentration ratio as r_1. It follows from the definition of a concentration ratio that $r_1 V_1 = V_1^*$. The corresponding symbols for the product class group are X, V^*, V, and r.

TABLE 14-8

	Product	Value of Shipments	Value of Shipments 4 Leading Companies	Concentration Ratios
Product Classes	x_1	V_1	V_1^*	r_1
	x_2	V_2	V_2^*	r_2
	x_3	V_3	V_3^*	r_3
Product Class Group	X	V	V^*	r

Proposition I. If four leading companies in a product class group are the same four leading companies in each of the component product classes, the weighted average of the product class concentration ratios is equal to the concentration ratio of the product class group.

Let r^* be the weighted average of the product class concentration ratios, and r be the concentration ratio for the product class group.

Prove: the conditions for $r^* = r$.

The value of shipments of a product class group V is the sum of the shipments in each of the component product classes. That is,

(14-1) $$V_1 + V_2 + V_3 = V$$

where the product class leaders are identical to the product class group leader, the value of shipments of the four leading companies in the product classes equals the value of shipments of the four leading companies in the product class group. That is,

(14-2) $$V_1^* + V_2^* + V_3^* = V^*$$

The weighted average of the product class concentration ratios in a product class group is

(14-3) $$\frac{r_1 V_1 + r_2 V_2 + r_3 V_3}{V_1 + V_2 + V_3} = r^*$$

Or

(14-4) $$\frac{V_1^* + V_2^* + V_3^*}{V_1 + V_2 + V_3} = r^*$$

From (14-1), (14-2), and (14-4) we know

(14-5) $$\frac{V^*}{V} = r^*$$

By definition, the product class group concentration ratio is

(14-6) $$\frac{V^*}{V} = r$$

Therefore, $r^* = r$, where the product class leaders are identical with the product class group leaders.

Proposition II. If the four leading companies in a product class group are *not* the same four leading companies in each of the component product classes, the weighted average of the product class concentration ratios will be *greater* than the concentration ratio of the product class group.

Prove: the conditions for $r^* > r$.

The sum of the value of shipments of the four leading companies in each of the product classes *exceeds* the value of shipments of the four leading companies in the product class group where the product class leaders are not the same as the product class group leaders. That is,

(14-7)
$$V_1^* + V_2^* + V_3^* > V^*$$

Dividing both sides of the inequality by V gives

(14-8)
$$\frac{V_1^* + V_2^* + V_3^*}{V} > \frac{V^*}{V}$$

Or

(14-9)
$$\frac{V_1^* + V_2^* + V_3^*}{V_1 + V_2 + V_3} > \frac{V^*}{V}$$

From (14-4) and (14-6), it follows

$$r^* > r$$

Therefore, $r^* > r$, where the product class leaders are *not* identical to the product class group leaders.

THE CONSTRUCTION OF MAXIMUM AND MINIMUM CONCENTRATION RATIOS. Since the actual shipments of each company are not disclosed by the Bureau of the Census, the precise changes in leadership among companies as broader classifications are formed are generally unknown. Without information concerning leadership changes, concentration ratios cannot be constructed accurately for broader groups from data pertaining to narrower product classifications. However, once assumptions are made as to changes in the leadership of companies, a value range can be established consisting of maximum and minimun concentration ratios.

A maximum concentration ratio for a product class group can be found by making the assumption that the leadership of the product classes is identical to the leadership of the product class group. Case I, Table 14-6, showed that the weighted average of the product class concentration ratios is equal to the value of the concentration ratio for the product class group when the company leadership is the same. In Case II, Table 14-7, where there was a change in leadership, we have

$$\text{Maximum value of group concentration ratio for Case II} = \frac{970}{1130} = 0.86$$

A minimum value of the concentration ratio for a product class group can be computed by making the following two assumptions: (1) the four leading companies in a product class which have a larger value of shipments than any other set of four leading companies in a product class group are assumed to produce only the item covered by their product class; and (2) if one set of four leading firms in a product class has a larger value of shipments than a set of four leading companies in another product class, then any individual company in the first set is larger than any individual company in the second set.[18]

The minimum concentration ratio for product class group X in Case II, Table 14-7, is found by dividing the value of shipments of the set of four leading companies with the largest value of shipments in a product class (namely, A, B, C, and D in x_1 with \$350) by the total shipments of all companies in the product class group (\$1130). That is,

$$\text{Minimum value of group concentration ratio for Case II} = \frac{350}{1130} = 0.31$$

The minimum value of the group concentration ratio for Case II is considerably lower than both the maximum value (0.86) and the actual value (0.81). The explanation lies in the fact that the market structure of Case II is extremely different from that envisioned by assumption (1). The set of four leading companies with the largest value of shipments in a product class includes A, B, C, and D from x_1 with \$350. Contrary to assumption (1), which was required in the construction of a minimum concentration ratio, these four companies have substantial shipments in the remaining product classes, x_2 and x_3.

Methodologically, the minimum concentration ratio is not diametric to the maximum concentration ratio. The maximum concentration ratio requires the assumption that all the product class leaders are identical to the corresponding product class group leaders. But the minimum concentration ratio does not require the antithesis: none of the product class leaders are identical to the product class group leaders. The latter condition would not be sufficient for a solution. The introduction of both assumptions (1) and (2) creates an artificial market structure in which the leaders of a product class are treated as producing goods in only one of the component product classes within a product class group.

---

[18]Kaysen and Turner, *Antitrust Policy*, pp. 275–80, and 297–98. Product class groups were consolidated and weighted averages of concentration ratios for the leading eight companies were computed with approximately the same assumptions (adjusted for eight leading companies).

PART III

Antitrust in a Multiple Product Context

SECTION E

Tying
Arrangements

CHAPTER FIFTEEN

An Introduction to Multiple Product Analysis

A multiple product firm may have difficulty in setting prices that will maximize total profits for those of its products interrelated in demand, because every price it sets for one of the products may affect the demand for the other product.[1] This pricing problem could begin an endless circularity in deciding between setting the price of one product which will then determine the price of the other product.

The traditional method for the determination of the profit-maximizing output for a single product firm equates marginal cost with marginal revenue. But this solution is generally inapplicable for the case of products interrelated in demand. The firm seeking to maximize joint profits from its related products cannot consider each market in isolation in making price and output decisions. The firm may be able to accumulate more profit by setting the prices of related products together than by setting the prices independently.

The Problem of Interrelated Demands

In the following analysis product A and product B are assumed to be complementary in demand, which will be defined to mean that a lower

[1] M. J. Bailey, "Price and Output Determination by a Firm Selling Related Products," *American Economic Review*, Vol. XLIV (March, 1954), 82–93; M. W. Reder, "Inter-Temporal Relations of Demand and Supply Within the Firm," *Canadian Journal of Economics and Political Science*, Vol. VII (March, 1941), pp. 25–39; R. H. Coase "Monopoly Pricing with Interrelated Costs and Demands," *Economica*, N.S. Vol. XIII (November, 1945), 278–95; W. S. Bowman, Jr., "Tying Arrangements and the Leverage Problem," *Yale Law Journal*, Vol. LXVII (November, 1957), 19–36.

price for at least one of the products will cause the demand not only for this product to increase, but also the demand for the other product. In Table 15-1 every 50-cent decrease in the price of B increases by 100 the amount of A that can be sold; every 50-cent decrease in the price of A increases by 200 the amount of B that can be sold.[2] Each unit of A or B is assumed to cost $2.00 and to be produced under conditions of constant cost. As a result of these interrelations in demand, every price change in product A will affect the demand for product B, and *vice versa.*

A set of demand curves can be constructed for product A for each price change in product B. In Fig. 15-1(I) the demand curve for A, when the

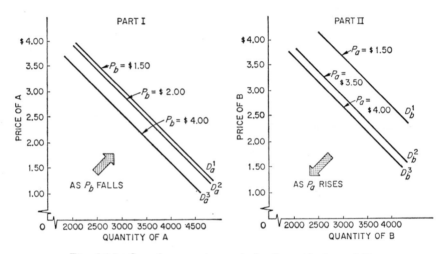

Fig. 15-1. *Complementarity and the Interrelation of Demand Curves*

price of B is $4.00, is D_a^3. The demand curve shifts rightward to D_a^2 when the price of B is lowered to $2.00; it again shifts rightward to D_a^1 when the price of B falls to $1.50. A set of demand curves for product B, which is dependent upon the price of product A, is depicted in Fig. 15-1(II). As the price of product A rises from $1.50 to $3.50 to $4.00, the demand curve for B shifts leftward toward the origin from position D_b^1 to D_b^2, and finally to D_b^3.

The profit resulting from the different price combinations of product A are given in matrix form in Table 15-1. The prices are assumed, for purposes of simplicity, to move only in intervals of 50 cents. The profit

[2]The numerical example is from Bowman, "Tying Arrangements and the Leverage Problem," p. 26.

TABLE 15-1

DEMAND CURVES FOR PRODUCT A AND FOR PRODUCT B

Demand Curves for Product A				Demand Curves for Product B			
P_a	D_a^1	D_a^2	D_a^3	P_b	D_b^1	D_b^2	D_b^3
$4.50	1600	1500	1100	$4.50	2200	1400	1200
4.00	2100	2000	1600	4.00	2700	1900	1700
3.50	2600	2500	2100	3.50	3200	2400	2200
3.00	3100	3000	2600	3.00	3700	2900	2700
2.50	3600	3500	3100	2.50	4200	3400	3200
2.00	4100	4000	3600	2.00	4700	3900	3700
1.50	4600	4500	4100	1.50	5200	4400	4200

D_a^1 assumes $P_b = \$1.50$ D_b^1 assumes $P_a = \$1.50$

D_a^2 assumes $P_b = \$2.00$ D_b^2 assumes $P_a = \$3.50$

D_a^3 assumes $P_b = \$4.00$ D_b^3 assumes $P_a = \$4.00$

matrix for A shows the total profit which can be earned from product A at a given price for product B. For instance, when the price of B is fixed at $1.50, the applicable demand curve for product A is D_a^1. See Table 15-1. D_a^1 shows that at a price for A of $4.00, there will be 2100 units demanded. The total cost ($2.00 per unit) of producing these units is (2100 × $2.00) or $4200; the total revenue is (2100 × $4.00) or $8400; and the total profit is the difference, $4200. This amount is the highest profit in the matrix for A in Table 15-2, and indicates that profits for product A are maximized when the price of B is set at $1.50 and the price of A is $4.00.

The profit matrix for B shows that the highest profit for B is $5500, which requires the price of A to be set at $1.50, and the price of B to be $4.50. Thus, different price combinations exist for maximizing either the profits for product A or the profits for product B. A seller that has the ability to set both of these prices would seek, therefore, to maximize his joint profits from both markets taken together rather than separately. The joint profits are shown in Table 15-2 by the profit matrix for A + B, where the corresponding elements for the separate matrices for A and B are added together. The highest amount of profit in this matrix is $6950, which results when the price of B is $4.00 and the price of A is $3.50. In contrast, the joint profits from A and B when profits from product A are maximized alone by the firm are $2100 ($P_a = \$4.00$ and $P_b = \$1.50$). Product A's profits are maximized at $4200, but a loss of $2100 is incurred for product B, leaving a net profit to the firm for A and B jointly, of $2100. Similarly, when product B's profits are maximized alone ($P_a = \$1.50$ and $P_b = \$4.50$), the joint profits are only $3500, since $2000 is lost in the sale of product A in obtaining the $5500 profit from the sale of product B.

TABLE 15-2

Profit Matrix for A

		P_a						
		$1.50	2.00	2.50	3.00	3.50	4.00	4.50
	$1.50	−2300	0	1800	3100	3900	4200*	4000
	2.00	−2250	0	1750	3000	3750	4000	3750
	2.50	−2200	0	1700	2900	3600	3800	3500
P_b	3.00	−2150	0	1650	2800	3450	3600	3250
	3.50	−2100	0	1600	2700	3300	3400	3000
	4.00	−2050	0	1550	2600	3150	3200	2750
	4.50	−2000	0	1500	2500	3000	3000	2500

Profit Matrix for B

		P_a						
		$1.50	2.00	2.50	3.00	3.50	4.00	4.50
	$1.50	−2600	−2500	−2400	−2300	−2200	−2100	−2000
	2.00	0	0	0	0	0	0	0
	2.50	2100	2000	1900	1800	1700	1600	1500
P_b	3.00	3700	3500	3300	3100	2900	2700	2500
	3.50	4800	4500	4200	3900	3600	3300	3000
	4.00	5400	5000	4600	4200	3800	3400	3000
	4.50	5500*	5000	4500	4000	3500	3000	2500

Profit Matrix for A + B

		P_a						
		$1.50	2.00	2.50	3.00	3.50	4.00	4.50
	$1.50	−4900	−2500	600	800	1700	2100	−2000
	2.00	−2250	0	1750	3000	3750	4000	3750
	2.50	−100	2000	3600	4700	5300	5400	5000
P_b	3.00	1550	3500	4950	5900	6350	6300	5750
	3.50	2700	4500	5800	6600	6900	6700	6000
	4.00	3350	5000	6150	6800	6950*	6600	5750
	4.50	3500	5000	6000	6500	6500	6000	5000

*Asterisk indicates the highest amount of profit in a matrix.

A Loss Leader Model

A seller of complementary products may in some situations be able to earn higher joint profits by pricing one product below cost. The joint profits resulting from pricing product A at cost ($2.00) and product B at

$2.50 are $2000 in the profit matrix for A + B in Table 15-2. If the price of A is dropped 50 cents below cost to $1.50, and the price of B is raised to $4.50, joint profits will increase $1500 to $3500. The rationale for the loss leader is apparent in this case: The profits lost in the pricing of one product below cost are more than compensated by additional profits earned by a related product offered by the same seller.

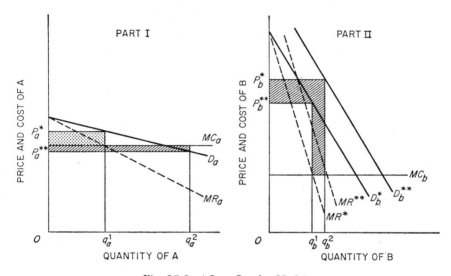

Fig. 15-2. *A Loss Leader Model*

Figure 15-2 describes a loss leader model. In (I) the price of product A is dropped from P_a^* to P_a^{**}, which is below cost. At P_a^{**} not only is a former profit in product A eliminated, which is measured by the shaded area above the marginal cost curve (MC_a), but an actual loss is incurred, which is measured by the shaded area below the marginal cost curve.

Figure 15-2(II) shows that the demand curve for product B shifts rightward from D_b^* (when the price of A was P_a^*) to D_b^{**} (when the price of A falls to P_a^{**}). The shaded area indicates that increased profits result in the B market as the price of A is reduced below cost. In this particular case the increased profits in the B market can be seen by inspection to exceed the profits lost in the A market by the "loss leader."[3]

Only the demand curves for product B in Fig. 15-2(I) shifted as a result of a change in price of one of the products. The interrelations in demand

[3]The loss leader is analyzed mathematically in C. F. Roos, *Dynamic Economics,* Monograph No. 1 of the Cowles Commission for Research in Economics (Bloomington, Ind.: Principia Press, 1934), pp. 128–47. Also see R. G. D. Allen, *Mathematical Analysis for Economists* (London: Macmillan & Co., Ltd., 1956), p. 362.

were restricted to one direction: from product A to product B. In contrast, Fig. 15-1 showed complementarity operating between the products in both directions: Price changes in A shifted the B demand curves, and price changes in B shifted the A demand curves. Thus, in approaching the problem of interrelated demands one must examine both the effects of price changes of product A on product B, and of product B on product A.[4] Nevertheless, in the next model, to simplify the analysis, it will again be assumed that changes in the price of A affect the demand for B, but price changes in B have only inconsequential effects on product A.

A Subsidization Model

In Fig. 15-3(II) the demand curve for product B shifts from D_b^* to D_b^{**} as a consequence of the lowering of the price of product A. The average cost curve (AC_b) and the marginal cost curve (MC_b) are now U-shaped. Profits in the B market increase from $CabD$ to $BcdE$. The difference between these two profit areas is shaded $(BcdEDbaC)$ and will be referred to as the marginal profit area in the B market. The market for product B may become saturated after a certain point, with the result that a further lowering of the price of product A will no longer have a positive effect on the demand for product B.[5]

A diagrammatic device is employed in Fig. 15-3(I) which takes the above marginal profits made in the B market and uses them to subsidize product A.[6] This manipulation of profit from one product market to another might be justified by noting that the lower price for product A is the proximate cause for the increase in demand for complementary product B. Therefore, the subsidization of product A can be conceived as simply a return of the profits lost in the A market by setting the price of product A unduly low.

The demand curve for product A is labeled D_a in Fig. 15-3(I). The price of product A is dropped incrementally from P_a^0 (not shown) to P_a^*. The corresponding output, which can be expected to be sold at this price, is q_a^1.

---

[4]The problems involving the income effect or the constancy of the marginal utility of money will not be treated. Cf. J. R. Hicks, *Value and Capital*, 2nd ed. (Oxford: Clarendon Press, 1957), Chap. III, pp. 42–52; F. A. Hayek, "The Geometric Representation of Complementarity," *Review of Economic Studies*, Vol. X (1942–43), 122–25; and H. Schultz, "Interrelations of Demand," *Journal of Political Economy*, Vol. XLI (August, 1933), 468–512.

[5]In the case where products A and B are substitutes for each other, a lowering of the price of A will tend to decrease the demand for B, and cause a leftward shift in the demand curve for B. Marginal profits in the B market will then be negative for a decrease in the price of A.

[6]See Coase, "Monopoly Pricing with Interrelated Costs and Demands," pp. 278–95.

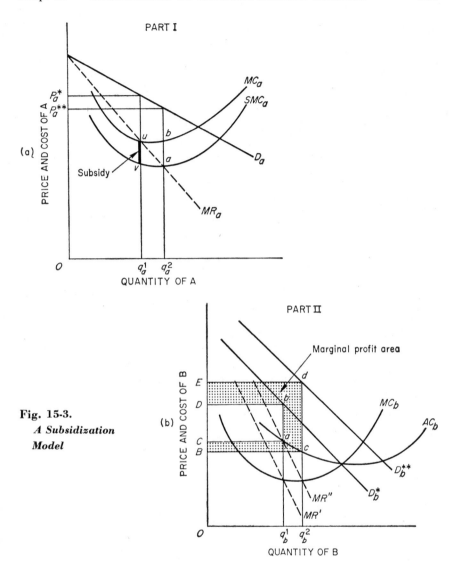

Fig. 15-3.
A Subsidization
Model

The basic rule for the diagrammatic device for portraying subsidization is the following: If the marginal profits in the product B market resulting from an incremental fall in the price of product A are positive, the amount is *deducted* from the marginal cost curve for product A at the corresponding output in terms of the demand curve for product A.[7]

The operation of the subsidization rule can be seen in the example

[7] If the change in profits earned in the B market is negative, such as where the products are substitutes, the amount is added to the marginal cost curve for product A.

involving products with complementary demands. In Fig. 15-3 a slight lowering of the price of product A to the level P_a^* in (I) causes a rightward shift in the demand curve for product B from D_b^* to D_b^{**} in (II). The shift in the demand curve for product B increases the profits earned by an amount measured by the shaded *marginal profit area*. These profits are subtracted from the marginal cost curve of the firm for product A. Specifically, the amount of profit given by marginal profit area is set equal to a line segment such as uv in (I), and is deducted from the marginal cost curve for product A at the output q_a^1. The latter output for product A is a coordinate on the firm's demand curve for product A at the incrementally changed price P_a^*.

A further lowering of the price of product A would produce an addition marginal profit area for product B, provided the firm's demand curve for product B again shifted rightward and profits were increased for the firm.

The continuance of this lowering of the price of A, and the transference of the resulting marginal profits from product B to product A give the locus of points describing the *subsidized marginal cost curve*, which is abbreviated as SMC_a.

A diagrammatic device permits the fiction that the additional profit from product B, when the price of the complementary demanded product A is lowered, can be used to lower the marginal cost curve of the complementary demanded product A. New equilibrium positions for the profit maximizing firm will result after product A is subsidized. Before subsidization the profit maximizing output for product A was at q_a^1, the level at which its marginal cost curve (MC_a) and marginal revenue curve (MR_a) intersect. After subsidization the profit-maximizing output advances to q_a^2, the output level at which the marginal revenue curve (MR_a) intersects the subsidized marginal cost curve (SMC_a). At this latter price-output combination, and in the absence of subsidization, the firm would sustain a loss measured by the triangle aub. Therefore, subsidization permits a firm that sells both products A and B to keep product A at a lower price than would be suggested in the absence of product B.[8]

[8]An alternative treatment takes the marginal revenue from one product market and adds or subtracts it, as the case may be, from the marginal *revenue* curve of the firm with respect to the second product market. Bailey, "Price and Output Determination," p. 83, states: "Since it is assumed that the sale of an additional unit of one commodity affects both its own price and the price obtainable for a given amount sold of the other commodity, it is useful to distinguish the net addition to revenue when both these effects are considered from marginal revenue in the ordinary sense, which depends only on the effect on one commodity's price of additional units of that commodity sold. The former concept will therefore be referred to as "differential revenue." This quantity will be a function of the amount sold of the 'other' commodity. . . . The solution of the output determination problem in this case here outlined is best approached by supposing the

A Price Discrimination Model

The problem of interrelated demands is also present when a firm sells during the same period of time identical products in separate markets at different prices.[9] Price discrimination will not be successful from an economic standpoint unless it is difficult to transfer units of the products from one market to the other. The buyer in the low-priced market will attempt to resell the purchased product in the higher-priced market until the price level of each market becomes equal except for transportation or other transfer costs.

A price discrimination model is shown in Fig. 15-4. The monopolist is assumed to sell a homogeneous product in two separate markets. The demand curve for the firm in market A, D_a, is drawn considerably steeper than the demand curve for the firm in market B, D_b. The price-discriminating monopolist maximizes its profits when the marginal revenues in from each of its markets are equal. Otherwise, it will pay the monopolist to sell more in the market where it derives a higher marginal revenue and less in the market where it derives a lower marginal revenue.

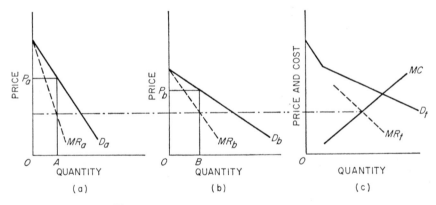

Fig. 15-4. *A Price Discrimination Model*

seller keeps one commodity continuously in equilibrium (by equating differential revenue to marginal cost) as he varies the amount sold of the other. Subject to this restraint he will select that output of the second commodity for which it also is in equilibrium, at which point he will be in full equilibrium."

[9]Stigler, *The Theory of Price*, rev. ed., pp. 214–18; Robinson, *Economics of Imperfect Competition*, pp. 179–208; F. Machlup, "Characteristics and Types of Price Discrimination," *Business Concentration and Price Policy*, Universities-National Bureau Committee for Economic Research (Princeton, N. J.: Princeton University Press, 1955), pp. 397–435; and E. W. Clemens, "Price Discrimination and the Multiple-Product Firm," *Review of Economic Studies*, Vol. XIX (1950–51), 1–11, reprinted in American Economic Association, *Readings in Industrial Organization and Public Policy*, pp. 262–76.

The horizontal addition of the marginal revenue curves MR_a and MR_b gives MR_t, and the horizontal addition of D_a and D_b gives D_t. The profit-maximizing output for the discriminating monopolist is determined by the intersection of the marginal cost curve for the entire output (MC) and the combined marginal revenue curve (MR_t). A horizontal dotted and dashed line connects all three diagrams in Fig. 15-4 at the level where the marginal revenue of the discriminating monopolist in market A is equal to its marginal revenue in market B, and its combined marginal revenue curve (MR_t) is equal to the marginal cost curve for the entire output (MC). It follows from the analysis that the profit-maximizing quantity in market A should be OA; and in market B, OB. At these respective outputs, the discriminating monopolist will charge OP_a in market A; and a lower price, OP_b, in market B.

The preceding multiple product models will be helpful in understanding the internal workings of tying arrangements and vertical integration. The next chapter develops the rationale for tying arrangements.

CHAPTER SIXTEEN

The Economic Rationale of Tying Arrangements

Tying arrangements are one of the most elementary market practices whereby a firm operates simultaneously in more than one market for the purpose of increasing its aggregate profit. The practice is, therefore, a useful starting point for analyzing the behavior of multiple product firms. The typical tying arrangement either conditions the sale of one commodity (tying good) on the sale of another (tied good), or conditions the lease of a machine on the use of supplies or services furnished by the lessor. The practice of tying goods together is implicit in other business practices, such as full-line forcing, where a seller presses his complete line of different products on a buyer predominantly interested in only a given product.

The economic motive or rationale for firms employing a tying arrangement is generally that total profits can be increased more by selling the items together than by selling them separately. There are five major situations in which a tying arrangement can increase the aggregate profits of the firm: (1) evasion of price regulation, (2) protection of goodwill, (3) economies of production or sale, (4) price discrimination, and (5) economic leverage. After a brief discussion of each of these cases, a detailed examination will be made of the role of leverage in tying arrangements.

Price Evasion

A prominent motive for employing tying arrangements during war years, when administrative price controls were imposed, was the evasion of price ceilings. Ceiling prices on rationed items prevented manufacturers and retailers from setting an otherwise higher profit-maximizing price. However, buyers could be coerced often to purchase under a tying arrangement an unregulated item. The portion of "lost profit" due to the ceiling on the tying good could be recouped by the higher price on the tied good.[1] Analogously, a firm not wanting to upset an oligopoly or administered price structure in one market might employ a tying arrangement as an alternative to changing its price.[2]

Protection of Goodwill

A manufacturer may tie a service contract, including repair parts, with the sale or lease of its machine in order to preserve the goodwill associated with its product. For example, a manufacturer of electronic equipment used on antenna sites of television stations tied the servicing of its equipment in the contract of sale, and offered as a justification of the tying arrangement that the industry was new and the equipment was so specialized that anyone not trained by the company and familiar with the particular equipment could cause tremendous damage to the whole antenna site.[3] In the event that the inferiority of outside service was imputed to the equipment, the firm's goodwill and future trade would be harmed. Similarly, a major automobile manufacturer was allowed to require its dealers not to use rival replacement parts in repairing automobiles.[4] But the protection of goodwill does not justify the use of tying arrangements when other lawful means could accomplish the same ends.[5] For example, I.B.M. was not allowed to tie the requirement for the purchase of its own tabulating cards with the leases of its computers. The Supreme Court held that the company could adequately safeguard its goodwill by conditioning its leases on the use of cards that met reasonably high specifications.[6] The legal distinction appears to turn on the *practicality* of employing

[1]Bowman, "Tying Arrangements and the Leverage Problem," pp. 19–36.

[2]M. L. Burstein, "A Theory of Full-Line Forcing," *Northwestern University Law Review*, Vol. LV (February, 1960), 67. For a mathematical treatment of tying arrangements see Burstein, "The Economics of Tie-In Sales," *Review of Economics and Statistics*, Vol. XLII (February, 1960), 68–73. Subsequent references to Burstein are to the former article.

[3]*United States* v. *Jerrold Electronics Co.*, 187 F. Supp. 545 (E.D. Pa., 1960), *affirmed per curiam*, 365 U.S. 567 (1961). The service contracts were allowed for several years until outside technicians were trained by the company.

[4]*Pick Mfg. Co.* v. *General Motors Corp.*, 80 F. 2nd 641 (7th Cir., 1935), *affirmed per curiam*, 299 U.S. 3 (1936).

[5]Hale and Hale, *Market Power: Size and Shape Under the Sherman Act.*, p. 273.

[6]*International Business Machines Corp.* v. *United States*, 298 U.S. 131 (1936). Also see United States, *Report of the Attorney General's National Committee to Study the Antitrust Laws* (Washington, D.C.: Government Printing Office, 1955), p. 139.

alternatives to a tying arrangement for the preservation of the integrity of a product. When there is a clear showing that a firm will suffer injury to its future trade unless it can adequately protect its product, and no feasible alternative other than a tying arrangement is available, the courts tend to permit the practice.

Economies of Production or Distribution

Economies in merchandising often underlie a company policy that requires a store to purchase its full line in order to obtain any one of its products. Economies of production through tying arrangements include almost all assembled products. A radio, for example, is theoretically a tying arrangement of tubes and parts. However, the functional necessity for all the parts in terms of a permanent construction excludes the radio from the tying arrangement nomenclature.[7] There may be cost advantages, such as in the planning and scheduling of production, which encourage manufacturers to produce an assembled product rather than segregated parts. Considerations such as these indicate how tying arrangements that encourage economies permit the firm to increase its profits through more efficient production.[8]

Price Discrimination.[9]

In two early patent cases the courts were faced with a patented machine licensed practically at cost with a restriction that the machine be used only with supplies furnished by the patent holder.[10] The patent holder

[7]D. Turner, "The Validity of Tying Arrangements Under the Antitrust Laws," *Harvard Law Review*, Vol. LXXXII (November, 1958), 50–75. Compare *Mercoid Corp.* v. *Mid-Continent Investment Co.*, 320., U.S. 661 (1944).

[8]Bowman, "Tying Arrangements and the Leverage Problem," p. 29.

[9]For a general discussion of price discrimination see Robinson, *The Economics of Imperfect Competition*, pp. 179–202; and Machlup, "Characteristics and Types of Price Discrimination," pp. 397–435.

[10]*Heaton Peninsular Button-Fastener Co.* v. *Eureka Specialty Co.*, 77 F. 288 (6th Cir., 1896) and *Henry* v. *A. B. Dick*, 224 U.S. 1 (1912). These decisions, which were rendered before the enactment of the Clayton Act in 1914, allowed the patentee to restrain another individual (called a contributory infringer) from selling unpatented supplies to its licensees. The decisions were later repudiated by the courts. See *Motion Picture Patents Co.* v. *Universal Film Mfg. Co.*, 243 U.S. 502 (1917), which overruled the *A.B. Dick* case, *supra*. The patent misuse doctrine, first stated in the *Motion Picture Patents* case, denies protection against direct and contributory infringement where the patentee employs a tying arrangement as a means for restraining competition in the unpatented product or supplies. Note *Morton Salt Co.* v. *Suppiger*, 314 U.S. 488 (1942); and *Attorney General's Report*, pp. 250–259.

made almost his entire profit not from the machine but from the *unpatented* supplies, which were buttons in one case, and mimeograph ink and paper in the other. Customers using the machines more intensively required a greater quantity of supplies, and thereby allowed the owner to derive a greater profit from them through the sale of supplies, which were priced above their marginal costs. Thus, the tying arrangement in effect required these customers to pay a higher price. In the words of Professor Burstein, "the tied good in these cases serves very much as a counting or metering device; the tying arrangement results in streams of payments flowing from the users of the machine to its seller (or lessor) with the rates of flow being directly proportional to the intensity of use of the machine. Those using the machine more intensively are paying more; *price discrimination* is being achieved."[11]

Where a meter system is not practical because of problems of enforcement and administration, the tying arrangement, as the only feasible method of price discrimination, allows the firm to earn greater total profits than would otherwise be possible. But the courts have rejected generally the defense that there exists no alternative profitable means for marketing the fruits of the patent other than a tying arrangement.[12]

Economic Leverage

"The essence of illegality in tying arrangements," in the words of the Supreme Court, "is the wielding of monopolistic leverage; a seller exploits his dominant position in one market to expand his empire into the next."[13] A firm by virtue of a tying arrangement increases its share of the tied-good market and gains the power to set the price of the tied product with respect to those customers purchasing its tying product. But the firm does not necessarily obtain the power to set the price in the general market for the tied product, which includes purchasers not accepting the tying arrangement. Therefore, the courts speak of a "limited" or "partial" monopoly in the tied good market.[14]

[11]Burstein, "A Theory of Full-line Forcing," pp. 64–65. Also see A. Director and E. H. Levi, "Law and the Future: Trade Regulation," *Northwestern University Law Review*, Vol. LI (May–June, 1956), 281–92, at p. 291; and G. W. Hilton, "Tying Sales and Full-Line Forcing," *Weltwirtschaftliches Archiv*, Vol. LXXXI (1958), 265–76.

[12]*B.B. Chemical Co.* v. *Ellis*, 314 U.S. 495 (1942).

[13]*Times-Picayune Publishing Co.* v. *United States*, 345 U.S. 594, 611 (1953).

[14]Burstein, "A Theory of Full-line Forcing," pp. 63–64, discards "the simple and natural view, so favored by the courts, that full-line forces and tie-in sales are primarily for the purpose of extension of monopoly into new markets," because, he argues, *full* monopolies seldom exist in the tied-good market. He asks, "Can it sensibly be accepted that G. S. Suppiger Co. tied salt to its salt dispensing machinery as part of a

Professor Bowman makes the distinction between leverage as a revenue-maximizing device and leverage as a monopoly-creating device. "The first involves the use of existing power. The second requires the addition of new power. . . . If the tying seller is maximizing his return on the tying product and the same output of the tied product can still be produced under circumstances consistent with competitive production of the tied product, no additional or new monopoly effect should be assumed."[15] The finding by both Professors Bowman and Burstein, that tying arrangements do not necessarily extend the tying product monopoly into a second monopoly over the tied-good market, is instrumental in their reaching substantially the same conclusion, namely, that the law should favor tying arrangements in certain cases where only incidental effects exist in the market for the tied product.

In the *Motion Picture Patents* case[16] the plaintiff held a patent covering a mechanism used in motion picture projectors for feeding film at a smooth and uniform rate. Projectors with this mechanism had a notice attached to them restricting the use of the machine to motion pictures obtained from a licensee of the patentee. The plaintiff-patentee was denied relief against the defendants, who were manufacturing motion pictures and exhibiting them in projectors embodying the plaintiff's patented feeding mechanism. The Supreme Court held that "it is not competent for the owner of a patent, by a notice attached to its machine, to, in effect, *extend the scope of its patented monopoly* by restricting the use of it to materials necessary in its operation, but which are no part of the patented invention. . . ."[17]

Although the plaintiff's argument was unsuccessful in the *Motion Picture Patents* case, it is important in the analysis of leverage and tying arrangements. The Court summarized the plaintiff's argument as follows:

It is argued as a merit of this system of sale under a license notice that the public is benefited by the sale of the machine at what is practically its cost, and by the fact that the owner of the patent makes its entire profit from the sales of the supplies with which it is operated. This fact, if it be a fact, instead of commending, is the

---

scheme to monopolize the American salt market? Did Morgan Envelope Co. tie its toilet paper to its dispenser as part of a grand scheme to monopolize the American bathroom tissue market? Why do we see again and again in the court reports cases involving the tying of rivets, staples, windshield wipers, repair parts, varnish, etc. when the tying monopolist's share of the market for the tied product remains miniscule? The game is afoot, and the extension-of-monopoly hypothesis is surely a rusty flintlock!" (footnotes omitted). References in the quotation are to *Morton Salt Co.* v. *Suppiger Co.*, 314 U.S. 488 (1942) and *Morgan Envelope Co.* v. *Albany Perforated Paper Co.*, 52 U.S. 425 (1893).

[15]Bowman, "Tying Arrangements and the Leverage Problem," pp. 19–20.

[16]*Motion Picture Patents Co.* v. *Universal Film Mfg. Co.*, 243 U.S. 502 (1917).

[17]*Ibid.*, p. 516 (italics added).

clearest possible condemnation of the practice adopted, for it proves that under color of its patent, the owner intends to and does derive its profit, not from the invention on which the law gives it a monopoly, but from the unpatented supplies with which it is used, and which are wholly without the scope of the patent monopoly, . . .[18]

Justice Holmes, in his dissent from the majority decision in the *Motion Picture Patents* case, contended that since the law gives the patentee the right to withhold his invention unconditionally from the public, he should be allowed the less severe alternative of *conditionally* withholding his patent. A typical condition would be that the patented machine can only be used in conjunction with unpatented supplies purchased from the patentee. Justice Holmes maintained that the tying arrangement allowed the patentee to obtain what he was rightfully entitled to under the patent law:

But there is no predominant public interest to prevent a patented teapot or film feeder from being kept from the public, because, as I have said, the patentee may keep them tied up at will while his patent lasts. Neither is there any such interest to prevent the purchase of the tea or films that is made the condition of the use of the machine. The supposed contravention of public interest sometimes is stated as an attempt to extend the patent law to unpatented articles, which of course it is not, and more accurately as a possible domination to be established by such means. But the domination is one only to the extent of the desire for the teapot or film feeder, and if the owner prefers to keep the pot or the feeder unless you will buy his tea or films, I cannot see in allowing him the right to do so anything more than an ordinary incident of ownership, ...[19]

The arguments of the majority and dissenting opinions in the *Motion Picture Patents* decision are presented in Fig. 16-1. Case I suggests a tying arrangement in which the firm earns no more profit from the tying product (Π_a) and the tied product (Π_b) than it could have earned by selling these products separately. Case II shows a tying arrangement in which the firm decides to take all profit in the tied-good market and sell the tying good at cost. The firm earns the same profit in the tied product B market ($\Pi_a + \Pi_b$) as it formerly earned on a combined basis in the product A market (Π_a) and the product B market (Π_b). Case III shows a firm earning by virtue of a tying arrangement additional profit (Π_*) that it could not have earned if the products were sold separately.

If the tying and tied products are sold in *fixed* proportions, such as one unit of product A always being tied to one unit of product B, the division of the joint demand into separate demand curves for the tying and tied products is not meaningful. It makes no difference to a purchaser of a pair of gloves to know that the left glove is the same price or more expensive

[18]*Ibid.,* pp. 516–17.
[19]*Ibid.,* p. 520.

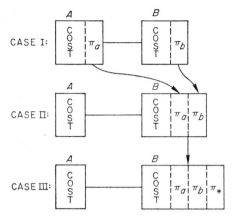

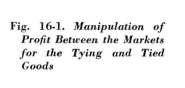

Fig. 16-1. *Manipulation of Profit Between the Markets for the Tying and Tied Goods*

than the right one. Consequently, demand analysis of the case of fixed proportions is more appropriately considered on an aggregate basis, rather than on a segmentation of markets with an imputation of prices for the component tying and tied goods. However, in the case of *variable* proportions the demands for the tying and tied goods must be considered separately, and their interaction must be analyzed comprehensively in order to ascertain the profit-maximizing position of the firm with respect to both products considered simultaneously.

The preceding chapter explained how a firm selling complementary products used in variable proportions can often achieve greater total profits from setting the prices together than by setting them separately. For example, if product A is sold by a monopolist and product B is sold by a great number of firms at a competitive rate of $2.00, the profit-maximizing price for product A is $4.00 in the "profit matrix for A" in Table 15-2. Under these conditions, the monopolist earns $4000, which is the maximum amount of profit obtainable from selling product A independently.

The monopolist of A cannot sell product B at a price over $2.00, since other sources of supply exist from which buyers may obtain this product at the $2.00 competitive rate. By imposing a tying arrangement, the monopolist of A can charge a price for product B (the tied good) in excess of the $2.00 rate. In the case of complementarity, the higher price for product B will cause a leftward shift in the demand curve for product A (the tying good). See Fig. 15-1(I). Thus, the firm will increase its profits from the sale of the tied good, by raising its price for this product above the competitive rate, but the firm will suffer a reduction of profits from the sale of the tying good. The tying arrangement will be an economically rational mode of conduct, provided the decrease in profits from the sale of the tying good is more than compensated by increased profits from the sale of the tied good.

The highest possible profit which a firm can earn by selling products A and B under a tying arrangement is $6950, which is marked by an asterisk in the "profit matrix for A + B" in Table 15-2. This amount of profit is earned by the firm when the price of the tying good (P_a) is $3.50 and the price of the tied good (P_b) is $4.00. It is clear that this profit exceeds the $4000 amount earned when the firm did not use a tying arrangement. The additional profit of $2950 is designated Π_* in Case III of Fig. 16-1, and is considered an exercise of economic leverage.[20]

The term "leverage," in the words of Professor Bowman, "specifically describes the establishment of a new or second monopoly. The existence of such leverage depends upon the effect of the tying arrangement on the output of the tied product. If the tying seller is maximizing his return on the tying product, and the same output of the tied product can still be produced under circumstances consistent with competitive production of the tied product, no additional or new monopoly effect should be assumed."[21] In the case of complements used in variable proportions, the output of the tied good for use with the tying good will be less than it would be if the price or output of the tying good were changed and the tied good were sold competitively. The restriction in the supply of the tied good is deemed an exercise of economic leverage.

The power held over a tied good in the complementarity case can be seen as an incident of the monopoly of product A, which carries a certain amount of power over product B for its uses with product A. The additional profits (Π_*) earned by the firm in tying together products with complementary demands used in variable proportions, can be considered, to paraphrase Justice Holmes, as giving domination or monopoly in the tied-good market only to the extent of the desire for the patented film feeder or teapot in the tying-good market. The Holmes' position in effect claims that the holder of a tying-good monopoly is entitled, as an incident of his ownership, to *all* the additional Π_* profit resulting from complementarity with a tied good. On the other hand, it could be argued in the complementarity case, that since the tying monopolist of product A could have earned none of the Π_* profit without the extended power to price the tied product B, the monopolist is entitled to *none* of the additional Π_* profits.

---

[20]The additional amount of profits for Professor Bowman is slightly less since he sets P_b equal to $3.50 rather than $4.00. It should be noted that if the firm could discriminate in price between different customers, the level of profit from the sale of product A alone might exceed $4000. However, this conduct is not considered "leverage" by Professor Bowman, since no control over the tied good is involved. See Bowman, "Tying Arrangements and the Leverage Problem," p. 25.

[21]*Ibid.*, p. 20. Reprinted by permission of the Yale Law Journal Company and Fred B. Rothman & Company. Footnotes omitted from quotation.

The determination of the maximum amount of profit which can be achieved from product A alone requires only a single product analysis. The presence of interrelated demands, however, requires a multiple product analysis for finding the maximum joint profit potential of the tying and tied products.

CHAPTER SEVENTEEN

The Per Se *Rule and* Tying Arrangements

Four market practices are listed generally as *per se* violations of the antitrust laws: price fixing, division of markets, group boycotts, and tying arrangements.[1] But the standards of proof associated with each of these market practices are quite distinct. Examination of tying arrangement cases discloses the legal and economic difficulties existing within the confines of a given type of *per se* violation.

The Supreme Court summarized the present standard of *per se* illegality applying to tying arrangements in the *Northern Pacific* case,[2] which involved a railroad company's "preferential routing" clause requiring lessees of its land to ship over its railroad all commodities produced on the land provided that its rates were equal to those of competing carriers:

> They are unreasonable in and of themselves whenever a party has sufficient economic power with respect to the tying product to appreciably restrain free competition in the market for the tied product and a 'not insubstantial' amount of interstate commerce is affected.

The Court appears to be stating the following equation for finding tying arrangements *per se* violations of the antitrust laws.

(1) Economic power in the market for the tying goods, *plus*
(2) substantial commerce in the tied goods, *equals*
(3) a *per se* violation of the antitrust laws.

[1] This chapter is taken from my article, "Market Power and Tying Arrangements," *Antitrust Bulletin*, Vol. VIII (July–August, 1963), 653–67.

[2] *Northern Pacific Railway Co.* v. *United States*, 356 U.S. 1, 6 (1958).

When this apparently straightforward *per se* equation is applied by courts to cases involving tying arrangements, a brief answer is seldom forthcoming. Indeed, the evidence required for part (1) of the equation suggests a discussion of the available economic evidence in what might appear to be a *rule of reason* approach.

This confrontation of the *rule of reason* and *per se* doctrines in the law of tying arrangements was present in *S. Kriete Osborn* v. *Sinclair Refining Co..*[3] The defendant argued that the record lacked evidence of its economic power in the tying-good market for gasoline, and, therefore, it could not have restrained commerce in the markets for the tied goods consisting of tires, batteries, and accessories. In refusing to hear further evidence beyond the finding that the defendant owned over 10 per cent of the gasoline stations in the state where the tying arrangement was enforced, the Circuit Court stated:

> If all the industry-wide economic data had to be shown for which Sinclair argues, it would convert tie-in cases into "rule of reason" cases. . . .[4]

The Extreme Form of the Per Se Test

In the extreme form of the *per se* doctrine, there is no need to examine the purpose or justification for the actions of the defendant. In the words of Justice Black,

> . . . there are certain practices which because of their pernicious effect on competition and lack of any redeeming virtue are conclusively presumed to be unreasonable and therefore illegal without elaborate inquiry as to the precise harm they have caused or the business excuse for their use. This principle of per se unreasonableness not only makes the type of restraints which are proscribed by the Sherman Act more certain to the benefit of everyone concerned, but it also avoids the necessity for an incredibly complicated and prolonged economic investigation into the entire history of the industry involved, as well as related industries, in an effort to determine at large whether a particular restraint has been unreasonable — an inquiry so often fruitless when undertaken.[5]

The tying arrangement is classified by Justice Black as an example of *per se* unreasonableness. Therefore, it might be concluded that once a contract containing tying clauses is introduced and accepted in evidence, a *per se* violation of the antitrust laws is established. But the courts are following a different standard of illegality, since there invariably is made an inspection of both the degree of market power over the tying good, and the substantiality of commerce affected in the market for the tied good.

[3]286 F. 2nd 832 (4th Cir., 1961), *cert. denied*, 366 U.S. 963 (1961).
[4]*Ibid.*, p. 841.
[5]*Northern Pacific Railway Co.* v. *United States*, 356 U.S. 1, 5 (1958).

The Per Se *Test as a Procedural Guide*

Part of the difficulty in answering the question of the amount of market data to admit in cases involving *per se* violations stems from a failure to recognize that *per se* and *rule of reason* are merely relative standards for classifying the extent of proof required in antitrust cases.[6] The two phrases should not be seen as absolute polar concepts referring, with respect to the former, to the admission of almost no evidence and, with respect to the latter, to the opening of the floodgates for all available economic evidence. Rather, the concepts should be employed as informal procedural guides indicating the quantum of evidence required in a given case.

Indicia of Economic Leverage

The purported *per se* analysis of the Supreme Court decisions reflect certain vestiges of a *rule of reason* inquiry into the markets for the tied and tying goods. The courts declare standards of illegality that cannot be ascertained without an examination of various market factors. In order to make a fair appraisal of leverage, the courts must look at economic evidence for the empirical content of words such as "dominance," "exploitation," "leverage," or "market," which appear in the previously discussed Supreme Court rule that, ". . . the essence of illegality in tying arrangements is the wielding of monopolistic leverage; a seller exploits his dominant position in one market to expand his empire into the next."[7]

One concept is fundamental to an economic analysis of tying arrangements: Leverage cannot be wielded over the market for the tied good without the existence of substantial economic power over the tying-good market. The following indicia of economic power over the market for the tying good should be useful in determining whether there exists a "wielding of monopolistic leverage." These indicia also illustrate the breadth of evidence present in tying arrangement cases.

MARKET DOMINANCE IN THE MARKET FOR THE TYING GOOD. The phrase "market dominance" is described by the Supreme Court as referring to

---

[6]Cf. W. L. Baldwin and D. McFarland, "Some Observations on 'Per Se' and Tying Arrangements," *Antitrust Bulletin*, Vol. VI (July–December, 1961), 433–39, and "Tying Arrangements in Law and Economics," *ibid.*, Vol. VIII (September–December, 1963), pp. 743–80. Also see J. C. Stedman, "Tying Arrangements," *American Bar Association Section of Antitrust Law*, Vol. XXII (April, 1963), 64–73; Phillips, *Market Structure, Organization, and Performance*, pp. 199–242; and W. B. Lockhart and H. R. Sacks, "The Relevance of Economic Factors in Determining Whether Exclusive Arrangements Violate Section 3 of the Clayton Act," *Harvard Law Review*, Vol. LVX (April, 1952), 919–42.

[7]*Times-Picayune Publishing Co.* v. *United States*, 345 U.S. 594, 611 (1953).

"some power to control price and to exclude competition."[8] The presence of dominance in the market for the tying goods forebodes almost certain illegality for the practices of the defendant, provided a substantial amount of commerce is affected in the tied-good market. However, the prerequisite economic power over the tying-good market for illegality can be considerably less than market domination. "Even absent a showing of market dominance, the crucial economic power may be inferred from the tying product's desirability to consumers or from the uniqueness in its attributes."[9]

DESIRABILITY OF THE TYING GOOD. Since customers will hardly ever purchase a product which appears undesirable to them, the equating of economic power with the desirability of a product is a circular way of invariably finding the crucial market power in the tying good. For example, in *United States* v. *Jerrold Electronics Co.*,[10] which permitted, for a temporary period of time, a tying arrangement of service contracts with community television antenna systems, the District Court stated:

Jerrold's highly specialized head end equipment for antennas was in great demand — in fact it was the only equipment available which was designed to meet all of the varying problems arising at the antenna site. This placed Jerrold in a strategic position and gave it the leverage necessary to persuade customers to agree to its service contracts. This leverage constitutes "economic power" sufficient to invoke the doctrine of per se unreasonableness.[11]

UNDESIRABILITY OF THE TIED GOOD. The "coercion theory" of tying arrangements focuses on the comparative bargaining power of the parties. In the usual tying arrangement a customer is required to take a product or brand which he does not necessarily want in order to secure one which he desires.[12] "By conditioning his sale of one commodity on the purchase of another, a seller coerces the abdication of buyers' independent judgment as to the 'tied' product's merits . . ."[13]

If the focus is changed from the tied good in isolation to a combination of the tying good and the tied good, the conclusion that the purchaser must necessarily be harmed is no longer clear. The purchaser must weigh the positive utility derived from the potential purchase of the tying good

[8]*United States* v. *Loew's Inc.*, 371 U.S. 38, 45 (1962).

[9]*Ibid.*, p. 45. Also see Turner, "The Validity of Tying Arrangements Under the Antitrust Laws," pp. 50–75.

[10]187 F. Supp. 545, 555 (E.D. Pa., 1960), *affirmed per curiam*, 365 U.S. 567 (1961).

[11]*Ibid.*, p. 567.

[12]Hale and Hale, *Market Power: Size and Shape Under the Sherman Act*, pp. 44–58 and 267–74.

[13]*Times-Picayune Publishing Co.* v. *United States*, 345 U.S. 594, 604 (1953).

as well as the tied good, and deduct, in the rare case, the negative utility from a useless tied good. The net utility derived from the potential purchase must exceed the utility foregone by the expenditure for the combined purchase price of the two items. If the purchaser does not like the combination, he can reallocate his income to the purchase of other items.

The case of a dealer being subjected to a tying arrangement can be distinguished from the consumer facing a tying arrangement involving a trivial expenditure. In *Standard Oil Co. (Calif.)* v. *United States*, commonly referred to as *Standard Stations*,[14] there were 5937 gasoline stations, constituting 16 per cent of the relevant market, which entered into exclusive requirements contracts with Standard Oil of California. Since the lease of a gas station generally commits the average proprietor to a substantial amount of his savings, it would be unwise for him to risk his whole business by not complying with the tying arrangements imposed by the lessor-supplier. A related area involves the sale of tires, batteries, and accessories (TBA) to dealers by the major oil companies.[15] The coercion exerted on a lessee or franchise holder is of far greater magnitude than the pressure found in the consumer tying arrangements, such as where an individual is required to purchase an undesirable cologne with a favorite shaving lather.

The coercion theory is also suggested by the Supreme Court's analysis in the *Loew's* case.[16] Large distributors of feature motion pictures were found to have violated Sec. 1 of the Sherman Act by their practice of block booking. The gist of the offense was seen as the forcing of small independent television stations into acceptance of inferior films along with desirable pictures.

In contrast, the Supreme Court in the *Tampa Electric* case[17] allowed a long-term requirements contract for one million tons of coal annually for a period of 20 years. Both parties were extremely large concerns, and there was evidence that the contract was negotiated at the customer's behest to insure a sufficient supply of coal for a newly constructed electric power plant. Although the Court did not rest its conclusion solely on this finding, and the case did not involve a tying arrangement, the attention paid to the relative strength of the parties indicates that the "coercion

---

[14]337 U.S. 293 (1949). The decision is also noteworthy for the controversy which arose over its doctrine of "quantitive substantiality." See United States, *Report of the Attorney General's National Committee to Study the Antitrust Laws*, pp. 141–49.

[15]See *Osborn* v. *Sinclair Refining Co.*, 286 F. 2nd 832 (4th Cir., 1960), *cert. denied*, 366 U.S. 963 (1961) and *Goodyear Tire & Rubber Co.* v. *Federal Trade Commission*, 331 F. 2nd 394 (7th Cir., 1964), *affirmed* 381 U.S. 357 (1964).

[16]*United States* v. *Loew's Inc.*, 371 U.S. 38 (1962).

[17]*Tampa Electric Co.* v. *National Coal Co.*, 365 U.S. 220 (1961).

theory" is part of the prerequisite analysis for the broader category of exclusive arrangements.

The undesirability of the tied product to the buyer is sometimes obvious from the initial facts. In these cases the Court presumes the existence of economic power over tying goods. For example, when a buyer suffers economic detriment from the tying arrangement because he is precluded from purchasing a tied product at better terms or of a better quality elsewhere, economic coercion can be inferred even without any direct showing of market dominance.[18]

PATENTS OR COPYRIGHTS COVERING THE TYING GOOD. The courts have condemned any attempt by the patentee to extend a patent beyond his invention into markets for unpatented goods. The patentee is seldom attempting to monopolize the market for the tied good, and in some instances, appears to be sacrificing some of his potential profit from the tying-good market and making it up in the market for the tied good. Consequently, neither monopoly power nor profits are necessarily increased by the patentee tying unpatented goods to his patent.

Tying arrangements between patented and unpatented items are presumed to be illegal under present antitrust decisions. This presumption grew out of the doctrine holding that a patentee who utilizes tying arrangements to sell supplies and related machinery would be denied relief against infringement of his patent.[19] Implicit in the presumption is the belief that since a patent or copyright is a statutory monopoly, it follows that each must also be a market monopoly. But all patents do not confer substantial or even significant market power. Nevertheless, the law today is that the "requisite economic power is presumed when the tying product is patented or copyrighted."[20]

BARRIERS TO ENTRY. One of the first cases to be brought under Sec. 3 of the Clayton Act raised the issue of barriers to entry as a factor to be considered in tying arrangements. In *Federal Trade Commission* v. *Sinclair Refining Co.*,[21] the Supreme Court allowed Sinclair as well as thirty other

[18]See the dissenting opinion of Justice Harlan in *Northern Pacific Railway Co.* v. *United States*, 356 U.S. 1, 16 (1958).

[19]See *Motion Picture Patents Co.* v. *Universal Film Mfg. Co.*, 243 U.S. 502 (1917); *Carbice Corp.* v. *American Patents Development Corp.*, 283 U.S. 27 (1931); *Leitch Manufacturing Co.* v. *Barber Co.*, 302 U.S. 458 (1938); *Ethyl Gasoline Corp.* v. *United States*, 309 U.S. 436 (1940); *Morton Salt Co.* v. *G. S. Suppiger Co.*, 314 U.S. 488 (1942); *Mercoid Corp.* v. *Mid-Continent Investment Co.*, 320 U.S. 661 (1944).

[20]*United States* v. *Loew's, Inc.*, 371 U.S. 38, 45 (1962).

[21]261 U.S. 463 (1923).

refiners to continue the practice of leasing underground tanks to gasoline stations at a minimal rental, upon the condition that the equipment should be used only for the storage of gasoline supplied by the lessor. The Court was impressed by the lowering of barriers to entry at the retail level. The practice of leasing allowed an individual to open a gasoline station with a comparatively small capital investment. But the Court failed to note that this same leasing practice tended to raise the barriers to entry at the gasoline distributor level.

Barriers to entry have been viewed by some writers as the principal evil of tying arrangements. In the words of Professors Turner and Kaysen:

> A tie-in always operates to raise the barriers to entry in the market of the tied good to the level of those in the market for the tying-good: the seller who would supply the one, can do so only if he can also supply the other, since he must be able to displace the whole package which the tying seller offers. Developing a substitute for the tying product may be very difficult, if not impossible. Thus tying tends to spread market power into markets where it would not otherwise exist: for example, few firms are prepared to supply machines like those of IBM, whereas many may be prepared to supply punch cards.[22]

The lowering of barriers to entry is one of the few exceptions to the general proscription against tying devices. In *Brown Shoe Co.* v. *United States*[23] the Supreme Court stated, "unless the tying device is employed by a small company in an attempt to break into a market, cf. *Harley-Davidson Motor Co.*, 50 F.T.C. 1047, 1066, the use of a tying device can rarely be harmonized with the strictures of the antitrust laws, which are intended primarily to preserve and stimulate competition."

EXCLUSIVENESS OF TYING ARRANGEMENTS. The finding of sufficient economic power over the tying good market may be reflected by the scope and number of the tying arrangements employed by the seller. A tie-in will not escape condemnation because the buyer is not obligated to obtain all of his requirements of the tied product from the seller. As the degree of exclusiveness increases, the need for evidence proving economic power over the tying goods is considerably diminished.

The greatest degree of exclusiveness in tying arrangements is found in cases of full-line forcing, where the buyer must obtain a complete line of related goods, or none at all, from a single seller. In *United Shoe Machinery* v. *United States*,[24] the lessor had the right to cancel the machine leases

---

[22]Reprinted by permission of the publishers from Carl Kaysen and Donald F. Turner, *Antitrust Policy* (Cambridge, Mass: Harvard University Press), copyright 1959 by the President and Fellows of Harvard College, p. 157.

[23]370 U.S. 294, 330 (1962).

[24]258 U.S. 451 (1922).

in the event that competing shoe machines were employed on the same item being processed through one of its machines. Competing suppliers were, as a practical matter, completely foreclosed from those factories leasing machines from United Shoe.

A manufacturer may lease a machine to a customer with a provision in the contract requiring the customer to use only the supplies of the manufacturer in the particular machine. These tying arrangements do not completely cut off the customer from access to competing product markets, since the customer can use the supplies obtained from different manufacturers in other machines. Nonetheless, the practice is generally condemned.[27]

Finally, the degree of exclusiveness should be considered in "qualified tying arrangements," which require the tied good to be purchased only if it sells at the same or a lower price as goods of the same quality sold by competing suppliers. This type of clause was contained in the leases in *International Salt Co. v. United States*,[28] where the defendant argued that the tying arrangements were inoffensive restraints because they allowed lessees to buy salt from other suppliers when offered at a lower price. The Supreme Court rejected the argument by stating that the "provision does, of course, offer a measure of protection to the lessee, but it does not avoid the stifling effect of the agreement on competition. The appellant had at all times a priority on the business at equal prices."[29]

ENFORCEMENT OF TYING CLAUSES. The fact that tying clauses in a contract are not always enforced is an insufficient defense. The record in the *United Shoe* case disclosed many instances where the tying provisions were not enforced. But the Court felt that the potential harm from their enforcement, which would result in the cancellation of the machinery leases, was sufficient to insure compliance from most of the lessees. In the words of the Court, "The power to enforce them is omnipresent, and their restraining influence constantly operates upon competitors and lessees."[30]

A significant element in enforcement is not the degree of actual insistence upon compliance with the terms of the tying arrangement, but the dire consequences flowing from cancellation of the contract. A shoe manu-

[27]*Signode Steel Strapping Co. v. Federal Trade Commission*, 132 F. 2nd 48 (4th Cir., 1942); *Judson L. Thomson Mfg. Co. v. Federal Trade Commission*, 150 F. 2nd 952 (1st Cir., 1945), *cert. denied* 326 U.S. 776 (1945). But see *Federal Trade Commission v. Sinclair Refining Co.*, 261 U.S. 463 (1923) for an exception when the element of "goodwill" is recognized.

[28]332 U.S. 392 (1947). Also see *Northern Pacific Railway Co. v. United States*, 356 U.S. 1 (1958).

[29]*Ibid.*, p. 397.

[30]258 U.S. 451, 458 (1922).

facturer would have difficulty staying in business in 1920 without access to any of the machines made by United Shoe. The trial court in the United Shoe case found that the defendant controlled over 95 per cent of the business of supplying shoe machinery.[31]

*   *   *

The legal and economic standards of proof observed in tying arrangement cases are far more flexible than the phrase *per se* suggests. Courts generally inspect the degree of market power over the tying goods, as well as the amount of commerce affected in the market for the tied goods, before passing on whether the tying arrangement tends to lessen competition. In the majority of tying arrangement cases the initial facts have indicated, without the need for further investigation, the presence of substantial market power over the tying goods. However, where the existence of market power is not clear, the courts have examined various indicia of economic leverage.

[31]*Ibid.*

CHAPTER EIGHTEEN

The Pure Theory
of Vertical Integration

The degree of vertical integration of a firm depends upon the extent to which it carries on the productive process from the extraction of raw materials to the transformation of these materials into a final product. Until a firm can achieve a level of volume high enough to justify its own manufacture of an input, it must make purchases from outside firms. Even in cases where a firm can produce an input with the same cost advantages achieved by a supplier, the firm may decide against assuming the capital investment and management problems associated with the input industry.

The economic rationale for a firm to integrate forward by acquiring its customers or building similar facilities, or to integrate backward toward the suppliers of its inputs is analyzed in this chapter. A model of a firm which uses two inputs, A and B, in order to produce a final product, X, is developed. Equilibrium positions of the firm are compared under various assumptions as to the market structure of the input and output industries. The focus of the analysis is on whether a firm with a monopoly over an input has an incentive, in economic theory, to integrate forward to a purely competitive final product industry; or whether a firm with a monopoly over a final product has an incentive to integrate backward to a purely competitive input industry.

Assume that inputs A and B are produced under conditions of pure competition and are available in perfectly elastic supply to the firms in industry X. A, B, and X are all produced under constant costs. The marginal cost curve for X, MC_x, in Fig. 18-1 is obtained by summing for each unit of output the marginal costs of input A, MC_a, and input B, MC_b. For simplicity, the inputs are assumed to be combined in fixed

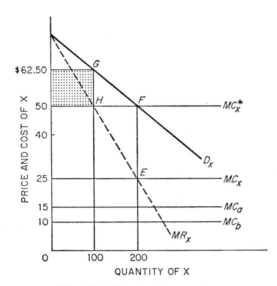

Fig. 18-1. *Vertical Integration*

proportions to yield a unit of the final product X. Hence, one unit of input A plus one unit of input B yields one unit of final product X. Input B should be treated as including the costs of the producer in transforming inputs A and B into output X, as well as a normal return. The demand curve is designated as D_x, and its corresponding marginal revenue curve as MR_x.[1]

Competitive Inputs and Monopolized Output

The profit maximizing output for a monopolist controlling industry X, with input industries A and B purely competitive, is given in Fig. 18-1 at point E, where the marginal cost and the marginal revenue curves for X intersect. The monopolist of X will maximize its profits by producing 200 units of product X and charging a price of $50. At this price and output level the monopolist of X will have a total revenue of $10,000, total costs of $5000, and a total profit of $5000.

Combined Monopoly of Inputs and Output

The profit maximizing output for a monopolist controlling input industries A and B as well as the final product industry X is also given by the

[1]The following discussion of this model is taken from Burstein, "A Theory of Full Line Forcing," p. 66. His discussion is, in turn, based upon a classroom presentation by Professor Milton Friedman.

intersection of MC_x and MR_x at point E. If the integrated monopolist can manufacture inputs A and B at the same cost as buying them, he will set imputed prices for these inputs equal to their former marginal costs when they were obtained from purely competitive outside industries. The combined monopolist of A, B, and X will earn the same total profit ($5000) in this situation as a monopolist of X where the industries A and B were purely competitive. Thus, a monopolist of a manufactured final product will have no profit incentive to enter by acquisition or internal growth purely competitive industries which supply its inputs.

Monopolized Input and Competitive Output

A firm that holds a monopoly over an input such as A, where input B and final product X are produced under purely competitive conditions, has no economic incentive to integrate horizontally to industry B or vertically forward to industry X. In this market structure the monopolist of A has the ability to extract all the potential profit from industry X by raising the price of input A. If the monopolist of input A in Fig. 18-1 raises its price to $40, a producer in industry X must accept this increased price for the input as a basic cost. If it is assumed that industry X is only one of many industries requiring input A, and its output is too small to influence the price policies of industry A, the maximum profit available to the monopolist of input A from industry X is $5000. The latter amount is equal to the total revenue from input A ($200 \times \$40 = \$8000$) less the total cost to produce this amount of input A ($200 \times \$15 = \$3000$).

Under the assumption of pure competition in industry X, there will be no abnormal profits earned in this industry, and the price of X will be equal to the marginal cost of X, MC_x^*. MC_x^* is at a level of $50, since each additional unit of X consists of one unit of input A ($40) plus one unit of input B ($10). The monopolist of input A is able to achieve all of the profit inherent in the production of X by charging $40 for each unit of input A.

The monopolist of input A may also earn profits from sales to final product industries other than X. However, if these profits from sales outside industry X are excluded, and the above assumptions are adhered to, it can be concluded that the same amount of profit is earned by a monopolist in the following market structures: (1) where a monopoly over a final product exists and the related input industries are purely competitive; (2) where a monopoly exists over both the final product industry and the related input industries; and finally, (3) where a monopoly exists over an input industry and the necessary remaining inputs and final product are produced in purely competitive industries.

Successive Monopolies

Successive monopolies are market structures in which a monopolist at one stage of production purchases materials from another monopolist at a higher stage of production. In terms of the preceding model, a monopolist of the final product X purchases one of its basic inputs, A, from another monopolist. Assume that the monopolist of X is one of a large number of purchasers from various industries which require input A, and the output of X is too small to influence pricing decisions of the monopolist of A. If the monopolist of input A raises its price to \$40, and input B sells at the purely competitive rate of \$10, the marginal cost curve for X will be at the \$50 level, or MC_x^*. The latter curve will intersect the marginal revenue curve for X, MR_x, at point H. The monopolist will charge a price for X of \$62.50 and will have an output of 100 units. The monopoly profit for X at this output is \$1250, total revenue is \$6250, and total costs are \$5000.

The monopolist of input A will receive from industry X a per unit profit of \$25 (or \$40 less \$15), and a total profit of \$2500 (100 × \$25). The aggregate profit for both the monopolists of input A and final product X is \$1250 + \$2500 or \$3750, which is less than the \$5000 profit earned in the previously discussed cases at the beginning of the chapter.

If the monopolist of input A and the monopolist of final product X would vertically integrate, or at least reach some type of agreement whereby the price of X is lowered from \$62.50 to \$50, their aggregate profits would increase to \$5000. Professor Bork reaches a similar conclusion as follows:

Where monopolies are integrated consumers will pay the monopoly price. But where the monopolies are in separate hands the higher monopolist may charge the full monopoly price to the lower who will in turn accept that price as a cost and further restrict output and raise price. The price as between the monopolists may be indeterminate, but the price to consumers will be higher than the single-monopoly price. Of course, the monopolists may negotiate and lower the price to consumers to the single-monopoly price in order to maximize the total profit to be split between themselves.[2]

Let us drop the initial assumption that the market for the final product X is too small to affect the pricing decisions of the monopolist of input A. Assume that the demand for input A is derived completely from the demand for the final product X. Marginal costs are no longer assumed to be horizontal; they are positively sloped. Under these conditions, it can be shown that successive monopolists will have a higher price and a lower output than a single vertically integrated monopolist.[3]

[2]R. Bork, "Vertical Integration and the Sherman Act: The History of an Economic Misconception," *University of Chicago Law Review*, Vol. XXII (Autumn, 1954), 196.

[3]F. Machlup and M. Taber, "Bilateral Monopoly, Successive Monopoly, and Vertical Integration," *Economica*, Vol. XXVII (May, 1960), 102.

Consider the case of successive monopolies in which a manufacturing monopolist sells to a retail monopolist.[4] In Fig. 18-2 the demand curve of

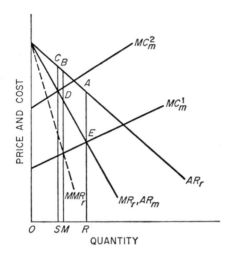

Fig. 18-2. *Successive Monopolies*

consumers which faces the retail monopolist is AR_r, and its corresponding marginal revenue curve is MR_r. The latter curve is also the demand curve of the retailer for the product of the manufacturer, provided the retailer has no monopolistic buying power. The manufacturer, with a marginal cost curve MC_m^1, will charge the retailer a price RE and offer an output of OR. The retailer, in turn, will charge at this output level a price RA to consumers.

If the manufacturer is stronger than the retailer, so that the latter must comply with the price terms set by the manufacturer, the manufacturer will have a marginal revenue curve such as MMR_r, which is *marginal* to the *marginal* revenue curve of the retailer. The manufacturer with a marginal cost curve MC_m^1 will produce OM of X, which will ultimately be the retailer's output; the manufacturer's price will be MD, and the retailer's price to consumers will be MB. The above relationship between successive monopolists, a retailer and a manufacturer, results in a higher price and a lower output in contrast to a single vertically integrated monopoly. The explanation lies primarily in the fact that the demand for the manufacturer's product is *derived* from the retailer's demand curve. Consequently, there will occur a "repeated marginalization" of the revenue curves of successive monopolists in determining their profit-maximizing outputs.

[4]See E. R. Hawkins, "Vertical Price Relationships," in *Theory in Marketing*, R. Cox and W. Alderson, eds. (Homewood, Ill: Richard D. Irwin, Inc., 1950), p. 183.

In the event the manufacturer attempts to sell its product directly to consumers, the relevant marginal revenue curve will not be MMR_r but MR_r, which is more elastic for the same quantities than the former curve. The manufacturer would thereby avoid the repeated marginalization of revenue curves. If the marginal costs of the manufacturer remain the same after assuming the retail function, the final price to consumers will fall from MB to RA, and the output to consumers will increase from OM to OR. The forward integration of the manufacturer will benefit the consumers with lower prices and higher output. However, where the manufacturer faces much higher costs, such as MC_m^2, when undertaking both vertical stages, the consumers may be left worse off than they were before vertical integration. Output will be restricted to OS, and the consumer price will be raised to SC, when the applicable marginal cost curve of the vertically integrated manufacturer is MC_m^2. Thus, a crucial factor in appraising the economic effects of vertical integration is whether the vertically integrated firm is more efficient in operating the stage that it supplants. If the costs of the manufacturer increase with vertical integration, but the marginal cost curve still intersects MR_r below point D, the consumer will enjoy the benefits of a lower price and higher quantity of the manufacturer's product as a result of vertical integration.

Professor Weintraub, after an analysis of successive monopolies, concludes: "Monopoly in the successive stages, therefore, will be more harmful to consumers than monopoly in but one stage. Hence fully integrated output will be superior from the consumer's standpoint even if there is some cost disadvantage attached to this development as compared to the economics of specialization."[5] Professor Machlup cautions against using the theoretical argument for vertical integration as if it were a reliable guide to public policy: " . . . joint profit maximization between monopolists, useful though it may be in mitigating the effects of horizontal combination, is not *the* ideal form of economic arrangement when there are possibilities of achieving greater degrees of competition in the several stages."[6] This broad question of competition and vertical integration is examined in the next chapter. Market practices associated with vertically integrated market structures are presented in terms of a number of leading antitrust law cases.

[5]Weintraub, *Price Theory*, p. 308. A similar conclusion is reached by A. C. Hoffman, "Large-scale Organization in the Food Industries," T.N.E.C. Monograph No. 35 (Washington, D.C.: Government Printing Office, 1940) and J. J. Spengler, "Vertical Integration and Antitrust Policy," *Journal of Political Economy*, Vol. LVIII (August, 1950), 347–52.

[6]Machlup and Taber, "Bilateral Monopoly, Successive Monopoly, and Vertical Integration," pp. 116–17.

CHAPTER NINETEEN

Market Practices Associated with Vertically Integrated Market Structures

The vertically integrated firm, by virtue of its multiple operations in production and distribution, may be able to use its market strength at one level of competition to further its interests at another. For example, such a firm may be able to affect the position of its own fabricators by charging an unduly high price for a raw material purchased by customers, who are nonintegrated competing fabricators. The nonintegrated fabricators would be caught in a "price squeeze" in attempting to meet the vertically integrated firm's price for the finished product where their raw material costs were higher than the imputed prices charged to the fabricating facilities of the vertically integrated firm.

In more complex market structures the vertically integrated firm may make purchases from the same companies to which it sells. For example, a firm may sell raw materials to a fabricator and also purchase fully fabricated products from the same company. In this market structure the vertically integrated firm might resort to the practice of reciprocity, whereby it would use its position as a buyer of fabricated products to press its sales of raw materials to independent fabricators. The competitive effects of market practices of vertically integrated firms, such as price squeezing and reciprocity, are analyzed in the settings of leading cases in this area of antitrust law.

The Foreclosure of Suppliers[1]

Complete or absolute foreclosure of competing suppliers by a firm employing either exclusive requirements contracts or vertical integration is present when a supplier obtains all outlets in a particular product market in order to deny competing nonintegrated suppliers any access to the market. In Fig. 19-1 there are four suppliers (A, B, C, and D) and one outlet.

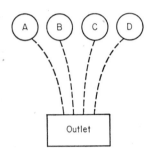

Fig. 19-1. *Absence of Foreclosure of Suppliers*

Since no firm is assumed to have any priority in the distribution of competing goods through the one outlet, the market structure reflects a total absence of foreclosure of suppliers.

The diametrically opposite market structure appears in Fig. 19-2. Firm A, through an exclusive requirements contract or vertical acquisition, pre-

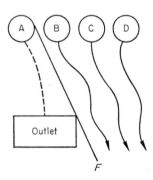

Fig. 19-2. *Absolute Foreclosure of Suppliers*

empts the business of the outlet and forecloses the competing suppliers (B, C, and D) from any access to the *sole* outlet. This absolute foreclosure of competitors is denoted by the straight line *F*. Given the market structure of four suppliers and one outlet, the absolute foreclosure of all competitors by a given firm will unquestionably violate the present antitrust

[1]This section includes excerpts from my article, "Vertical Integration and Economic Growth," *American Bar Association Journal*, Vol. L (June, 1964), 555–58.

laws. Firms B, C, and D cannot possibly survive in the present state of affairs. In other words, once one supplier acquires an outlet, which is distributing the products of competing suppliers, and then exerts pressure on the outlet to foreclose competing suppliers, the ousted suppliers must of necessity seek further outlets.

In *United States* v. *Maryland and Virginia Milk Producers Assn.*,[2] an association of milk dealers was required by the Supreme Court to divest the previously acquired assets of its leading competitor in the distribution of milk. The decision has been described as presenting "an unambiguous 'leverage' problem, i.e., the use of power at one level — distribution — to secure or strengthen power at another level — production."[3]

The defendant milk association (square X) in Fig. 19-3 accounted for approximately 86 per cent of all sales of fluid milk to all twelve of the milk

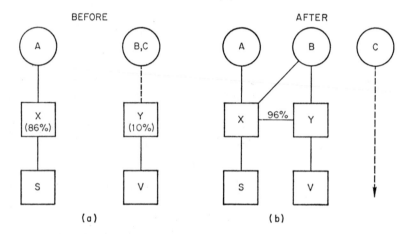

Fig. 19-3. *Foreclosure of Competing Suppliers*

dealers in the Washington metropolitan area. Embassy Dairy (square Y) was an independent concern not buying from the defendant association, but procuring its supply directly from farmers refusing to sell to the defendant association. Embassy accounted for 10 per cent of the fluid milk sales in the above market.

The association, by gaining control of Embassy, achieved 96 per cent of the Washington fluid milk market. This market position allowed the association not only to stop most of the inflow of lower-priced milk, but to use its apparent monopoly control over the retail market as leverage in

[2]362 U.S. 458 (1960).

[3]F. Kessler and R. H. Stern, "Competition, Contract, and Vertical Integration," *Yale Law Journal*, Vol. LXIX (November, 1959), 73.

forcing the remaining independent farmers, who formerly sold milk to Embassy, to join the association.

The independent dairy farmers, such as B and C in Fig. 19-3, had the choice after the acquisition of joining the association and having their milk sold in the Washington area, or refusing membership in the association and being forced to ship milk to other markets such as Baltimore, Maryland. The diagonal line in Fig. 19-3 connects some of the formerly independent farmers (circle B) with the association (square X). A few farmers, such as C, shipped their milk to other markets rather than accept membership in the association.

The "Squeezing" of Independent Fabricators

In *United States* v. *Aluminum Co. of America*[4] the sole domestic producer of virgin aluminum also engaged, along with several other manufacturers, in the fabrication operation of rolling aluminum ingots into sheets. The offense committed by Alcoa was the subsidization of sheet manufacturing, which was performed at a near loss, by the profits made at the higher level of ingot production. The Court of Appeals segregated the various technological levels of the integrated firm and treated each level as an independent operation, in an accounting sense, for estimating "fair price" and "fair profit."

Subsidization by Alcoa of some levels of operations by the profits or returns made at other levels was referred to as the act of "squeezing" independent fabricators. Figure 19-4 shows Alcoa as circle A, its manufacturing or rolling operation as square X, and finally its outlet or retail level as the square V. The other manufacturers of sheet who had to purchase ingots from Alcoa are represented by the square Y. These manufacturers sold rolled sheets through their outlets, square *S*, in competition with the Alcoa outlet, square V. Alcoa charged the competing fabricators a high price for ingots and, thereby, raised their raw material cost base. Alcoa also sold sheets through its own outlets at an exceptionally low price in hard competition with the other independent fabricators.

Since Alcoa was alleged to have set both the ingot and sheet prices, it had the power to determine for its competitors the profit spread between the raw material and the finished product. Alcoa was "squeezing" when it set the ingot price so high and the sheet price so low that the other manufacturers could survive only with great difficulty in the rolling operation. Alcoa was alleged to be using its profits from ingot sales to subsidize its rolling operations until, presumably, its competitors went under. Alcoa's

[4]148 F. 2nd 416 (2nd Cir., 1945). Also see 91 F. Supp. 333 (S.D.N.Y., 1950) for the remedial part of the case.

defense that it could not determine until the end of an accounting period whether it had made a profit or loss was rejected by the court.

Theoretically, one might argue that if Alcoa really had a pure monopoly it could sell ingots at an unusually high price and maximize its profits with-

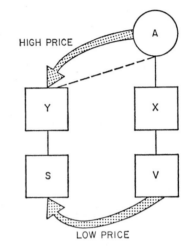

Fig. 19-4. *Squeezing Non-integrated Fabricators*

out entering the fabrication field. Alternatively, Alcoa could split this profit between ingots and fabrication in a manner analogous to the patent monopolist's reducing the profit in the patented tying good, and recovering it by charging higher prices for the tied good.

However, the Court of Appeals suggested that these alternative methods for making profits may be unlawful:

... that it was unlawful to set the price of "sheet" so low and hold the price of ingot so high, seems to us unquestionable, provided, as we have held, that on this record the price of ingot must be regarded as higher than a "fair" price. True, this was only a consequence of "Alcoa's" control over the price of ingot, and perhaps it ought not be considered as a separate wrong . . .[5]

The offense of Alcoa was not simply the charging of a high price for ingots, nor the coordinated charging of a low price for sheets. Rather, the offense was the continuation of this pricing policy *after* it had been put on notice that the survival of independent sheet rollers was in imminent danger. Only when the existence of independent or nonintegrated firms is at stake do the practices of subsidization or squeezing become open to question as tending to lessen competition.

[5]148 F. 2nd 416, 438 (1945).

The Squeezing Dilemma

In *Federal Trade Commission* v. *Standard Oil of Indiana*,[6] a price squeeze existed which was almost the reverse of that found in the *Alcoa* case. Instead of following the Alcoa pattern of selling at a high price to customers, and attempting to undersell them at the outlet level, Standard Oil sold gasoline at a high price to its own retailers, and sold at a low price to wholesale jobbers. In Fig. 19-5 Standard Oil is represented by circle *A*, its own retailers by square *V*, and competing wholesalers by square *X*.

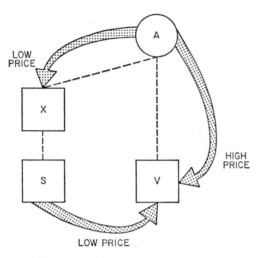

Fig. 19-5. *The Squeezing Dilemma*

The Federal Trade Commission charged that Standard Oil violated the provisions of the Robinson-Patman Act against price discrimination in granting lower prices exclusively to four jobbers in the Detroit area. The Commission maintained that the lower prices to the four jobbers were injurious competitively to retail dealers in Detroit who were buying directly from Standard Oil. The retailers who were able to buy at lower prices from these four jobbers could undercut retailers buying at higher prices directly from Standard Oil.

The Commission, in trying to enforce a decree compelling Standard Oil not to sell to its retail customers at a price higher than that charged by its

[6]340 U.S. 231 (1951). See J. McGee, "Price Discrimination and Competitive Effects: The Standard Oil of Indiana Case," *University of Chicago Law Review*, Vol. XXIII (Spring, 1956), 398–473; and Note, *Harvard Law Review*, Vol. LXVII (December, 1953), 294–317.

wholesale customers, was in effect ordering Standard to put a price squeeze on its integrated wholesale customers (square X).[7] Standard Oil faced the dilemma of either continuing its present pricing pattern, which was putting a price squeeze on its retail customers, or complying with the Commission's request and changing its pricing pattern into an Alcoa-type squeeze on wholesale customers. Standard Oil was able to avoid the Commission's order by proving that the lower prices granted to the four jobbers were made in good faith to meet the competition of other gasoline suppliers who were quoting the same or lower prices to the four jobbers.[8] The next chapter considers in greater detail the Robinson-Patman Act good faith "meeting competition" defense. At this stage of the analysis, the vertical structure existing in the *Standard Oil of Indiana* case is under scrutiny, rather than the legal provisions of the Robinson-Patman Act.

The Total Squeeze

The District Court in *United States* v. *Bethlehem Steel Corp.*[9] considered the position of fabricators who purchase their raw materials of *rope wire* from Youngstown, twist it, and then sell back to Youngstown the fully fabricated product of *wire rope*. Since Bethlehem fabricates wire rope, and could reasonably be expected in the future to sell large quantities to Youngstown, the District Court found that the merger of Bethlehem and Youngstown would tend to place the independent nonintegrated firm at a competitive disadvantage.

Youngstown is represented in Fig. 19-6 by circle Y, Bethlehem by circle B, and the two firms after the merger by circle B-Y. At first glance the independent fabricators, such as Z, appear to be threatened by an Alcoa-

[7]F. Rowe, *Price Discrimination Under the Robinson-Patman Act*, (Boston: Little, Brown & Company, 1962), pp. 217–19, 544; G. A. Birrell, "The Integrated Company and the Price 'Squeeze' under the Sherman Act and Section 2(a) of the Clayton Act, As Amended," *Notre Dame Lawyer*, Vol. XXXII (December, 1956), 21; A. E. Sawyer, *Business Aspects of Pricing Under the Robinson-Patman Act*, Trade Regulation Series (Boston: Little, Brown & Company, 1962); and H. Taggart, *Cost Justification* (Ann Arbor, Mich.: University of Michigan Press, 1959).

[8]*Federal Trade Commission* v. *Standard Oil*, 355 U.S. 396 (1958). Section 2 (b) of the Robinson-Patman Act, which covers the good faith "meeting competition" defense, provides in part: ". . . that nothing herein contained shall prevent a seller from rebutting the prima-facie case thus made by showing that his lower price or the furnishing of services or facilities to any purchaser or purchasers was made in good faith to meet an equally low price of a competitor, or the services or facilities furnished by a competitor."

[9]168 F. Supp. 576 (S.D.N.Y., 1958). Also see M. A. Adelman, "Economic Aspects of the Bethlehem Opinion," *Virginia Law Review*, Vol. XLV (June, 1959), 684; and L. S. Keyes, "The Bethlehem-Youngstown Case and the Market Share Criterion," *American Economic Review*, Vol. LI (September, 1961), 653.

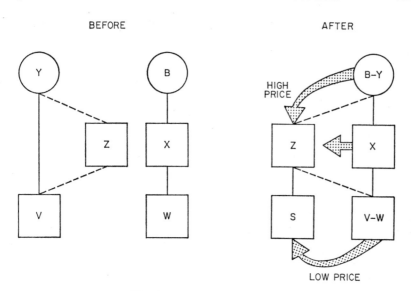

BEFORE   AFTER

Fig. 19-6. *The Total Squeeze*

type price squeeze if the proposed merger is consummated. The source of supply for *Z* would change from a noncompetitor (Youngstown) to a vertically integrated competitor (Bethlehem-Youngstown). Bethlehem-Youngstown could charge the independent fabricators a high price for rope *wire*, the basic raw material, and then undersell the independents with a low price for wire *rope*, the finished product. In the words of the District Court:

... the opportunities for a price squeeze on the independent are enhanced, since the supplier may shift his profit between rope wire and wire rope in such a manner as to narrow or eliminate the independent's margin or profit on wire rope. As to this latter disadvantage, for several years prior to the trial and at the same time of the trial the price of rope wire (the raw material) had been raised several times while the price of wire rope (the ultimate product) remained virtually constant. ... The evidence established that the independents were caught in a price squeeze.[10]

Unlike the price squeeze in the *Alcoa* case, where an integrated firm had almost complete control over the raw material supply for fabricators, the combination of Bethlehem-Youngstown did not have exclusive control over the raw material of rope *wire*. The independent fabricators could purchase their supplies of rope *wire* from a number of other steel firms. However, Youngstown was one of only six companies in the United States which sold the raw material of rope *wire* without also fabricating wire *rope*.

[10]168 F. Supp. 576, p. 612.

Youngstown was therefore one of the few suppliers which could not squeeze the independent fabricators of wire rope. The District Court concluded that "to remove Youngstown as a source of supply would render even more hazardous the competitive position of independents and might well mean the difference between their continued existence and their extinction."[11]

Youngstown, as a *seller* of the raw material rope wire, accounted for 12.5 per cent of the total rope *wire* shipments in 1955 consumed by companies which manufacture wire *rope* but do not produce their own wire. In the same year, Youngstown, as a *buyer*, purchased approximately 1.3 per cent of the shipments of the finished product of wire *rope*. Thus, Youngstown appeared to have an advantage in the rope *wire* market before its proposed merger with Bethlehem: It could use its position as a buyer of fabricated wire rope to influence its sales of wire to fabricators. This practice, known as "reciprocal buying," will be discussed in the next section.

Another competitive advantage of the proposed merger involved the loss of a significant customer to the independent fabricators. If Youngstown switched its purchases away from the independent fabricators and over to Bethlehem, the independents would be deprived of a significant customer. Since Bethlehem is a substantial producer of wire *rope*, a reasonable probability existed, in the opinion of the District Court, that Bethlehem would attempt to foreclose the independent fabricators from supplying the Bethlehem-Youngstown outlets with wire rope.

The elimination of Youngstown as a potential market for wire *rope* fabricated by independents is depicted in Fig. 19-6 by the arrow between squares X and Z. Before the merger, the independent fabricator Z supplied the Youngstown outlets V. After the merger, the Youngstown outlets would be combined with the Bethlehem outlets (square V-W). The amount of sales between the independent fabricator Z and the integrated outlet V-W would tend to decrease, in the opinion of the District Court, as the independent fabricators were excluded. These vertical features of the case contributed to the finding by the District Court that the proposed merger between Bethlehem and Youngstown would tend to lessen competition substantially and violate Sec. 7 of the Clayton Act.

Business Reciprocity

Business reciprocity may be present where companies encounter each other in the dual capacities of buyer and seller. Reciprocal buying, for instance, covers an arrangement between firms that "We will buy from

---

[11]*Ibid.*, p. 613.

you, if you will buy from us."[12] The willingness of each company to purchase from the other is conditioned on the expectation of reciprocal purchases.

Basically, all economic transactions in a society involve a degree of
reciprocity. A barter economy operates exclusively under a system of
reciprocity, whereby every seller must of necessity be a buyer. In antitrust
the practice of reciprocity generally includes an element of coercion: an
involuntary conditioning of the sale of one product on the purchase of
another.

In *Federal Trade Commission* v. *Consolidated Foods Corp.*,[13] the Federal
Trade Commission ordered the divestiture by Consolidated Foods, a large
diversified processor and seller of food products, of the assets of an acquired
company, Gentry, Inc., which was primarily engaged in the production of
dehydrated onion and garlic. The Supreme Court found that the effect of
the acquisition may be substantially to lessen competition in violation of
Sec. 7 of the Clayton Act.

Since Consolidated was a substantial purchaser of the products of food
processors, who in turn purchased dehydrated onion and garlic for use in
preparing and packaging their foods, the opportunity for reciprocal buying
was made possible by the acquisition. Gentry had in 1950, immediately
prior to the acquisition by Consolidated, about 32 per cent of the total
sales of the dehydrated garlic and onion industry and, together with its
principal competitor, Basic Vegetable Products, accounted for 90 per cent
of the total industry sales. The remaining 10 per cent was divided between
two other firms. In dehydrated onion sales, Gentry's market share rose
from 28 per cent in 1950 to 35 per cent in 1958. In dehydrated garlic sales,

---

[12]See D. Ammer, "Realistic Reciprocity," *Harvard Law Review*, Vol. XL (January–
February, 1962), 116–124; L. D. Asper, "Reciprocity, Purchasing Power, and Competition," *Minnesota Law Review*, Vol. XLVIII (1964), 522–55; B. Bock, "Mergers and Reciprocity," *Conference Board Record*, Vol. II (July, 1965), 27–36; C. Edwards, "Conglo-
merate Bigness as a Source of Power," in *Business Concentration and Price Policy*,
Universities-National Bureau Committee for Economic Research (Princeton, N. J.:
Princeton University Press, 1955), especially pp. 342–45; J. Ferguson, "Tying Arrange-
ments and Reciprocity: An Economic Analysis," *Law and Contemporary Problems*, Vol.
XXX (Summer, 1965), 552–580; M. Handler, "Gilding the Philosophic Pill — Trading
Bows for Arrows," *Columbia Law Review*, Vol. LXVI (January, 1966), 1–11; R. M.
Hausman, "Reciprocal Dealing and the Antitrust Laws," *Harvard Law Review*, Vol.
LXXVII (March, 1964), 873–86; A. Krash, "The Legality of Reciprocity under Section
7 of the Clayton Act," *Antitrust Bulletin*, Vol. IX (January–February, 1964), 93–100; L.
Sloane, "Reciprocity: Where Does the P. A. Stand?," *Purchasing*, November 20, 1961,
p. 71; and G. Stocking and W. Mueller, "Business Reciprocity and the Size of Firms,"
Journal of Business, Vol. XXX (April, 1957), 73–95.

[13]380 U.S. 592 (1964).

Gentry's market share fell during the same period from 51 per cent to 39 per cent of the industry total. The production of each of these two products more than doubled in the eight-year period following the acquisition.

The Federal Trade Commission rejected the argument made by Consolidated Foods that the decline in its share of the dehydrated garlic market proved the ineffectiveness of any practice of reciprocity. In the words of Commissioner Elman,

> We do not know that its share would not have fallen still farther, had it not been for the influence of reciprocal buying. This loss of sales fails to refute the likelihood that Consolidated's reciprocity power, which it has shown a willingness to exploit to the full, will not immunize a substantial segment of the garlic market from normal quality, price, and service competition.[14]

The Supreme Court agreed with the Federal Trade Commission that the acquisition may tend substantially to lessen competition as a result of the opportunity for reciprocity.

> We hold at the outset that the "reciprocity" made possible by such an acquisition is one of the congeries of anticompetitive practices at which the antitrust laws are aimed. The practice results in "an irrelevant and alien factor," . . . intruding into the choice among competing products, creating at the least "a priority on the business at equal prices."[15]

The *Consolidated Foods* case is depicted in terms of its vertically integrated market structure in Fig. 19-7. Circle *A* is the Gentry Division, which supplies dehydrated seasonings. Square *Z* is the independent food processor which purchases its seasoning requirements from Gentry, and then resells the processed item to Consolidated Foods, which acts as a distributor (square *X*).

The market setting in *Consolidated Foods* was different from that found in the *Bethlehem* case. First, the input of seasoning used by the processor *Z* was a small percentage of the total input cost of canned or packaged items. The supplier *A* could not squeeze the fabricator *Z* out of business, as alleged in the *Bethlehem* case, because the cost base of seasoning is but a minor part of the total cost base of the processed food items. In the *Bethlehem* case all the raw materials were furnished by the supplier to the fabricators of steel wire rope.

Second, the barriers to entry in the steel industry are not present in the dehydrated garlic and onion industry. In the *Bethlehem* case the independent wire rope fabricators could not be expected to undertake the construc-

---

[14]Docket No. 7000, Opinion of the Commission (November 15, 1962), p. 19 of the mimeographed text.

[15]380 U.S. 592, 594 (1964).

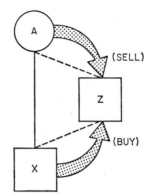

Fig. 19-7. *Reciprocal Buying*

tion of a steel mill in order to produce their own rope wire. There was evidence in the *Consolidated Foods* case that barriers to entry did not exist in the dehydrated spice industry; a new firm, Gilroy Foods, entered the industry during the litigation of the case. Hence, even though there were only a few suppliers of these seasonings, no one of these suppliers could raise its prices unduly high without encouraging the large food processors to enter the industry and manufacture their own dehydrated spices.

The market practice of reciprocal buying is closely related to tying arrangements. In a tying arrangement a powerful seller in the market for the tying good may use its strength in this market to coerce a buyer to accept the tied good. In contrast, the act of reciprocal buying consists of a market for the "tying good" which is dominated by a purchaser, rather than a seller. But the "tied good" continues in the same posture as part of a seller's market. Consolidated Foods allegedly used its leverage as a strong buyer of food products to coerce its weak suppliers (such as small processors) to purchase their requirements for dehydrated seasoning from its Gentry Division. In view of the number of firms and the vast size of the food distribution industry, it may be questioned whether Consolidated Foods had a dominant position sufficient to coerce suppliers to purchase from its Gentry division.

SECTION G

Price Discrimination

CHAPTER TWENTY

Selected Issues Under the Robinson-Patman Act

Price Discrimination Under Section 2(a)

LEGAL AND ECONOMIC DEFINITIONS OF PRICE DISCRIMINATION. A prerequisite for a finding of illegal price discrimination under Sec. 2(a) of the Robinson-Patman Act is a *price difference* resulting from sales by an individual seller of the same kind of goods at a lower price to one purchaser than to another. Section 2(a) of the Robinson-Patman Act provides in part:

> That it shall be unlawful for any person engaged in commerce . . . to discriminate in price between different purchasers of commodities of like grade and quality . . . where the effect of such discrimination may be substantially to lessen competition or tend to create a monopoly in any line of commerce . . .

Unless a price differential between two customers is established, a court will not consider the further legal issue of whether the price discrimination may injure competitors, or tend to lessen competition substantially or tend to create a monopoly.

Economic discrimination may occur even in the absence of a price differential. If two buyers of the same kind of goods are charged identical prices by a single seller, but the seller incurs different transportation, selling, or production costs in serving them, economic discrimination exists.[1] Thus,

[1] Rowe, *Price Discrimination Under the Robinson-Patman Act*, p. 29; J. Backman, "An Economist Looks at the Robinson-Patman Act," *American Bar Association Section of Antitrust Law*, Robinson-Patman Symposium, Vol. XVII (August, 1960), 343–59; M.A.

in order to know when there is price discrimination in an economic sense between two buyers, it is necessary to have information concerning not only the prices charged, but also the costs incurred by the seller.

PRIMARY-LINE AND SECONDARY-LINE COMPETITION. The Robinson-Patman Act was enacted in response to the complaints of independent wholesalers that chain stores were obtaining unwarranted lower prices, greater advertising and promotion allowances, and special discounts. These concessions could not be justified by lower costs as a result of the large volume purchases by the chain stores. Consequently, the independent wholesalers had to pay higher prices for their goods and operated under a competitive handicap. This plane of competition among *buyers* is referred to as "secondary-line" competition.

The Supreme Court has held that the Robinson-Patman Act is also applicable to "primary-line" competition, where *sellers* are injured by the discriminatory pricing practices of one of their competitors.[2] In *Federal Trade Commission* v. *Anheuser-Busch, Inc.*[3] the defendant was charged with violating Sec. 2(a) of the Robinson-Patman Act for lowering the price of its premium beer, Budweiser, to the same price level as regional beers in St. Louis, Missouri.[4] Budweiser, as a premium beer, is generally priced higher than beers of regional and local breweries. As a result of the promotional price cut, Budweiser sales advanced over 200 per cent during several months as compared to a similar period in the preceding

Adelman, "Effective Competition and the Antitrust Laws," *Harvard Law Review*, Vol. LXI (1948), 1289–1350, "Integration and Antitrust Policy," *ibid.*, Vol. LXIII (1949), 27–77, "The Consistency of the Robinson-Patman Act," *Stanford Law Review*, Vol. VI (1953), 3–22, and "Price Discrimination as Treated in the Attorney General's Report," *University of Pennsylvania Law Review*, Vol. CIV (1955), 222–42; Machlup, "Characteristics and Types of Price Discrimination"; and J. B. Dirlam and A. Kahn, "Price Discrimination in Law and Economics," *American Journal of Economics and Sociology*, Vol. XI (1952), 281–313.

[2]The courts have consistently found a violation of Sec. 2 (a) of the Robinson-Patman Act in cases where a company maintained a substantially lower price in one locality, while charging higher prices elsewhere, for the obvious predatory purpose of driving a specific competitor out of business. See *Moore* v. *Mead's Fine Bread Co.*, 348 U.S. 115 (1954); *E. B. Muller & Co.* v. *Federal Trade Commission*, 142 F. 2nd 511 (6th Cir., 1944); *Maryland Baking Co.* v. *Federal Trade Commission*, 243 F. 2nd 716 (4th Cir., 1957); and *Atlas Building Products Co.* v. *Diamond Block & Gravel Co.*, 269 F. 2nd 950 (10th Cir., 1959), *cert. denied* 363 U.S. 843 (1959).

[3]363 U.S. 536 (1960). Compare to *Utah Pie Co.* v. *Continental Baking Co.*, 386 U.S. 685 (1967).

[4]A problem arises when a price reduction of a "premium" image product matches a rival's price of a nonpremium good, so that in a marketing sense, the latter price is undercut. This aspect of the *Anheuser-Busch* case can be found in 54 F.T.C. 277 (1957). Also see *United States* v. *The Borden Company*, 383 U.S. 637 (1966).

year. There was no discrimination by Anheuser-Busch among its buyers within the St. Louis area; all the buyers were offered the same lower promotional price. The Supreme Court found, however, that Anheuser-Busch maintained higher prices for customers outside the St. Louis area, while charging lower prices for customers within St. Louis. Although there was no competition between the customers in these geographically distinct markets, the Supreme Court nevertheless held that Anheuser-Busch had discriminated in price when it charged different prices in the separate geographic areas.[5] This same concept of discrimination, which has reference to a price differential between separate geographic markets, rather than between separate customers in the same geographic market, is at the crux of the delivered price system cases, which are considered next.

DELIVERED PRICE SYSTEMS. There are several types of delivered price systems.[6] Under a single basing point system, a buyer is charged a price that includes both the cost of a good at a geographic location designated the basing point *plus* the transportation charges from the basing point to

[5]The Supreme Court, after deciding that price discrimination existed, remanded the case to the Circuit Court to consider whether the requisite injury to competition also existed for a finding of *illegality* under Sec. 2 (a). The Circuit Court found that the sharp increase in sales by Anheuser-Busch during the price promotional resulted in only a temporary improvement in its market position in St. Louis. Therefore, the Circuit Court concluded, there was no injury to competition, and dismissed the action against Anheuser-Busch. See *Anheuser-Busch, Inc.* v. *Federal Trade Commission*, 289 F. 2nd 835 (7th Cir., 1961).

[6]C. Kaysen, "Basing Point Pricing and Public Policy," *Quarterly Journal of Economics*, Vol. XLIII (1949), 289–314; reprinted in *Readings in Industrial Organization and Public Policy*, pp. 153–75; F. Machlup, *The Basing Point System* (Philadelphia: Blakiston Co., 1949); F. A. Fetter, "Exit Basing Point Pricing," *American Economic Review*, Vol. XXXVIII (1948), 815–27; C. D. Edwards, "The Effect of Recent Basing Point Decisions Upon Business Practices," *ibid.*, pp. 828–42; R. H. Bingham, "The Uniform Delivered Pricing Method in the Grocery Manufacturing Industry," *Journal of Marketing*, Vol. XIV (1949–50), 594–600; D. Dewey, "A Reappraisal of f.o.b. Pricing and Freight Absorption," *Southern Economic Journal*, Vol. XXII (1955–56), 48–54; J. S. McGee, "Cross Hauling — A Symptom of Incomplete Collusion Under Basing–Point Systems," *Southern Economic Journal*, Vol. XX (1953–54), 369–79; L. Marengo, "The Basing Point Decisions and the Steel Industry," *American Economic Review*, Vol. XLV (May Proceedings, 1955) 509–22; V. A. Mund, "The Development and Incidence of Delivered Pricing in American Industry," *Law and Comtemporary Problems*, Vol. XV (1950), 141–58; J. M. Clark, "Imperfect Competition Theory and Basing Point Problems," *American Economic Review*, Vol. XXXIII (1943), 283, "The Law and Economics of Basing Points," *ibid.*, Vol. XXXIX (1949), 430–48; G. W. Stocking, *Basing Point Pricing and Regional Development* (Chapel Hill, N.C.: University of North Carolina Press, 1954); G. J. Stigler, "A Theory of Delivered Price Systems," *American Economic Review*, Vol. XXXIX (1949), 1143–59; T.N.E.C. Monograph No. 42, *The Basing Point Problem* (Washington, D.C.: Government Printing Office, 1941); and Wilcox, *Public Policies Toward Business*, rev. ed., Chap. 10.

the buyer's place of business. In contrast, a company that does not engage in a delivered price system generally sells its product under an "f.o.b. mill price system": Each plant, or mill, quotes a price for its product "free on board" (f.o.b.) a carrier, such as a truck or railroad car, which is at or nearby the seller's plant. The seller bears the cost of loading its product from its door to the adjacent carrier, but the buyer bears the transportation costs from there on.

In the period 1905–24 the steel industry in the United States followed a single basing point system entitled "Pittsburgh-plus." This delivered price system established Pittsburgh as the single basing point, U.S. Steel's price for steel products in that city as the base price, and the transportation costs from Pittsburgh to any customer as the "plus" element. A customer was charged the Pittsburgh base price plus the railroad transportation charge from Pittsburgh, even though the steel product was delivered from a plant not located in the Pittsburgh area. If the buyer was located in Chicago and received delivery from a Chicago steel mill, he paid a delivered price that included "phantom freight" from Pittsburgh. The result of this delivered price system was that a steel buyer would be quoted an identical price, regardless of his location, by any steel supplier in the United States.

After 1924, as a result of a Federal Trade Commission suit against U.S. Steel, the steel industry abandoned the "Pittsburgh-plus" system, and established a *multiple* basing point system with Chicago, Birmingham, and Pittsburgh as the new bases.[7] Steel buyers in the East were still quoted a "Pittsburgh-plus" price; but buyers in the South were quoted a "Birmingham-plus" price, since Birmingham was a nearer basing point; buyers in the West took advantage of a "Chicago-plus" delivered price. In 1951 the members of the steel industry consented to a Federal Trade Commission order barring them from agreeing to refuse to sell and deliver any steel products at an f.o.b. mill price.[8]

A variant of multiple basing point pricing is called the "freight equalization system."[9] The most favorably located seller's mill to a given buyer generally serves as the basing point from which the actual freight to the buyer's plant is added. Any seller in the industry may "equalize" his delivered price with the base price plus freight charged by the competing seller nearest the buyer. Thus, by absorbing freight costs, more distant suppliers can match the price of the seller nearest the buyer, but the buyer faces identical delivered prices from different geographically located suppliers.

[7]8 F. T. C. (December 1, 1924).

[8]Federal Trade Commission Order No. 5508 (August 16, 1951).

[9]See *Bond, Crown & Cork Co.* v. *Federal Trade Commission*, 176 F. 2nd 974 (4 Cir., 1949).

In "zone pricing" the country is divided into a number of geographic areas and all buyers within a single zone receive the same delivered price; delivered prices may differ between zones.[10] If a seller is located in the center of a zone, and charges an average transportation cost to all buyers located in its zone, those buyers on the periphery of the zone will have the benefit of the seller absorbing part of their freight costs; those near the center will bear more than the actual transportation costs from the seller's mill.

From the point of view of the buyers within a delivered pricing zone, there is no price differential between the delivered prices they pay and those that their competitors within the same zone pay. But from the seller's side, there exists a wide variation in the net receipts resulting from sales to buyers at different distances from the seller's mill. The "mill net return," or the amount the seller receives for his product after deducting from the delivered price his transportation expenses, will be greater where the buyer pays a delivered price that includes "phantom freight" and less where the seller must absorb part of the freight costs. If the term "price" in Sec. 2(a) of the Robinson-Patman Act is construed as the seller's "mill net return," a delivered price system with freight absorption or "phantom freight" reflects the necessary price differential, even though all customers pay identical delivered prices regardless of their distance from a supplying mill. The prevailing view, however, is to interpret price as the actual amount the buyer must pay, i.e., the delivered price, rather than the "mill net return" received by the seller.[11]

The discriminatory aspects of a single basing point delivered price system under Sec. 2(a) of the Robinson-Patman Act were considered by the Supreme Court in *Corn Products Refining Co.* v. *Federal Trade Commission*,[12] and the companion case, *Federal Trade Commission* v. *A. E. Staley Mfg. Co.*[13]

In the *Corn Products* case the defendant operated a plant in Chicago which produced glucose used by candy manufacturers. When the company opened a new plant in Kansas City, it continued to maintain Chicago as its basing point. Both plants sold only at delivered prices, computed by adding to a base price at Chicago the published railroad rate to the point of delivery. The Supreme Court found that candy manufacturers located

---

[10]*Milk and Ice Cream Can Institute* v. *Federal Trade Commission*, 152 F. 2nd 478 (7th Cir., 1946).

[11]*In the Matter of National Lead Co.*, 49 F.T.C. 791 (1953); *In the Matter of Chain Institute, Inc.*, 49 F.T.C. 1041 (1953); and United States, *Report of the Attorney General's National Committee to Study the Antitrust Laws*, pp. 216–17.

[12]324 U.S. 726 (1945).

[13]324 U.S. 746 (1945). For a discussion of these companion cases, see Neale, *The Antitrust Laws of the U.S.A.*, pp. 254–58.

near Kansas City had to pay "phantom freight" from Chicago even though they received their glucose shipments from the new Kansas City plant. If the Chicago base price of Corn Products was $20 and the unit railroad cost to Kansas City was $3, the candy manufacturers located in Kansas City would pay a delivered price of $23 even though they received their shipments from the Kansas City plant. Since the Kansas City customers were found to be competitors of the Chicago customers, the discrimination appeared to be prima facie unlawful.

The delivered price of shipments from the Chicago plant could be cost justified, since they were proportional to the freight costs incurred in shipping to different geographic locations. The deliveries from the Kansas City plant were not cost justified. For example, if a customer was located between Kansas City and Chicago and received its glucose shipments from Kansas City, his delivered price would include the Chicago base price plus freight from Chicago to his destination. This delivered price would be *lower* than the delivered price at the door of the Kansas City plant.[14] This is the reverse of cost justification: The delivered price at the buyer's plant is lower than it would be if it was picked up by the buyer at the factory from which it is shipped.

In the *Staley* case, a smaller glucose manufacturer located in Decatur, Illinois, which was two hundred miles from Chicago, followed the "Chicago-plus" basing point system of Corn Products. When Staley sold glucose to candy manufacturers in Chicago, it absorbed the freight from Decatur to the Chicago basing point; however, Staley gained "phantom freight" when it sold its product to customers situated closer to Decatur than Chicago. Basically, Staley accepted Corn Products as the glucose price leader and followed its prices in all markets. The Court held that Staley could not justify the adoption of a competitor's basing point price system under Sec. 2(b) as a good faith attempt to meet the latter's equally low price.

The Supreme Court found that the single basing point system followed by Staley and Corn Products was illegal under Sec. 2(a) of the Robinson-Patman Act. Price discrimination resulted because the basing point was different from the point of production; customers paid different delivered prices, and these discriminatory prices could not be cost justified. Furthermore, the discriminatory prices were found to result in competitive injury between customers purchasing from the Chicago plant and those purchasing from the Kansas City plant.

----

[14]Since every shipment from Kansas City to customers in the direction of Chicago was sold at a delivered price lower than the price at the door of the Kansas City factory, it might be argued that there was no "phantom freight." The explanation for this apparent anomaly is in the differential between the two factory door prices. The "phantom freight" from Chicago to Kansas City has been used to raise the price at the door of the Kansas City factory to $23 in contrast to the Chicago price of $20.

The Supreme Court in the *Corn Products* case accepted the finding of the Federal Trade Commission that the candy manufacturers in Kansas City competed with those in Chicago; and the price differentials on glucose would affect their costs as well as the final prices of candy. Small differences in raw material costs were, in the opinion of the Federal Trade Commission, "enough to divert business from one manufacturer to another." Thus, there was competitive injury at the buyer level between candy manufacturers. Finally, the Court rejected the defense in the *Staley* case that it was meeting in good faith the equally low price of a competitor within the meaning of Sec. 2(b). The Court held that Staley never attempted to establish independently a nondiscriminatory price system, but rather the company followed the delivered price system of Corn Products.

If the candy manufacturers located near Kansas City had no alternative source of supply for glucose than Chicago, Corn Products could charge a high f.o.b. price at their Kansas City plant. The candy manufacturers were not necessarily entitled to the cost savings resulting from Corn Products' locating a new plant in Kansas City. Neither was the public necessarily entitled to lower candy prices resulting from lower raw material costs, if Corn Products chose to pass on its cost savings to the candy maker, who, in turn, chose to pass on these cost savings to consumers. Rather, it can be argued, a company constructing a new plant or warehouse should receive, in the short run, the resulting profit from cost savings.

A related question raised by these two cases is: How were the candy manufacturers competitively injured by the price policies of the glucose manufacturers? Consider the position of the candy manufacturers located nearby or in Kansas City before Corn Products built its new plant. The candy manufacturer had a higher raw material cost for glucose than a company located in Chicago. Therefore, if the candy manufacturer wanted to sell its product primarily in Chicago, it should have located near its source of supply and major market. However, a candy manufacturer desiring to sell its product primarily in Kansas City would have to choose between locating near its source of supply (Chicago) or near its sales outlet (Kansas City). If the company decided to locate in Kansas City, it would have to bear the cost of having glucose shipped from Chicago, but the company would save on transportation costs in shipping finished candy to its customers in Kansas City.

Consider the market structure in the *Corn Products* case *after* the Kansas City plant was constructed. If Corn Products continued to use a Chicago-plus delivered pricing system, the candy manufacturers would not be any worse off than they were before the Kansas City plant was constructed. Of course, if the Kansas City candy makers could get glucose at a lower price, they could extend the geographic area of their sales and meet more effectively the competition from Chicago candy manufacturers. Or, alternatively, the Kansas City candy makers could maintain the same price and sales volume for their candy and earn higher profits resulting from lower costs for glucose. If Corn Products is not an adjudged illegal monopoly, there is no apparent reason why the Kansas City candy makers are entitled to a lower cost base in preference to a higher profit margin for the Corn Products' plant located in Kansas City.

The later delivered pricing cases were brought by the Government also under Sec. 5 of the Federal Trade Commission Act as "unfair methods of competition." In the *Cement Institute* case[15] the Supreme Court found an industrywide multiple basing point system in the sale of cement a twin violation of Sec. 5 of the Federal Trade Commission Act and Sec. 2(a) of the Robinson-Patman Act. Under the auspices of the Cement Institute, a trade association, a concerted program of reprisals and boycotts was established for enforcing strict adherence to the delivered price system. The focus in delivered pricing cases changed from price discrimination to a theory that the concurrent use by competing companies in an industry of a delivered price system is partial, if not conclusive, evidence of concerted action that unfairly restrains trade.

The Meeting Competition Defense Under Sec. 2(b)

THE MEETING COMPETITION PROVISO AS AN "ABSOLUTE" DEFENSE. The *Standard Oil of Indiana* decision, discussed in the preceding chapter, established that the good-faith meeting of a competitor's price was an absolute defense under 2(b) of the Robinson-Patman Act to a charge of price discrimination, irrespective of findings as to competitive injury.

Section 2(b) provides in part:

That nothing herein contained shall prevent a seller from rebutting the prima-facie case thus made by showing that his lower price or the furnishing of services or facilities to any purchaser or purchasers was made in good faith to meet an equally low price of a competitor. . . .

The Supreme Court held that once the defendant was able to show that his lower price did not undercut competitors, but merely met their equally low price, he would be excused, regardless of the competitive effects of his lower price.

[15]*Federal Trade Commission* v. *Cement Institute*, 333 U.S. 683 (1948). Also see *Federal Trade Commission* v. *National Lead Co.*, 352 U.S. 419 (1957). Cf. *Triangle Conduit & Cable Co.* v. *Federal Trade Commission*, 168 F. 2nd 157 (1948), *Clayton Mark & Co.* v. *Federal Trade Commission*, 336 U.S. 956 (1949); and *Bond Crown & Cork Co.* v. *Federal Trade Commission*, 176 F. 2nd 974 (1949).

In the earlier proceedings of the *Standard Oil of Indiana* case, the Federal Trade Commission took a contrary position: Once it was established that the discriminatory prices charged by Standard Oil were competitively injurious to retail dealers who bought from Standard directly, a violation of the Robinson-Patman Act should be conclusively established. Furthermore, the Commission argued, an affirmative finding of injury should bar the seller from raising the defense that his prices were quoted in good faith to meet a competitor's equally low price.

The position of the Commission in the *Standard Oil of Indiana* case was criticized as follows by Frederick Rowe, a leading authority on the Robinson-Patman Act:

Hence Section 2(b) remained available to a seller only when he did not need it (i.e., when the FTC had already lost its case by failing to prove competitive injury), but became unavailable in the only eventuality requiring its use (i.e., when the FTC's proof of competitive injury established a prima facie violation).[16]

The Supreme Court decision in 1951 ruled against the Federal Trade Commission's position, and thereby refused to "weigh the potentially injurious effect of a seller's price reduction upon competition at all lower levels against its beneficial effect in permitting the seller to meet competition at its own level."[17] In other words, the Court resolved the conflicting goals of avoiding injury to competitors and encouraging competition in favor of the latter. Standard Oil could legally discriminate in price to customers, provided that the lower price met in good faith an equally low price of a competitor. The fact that other competitors might be injured in the process was not relevant, since the meeting competition proviso of Sec. 2(b) was deemed an *absolute* defense.

RETAINING VERSUS OBTAINING NEW CUSTOMERS. In *Sunshine Biscuits, Inc.* v. *Federal Trade Commission*[18] the Federal Trade Commission argued that the defense of meeting competition under Sec. 2(b) of the Robinson-Patman Act should be limited to a seller acting in self-defense against competitive price attacks, and should *not* apply to a seller reducing prices to obtain new customers.

This particular issue did not arise in the preceding *Standard Oil of Indiana* case, since the lower prices granted were made only to retain existing customers. The Circuit Court held in the *Sunshine Biscuit* case

[16]Rowe, *Price Discrimination Under the Robinson-Patman Act*, p. 218.

[17]340 U.S. 231 Also see 355 U.S. 396 (1958).

[18]306 F. 2nd 48 (7th Cir., 1962). Also see *Standard Motor Products, Inc*, v. *Federal Trade Commission*, 265 F. 2nd 674 (2nd Cir., 1959), *cert. denied*, 361 U.S. 826 (1959).

that the meeting competition defense should not be limited to defensive cuts in price to retain old customers:

... (if) sellers could grant good faith competitive price reductions only to old customers in order to retain them, competition for new customers would be stifled and monopoly would be fostered.[19]

The Federal Trade Commission declined to seek Supreme Court review of the Circuit Court decision that set aside its order. In a public statement the Commission stated that "its decision not to seek Supreme Court review in this case does not reflect a change of position by the Commission on the question of the law involved."[20]

MEETING PRICES OF THE SELLER'S COMPETITORS OR HIS CUSTOMERS' COMPETITORS In *Sun Oil* v. *Federal Trade Commission*[21] the Supreme Court rejected the meeting competition defense raised by Sun Oil. Sun Oil lowered its price only to McLean, one of a number of independent dealers operating Sunoco service stations in Jacksonville, Florida. Sun Oil made the discriminatory price allowance to McLean in order to enable him to meet the lower price of a competitive private brand gasoline, Super Test, sold by an independent retail dealer.

The defense argued that McLean was merely a "conduit" in marketing the products of Sun Oil. Therefore, as a practical matter Sun Oil was competing at the retail level with Super Test. The Supreme Court disagreed, holding that the lower price which must be met refers to the price of a competitor of the seller who grants the discriminatory price (such as another refiner-supplier); it does not refer to the price of a competitor (such as Super Test) of the buyer who receives the discriminatory price allowance. Hence, if Sun Oil as a wholesale supplier reduced its price to McLean when another wholesale supplier attempted to obtain McLean as a retail customer, the meeting competition defense would be allowed. However, when Sun Oil lowered its price to McLean sufficiently to allow McLean to reduce his price to meet a competitive retail price of Super Test, a gasoline station located across the street, the meeting competition defense was not allowed, since Sun Oil was not meeting the price of one of its own competitors, but was trying to meet the price of a competitor of its customer.

In the *Sun Oil* case the Supreme Court assumed, contrary to the Circuit

---

[19]*Ibid.*, p. 52. Also see J. W. Markham, "Antitrust Trends and New Constraints," *Harvard Business Review*, Vol. XLI (May–June, 1963), 84–92.

[20]Federal Trade Commission, *News Summary* (November 30, 1962). There was evidence in the case that Sunshine was not necessarily obtaining new customers, but rather was gaining the former customers of two companies which it had recently acquired.

[21]371 U.S. 505 (1963).

Court, that Super Test was engaged solely in retail operations and that it was not the beneficiary of any enabling price cut from its own supplier. "Were it otherwise," in the words of Supreme Court Justice Goldberg, "*i.e.*, if it appeared either that Super Test were an integrated supplier-retailer, or that it had received a price cut from its own supplier — presumably a competitor of Sun — we would be presented with a different case, as to which we neither express nor intimate any opinion."[22]

The economic effects that were alleged as inevitable, if discriminatory price concessions such as Sun Oil made to McLean were not permitted, are noteworthy. Sun Oil argued that the Court's interpretation of the Robinson-Patman Act would harm rather than protect small independents such as McLean:

... the limited resources available to McLean bar his survival in a gasoline price war of any duration. McLean's small margin of profit, his relative inability to lower his retail price because (it is) a direct function of the price he pays his supplier, here Sun, and other factors make his continued independent existence in a present-day price war wholly dependent upon receipts of aid — in the form of a price reduction — from his supplier.[23]

Second, the Commission maintained that the nearby Sunoco service stations would be injured by virtue of McLean's discriminatory price concession. The Commission found that neighboring Sunoco dealers were able to identify customers who, apparently retaining a preference for Sun Oil products, shifted their patronage from the competing stations to McLean. The defense asserted "that the harm to competitors of McLean must be suffered as a consequence of the very competition which is the pervasive essence of our overall antitrust policies."[24] The Supreme Court was, therefore, faced with the dilemma that the protection of McLean would be detrimental to the Sun Oil and Super Test competitors of McLean, and *vice versa*. In the words of the Court,

... the mere recognition that harm sometimes may be a by-product of competition is the beginning, not the end, of analysis. Whatever the result here, someone may be hurt — to allow Sun to pursue its discriminatory pricing policy will, as has been indicated, harm other Sun dealers who compete with McLean; to prevent Sun from making discriminatory price allowances, it is asserted, will injure the McLeans of the competitive world.[25]

Third, the Court noted that there would be economic effects on the pricing behavior of gasoline dealers if Sun Oil were not permitted to grant a

[22]*Ibid.*, p. 512.
[23]*Ibid.*, p. 518.
[24]*Ibid.*, p. 519.
[25]*Ibid.*

discriminatory price concession to its customer McLean. In the words of the Court,

> While allowance of the discriminatory price cut here may provide localized and temporary flexibility, it inevitably encourages maintenance of the long-range and generalized price rigidity which the discrimination in fact protects. So long as the wholesaler can meet challenges to his pricing structure by wholly local and individualized responses, it has no incentive to alter its overall pricing policy. Moreover, as indicated, the large supplier's ability to "spot price" will discourage the enterprising and resourceful retailer from seeking to initiate price reductions on his own. Such reasoning may be particularly applicable in the oligopolistic environment of the oil industry.
>
> We see no reason to permit Sun discriminatorily to pit its greater strength at the supplier level against Super Test, which, so far as appears from the record, is able to sell its gasoline at a lower price simply because it is a more efficient merchandiser, particularly when Super Test's challenge as an "independent" may be the only meaningful source of price competition offered the "major" oil companies, of which Sun is one.[26]

Finally, Sun Oil argued that if it were denied the meeting competition defense, it would be forced vertically to integrate further into the retail distribution of gasoline. The Court summarized the defendant's position as follows:

> Sun asserts that the only course realistically open to it is to change the nature of its distribution system by effecting some sort of further vertical integration, all at the expense and to the detriment of the very independent merchants — the individual station operators — whom the Robinson-Patman Act was intended to preserve and protect. It may be that active pursuit of such a course by Sun, involving the elimination of independent retail dealers, would be a greater evil than allowance of discriminations such as are here involved; such a broad determination of economic policy, however, is not for us to make here.[27]

Price Discrimination and Competition

FUNCTIONAL DISCOUNTS AND COMPETITIVE INJURY. The Robinson-Patman Act permits a seller to grant a functional discount as compensation to those of its customers who perform distribution functions such as storage, delivery, or promotions. For example, a manufacturer may grant a functional discount to a wholesaler who performs a storage function which would otherwise have to be borne by the manufacturer. In this setting, the retailers and the wholesalers are on separate planes of competition.

The functional discount presents a more complex problem in cases where purchasers do not follow the traditional role of wholesaler or retailer,

---

[26] *Ibid.*, p. 523 (footnote omitted).

[27] *Ibid.*, pp. 527–28.

but rather perform dual distribution functions of both wholesaling and retailing. Preferential price treatment to a purchaser, in his role of a wholesaler, may appear to confer a competitive advantage on his retail activities. Competing retailers may complain that the combined wholesaler-retailer is obtaining his goods at a lower cost and hence has a competitive advantage.[28]

If the wholesaler-retailer performs a distribution function, such as storage, that similar buyers do not perform, and is allowed to receive compensation that precisely offsets the costs for performing this function, there is no economic discrimination. The cost bases of retailers and wholesaler-retailers would appear to be approximately equal after the additional investment cost of the wholesaler-retailer is included in the computation. In contrast, a competitive advantage exists where a wholesaler-retailer receives a preferential discount above the level of reimbursement for the cost of performing additional distribution functions.

Unless recognition is given to these additional distribution functions performed by purchasers, there will be no incentive for retailers to integrate backwards and perform distribution functions themselves. Wholesalers will be insulated from the potential competition of their customers who would otherwise enter the wholesaling field, where they believed they could perform this function more effectively themselves.

THE REQUIREMENT OF "LIKE GRADE AND QUALITY." In *United States v. The Borden Company*[29] the Supreme Court held that evaporated milk sold under the Borden national brand name and physically identical and equal in grade with evaporated milk sold by Borden under various private brands was of "like grade and quality" under Sec. 2(a) of the Robinson-Patman Act. The fact that the Borden national brand had more customer appeal and could command a higher price in the market place was not deemed relevant.

The Federal Trade Commission has taken a different, but not necessarily inconsistent, position toward "like grade and quality" in Sec. 2(b) cases where the issue involves meeting an equally low price of a competitor. In the *Anheuser-Busch* case[30] the Federal Trade Commission ruled that

[28]Compare *Mueller Company* v. *Federal Trade Commission*, 323 F. 2nd 44 (7th Cir., 1963) and *General Foods Corp.* 52 F.T.C. 798 (1956) with *Doubleday & Co.*, 52 F.T.C. 169 (1955). Also see Rowe, *Price Discrimination Under the Robinson-Patman Act*, pp. 180–95; *Report of the Attorney General's National Committee to Study the Antitrust Laws*, pp. 202-9 and J. Van Cise, "How to Quote Functional Prices," *Section on Antitrust Law*, Symposium, New York State Bar Association (New York: Commerce Clearing House, Inc., 1957).

[29]383 U.S. 637 (1966).

[30]54 F.T.C. 277 (1957).

"premium" beers were different in terms of "like grade and quality" from regional beers, even though the premium image resulted from advertising rather than differences in the physical properties of beer. The Commission found that Anheuser-Busch, in lowering the price of its premium beer, Budweiser, to the level of regional beers, was not meeting an equally low price of a competitor, but was undercutting its competitor's price. Similarly, in the earlier proceedings of the *Standard Oil of Indiana* case,[31] the Federal Trade Commission rejected the meeting competition defense raised by Standard Oil because the off-brand gasoline (Fleet Wing), whose price Standard Oil was meeting, was not the same grade as Standard's major brand of gasoline (Red Crown). The off-brand was deemed to be an inferior grade to the generally premium priced Standard Oil brand, because in the eyes of consumers it was merely a local brand without a high degree of public acceptance. In terms of chemical analysis both brands were identical. In the *Borden* case[32] the Supreme Court noted that evidence showing greater advertising, promotion, and other distribution costs for a branded product could still be introduced by Borden under the "cost justification" and "injury to competition" defenses.

The dissent in the *Borden* case urged that a market acceptability test should be followed in which the Court would take into consideration under Sec. 2(a) all commercially significant distinctions which affect market value, whether they be physical or promotional.[33] Citing Professor Chamberlin's *Theory of Monopolistic Competition*,[34] Justice Stewart, speaking for the dissent, stated:

There is nothing intrinsic to the concepts of grade and quality that requires exclusion of the commercial attributes of a product from their definition. The product purchased by a consumer includes not only the chemical components that any competent laboratory can itemize, but also a host of commercial intangibles that distinguish the product in the market place. The premium paid for Borden brand milk reflects the consumer's awareness, promoted through advertising, that these commercial attributes are part and parcel of the premium product he is purchasing.[35]

---

[31] 49 F.T.C. 923 (1953). Also see *Minneapolis-Honeywell Regulator Co.*, 44 F.T.C. 351 (1948) and *Gerber Products Co.* v. *Beech-Nut Life Savers Co.*, 160 F. Supp. 916 (S.D.N.Y., 1958).

[32] 383 U.S. 637 (1966).

[33] Also see Rowe, *Price Discrimination Under the Robinson-Patman Act*, pp. 62–76; R. Cassady, Jr. and E. T. Grether, "The Proper Interpretation of 'Like Grade and Quality' Within the Meaning of Section 2(a) of the Robinson-Patman Act," *Southern California Law Review*, Vol. XXX (April, 1957), 241–79; C. E. Hopfl, "What Goods are 'Of Like Grade and Quality'?" *American Bar Association Journal*, Vol. LII (December, 1966), 1133–36; and J.E. Sheehy, "Like Grade and Quality," *American Bar Association Section of Antitrust Law*, Vol. XXX (April, 1966), 2–7.

[34] 8th ed., p. 56.

[35] 383 U.S. 637, 649–50 (1966).

The structural settings of the Sec. 2(a) and Sec. 2(b) cases are different when the courts are confronted by the issue of "like grade and quality." In the Sec. 2(a) cases, such as *Borden*, the defendant is selling the two products whose prices and physical characteristics are being compared. In the Sec. 2(b) cases, such as *Anheuser-Busch*, the perspective on discrimination is between products of *different* sellers: the premium national beer versus regional and local beers.

In the Sec. 2(b) cases the fundamental issue is one of meeting competition. All competitive attributes of a product resulting from advertising and consumer acceptance become essential to the issue. In contrast, Sec. 2(a) cases are not directly considering meeting or injuring competition, but rather are facing the threshold jurisdictional question of whether price discrimination exists. The policy issue in Sec. 2(a) cases, such as *Borden*, is whether to confront the issue of economic factors inherent in brand names and national advertising *initially*, in determining the jurisdictional question of like grade and quality, or to await for the issue to be raised later under a meeting competition or cost justification defense.

The latter procedure places the multiple-product firm, which distributes both brand and private label goods, in the difficult role of treating products that it considers different in a marketing sense as equal in terms of law. Instead of pricing its private labels according to market demand conditions, a company must relate the price of its private brands to its premium brands in order to raise successfully a "cost justification" defense under Sec. 2(a). The dissent in the *Borden* case recognized this problem in noting that "the cost ratio between Borden's premium and private label products is hardly the most significant factor in Borden's pricing decisions and market return of those products."[36] The price flexibility of private brands is, therefore, reduced by the Robinson-Patman Act treatment of brand and private label products of physically identical products as "like grade and quality."

PRICE DISCRIMINATION AS A COMPETITIVE FORCE. The competitive process presupposes a degree of both injury and discrimination as purchasers select some sources of supply and reject others. Aggressive buyers can obtain on occasion a price concession or similar benefit from a seller, by playing one seller against the other, and subtly requiring each to meet the competition of the other. These buyers can be an effective competitive force when their price-chiseling techniques result in disrupting an otherwise inflexible price structure. "In such a context, a discriminatory price cut discreetly granted to a large customer may be the crack that tends to spread to others and finally crumble an industry's rigid price wall."[37]

---

[36]*Ibid.*, p. 659.

[37]Rowe, *Price Discrimination Under the Robinson-Patman Act*, p. 27.

Aggressive sellers may seek to extend their sales by invading more distant geographic areas or by promoting their product through lower prices in a particular market. In the first instance, a firm charging the same prices in two geographic areas may be earning a lower profit margin on its sales in the more distant market. Despite the identity of prices, there will be economic discrimination as a result of the different profit margins earned in each market. In the second case, where the geographic pricing is different, there can be both legal and economic discrimination.

A lower price policy by a firm in a particular geographic area may be an indicia of healthy business rivalry. Higher profit margins and prices of other sellers may be lowered through the force of price competition. Competitors will be injured to the extent that the firm initiating the price cut will gain sales at the expense of others. Thus, on a temporary basis, price discrimination may encourage price flexibility and serve as a vital stimulus to the competitive behavior of firms. To quote Professor Adelman: *"Sporadic, unsystematic* discrimination is one of the most powerful forces of competition in modern industrial markets."[38]

On a protracted basis, price discrimination may wreak havoc of competitors and destroy competition. Predatory conduct of this variety is condemned by the Robinson-Patman Act. But the danger in administering this Act is that an overzealous concern with predatory pricing may place the protection of competitors above the encouragement of competition. Professor Markham has noted that some injury to competitors is an inevitable outcome of competition: "The natural, normal, and predictable consequence of a competitive strategy used successfully by one firm is a disadvantage — momentary or enduring — to those firms with which it competes."[39] Fear of Robinson-Patman reprisal may cause a company to use softer competitive tactics, since the line is often vaguely drawn between aggressive pricing in a strongly competitive market and predatory pricing to destroy a competitor.

[38]Effective Competition and the Antitrust Laws," p. 1331.
[39]Antitrust Trends and New Constraints," p. 90.

CHAPTER TWENTY-ONE

Background of the Antimerger Act (1950)

Extension of Coverage to Asset Purchases

Section 7 of the Clayton Act, as enacted in 1914, prohibited the acquisition by one corporation of the stock of another corporation when such acquisition would result in a substantial lessening of competition between the acquiring and acquired companies or tend to create a monopoly in any line of commerce. The pertinent provisions of the original Sec. 7, before its amendment in 1950, read as follows:

No corporation engaged in commerce shall acquire, directly or indirectly, the whole or any part of the stock or other share capital of another corporation engaged also in commerce, where the effect of such acquisition may be to substantially lessen competition between the corporation whose stock is so acquired and the corporation making the acquisition, or to restrain such commerce in any section or community, or tend to create a monopoly of any line of commerce.

The above Act did not bar the acquisition by one corporation of the *assets*, not stock, of another corporation.[1] The Government had to resort to the Sherman Act in order to challenge asset acquisitions. In *United States* v. *Columbia Steel Co.*,[2] the Government failed in its action under Secs. 1 and 2 of the Sherman Act to stop the cash purchase by United States Steel Corporation, which controlled approximately 13 per cent of the total structural steel products in an 11-state area on the West Coast, of the

[1]*Arrow-Hart & Hegeman Electric Co.* v. *Federal Trade Commission*, 291 U.S. 587 (1934).
[2]334 U.S. 495 (1947).

242

assets of Consolidated Steel Corp., an independent steel fabricator with approximately 11 per cent of the above structural steel market.

Senator Kefauver viewed the *Columbia Steel* case as a dramatic example of the inability of the Sherman Act to cover asset purchases which contribute to increases in undue economic concentration.[3] One of the major changes accomplished by the 1950 Celler-Kefauver Antimerger Act amendment to Sec. 7 of the Clayton Act was to "plug the loophole" in the statute which permitted asset acquisitions. The 1950 amendment, which added the words "shall acquire the whole or any part of the assets" of another corporation, explicitly brought within the coverage of Sec. 7 of the Clayton Act acquisitions of assets, as well as stock.

Extension of Coverage to Vertical and Conglomerate Mergers

A second major change intended by the 1950 amendment was to make clear that Sec. 7 of the Clayton Act applied not only to horizontal mergers between actual competitors, but also to vertical and conglomerate mergers. In the 35-year period from 1914, when the Clayton Act was enacted, to 1949 the Government did not invoke Sec. 7 against vertical acquisitions. The Federal Trade Commission had stated that Sec. 7 did not apply to vertical acquisitions.[4]

The 1950 amendment served to delete the following language, which was generally believed to limit Sec. 7 to horizontal mergers: "between the corporation whose stock is so acquired and the corporation making the acquisition." As Sec. 7 presently stands, its provisions apply not only to horizontal mergers between actual competitors, but also to vertical and conglomerate mergers whose effect may tend to lessen competition in any line of commerce in any section of the country.[5]

The Supreme Court has held, since the adoption of the 1950 amendment, that the original 1914 version of Sec. 7 of the Clayton Act did apply to vertical acquisitions, notwithstanding the fact that it was never resorted to until 1949. In *United States* v. *E. I. duPont de Nemours and Company*[6] the Supreme Court found that the purchase by duPont in 1917–19 of a 23 per

---

[3]United States, *Hearings before a Subcommittee of the Senate Committee on the Judiciary on Corporate Mergers and Acquisitions*, 81st Cong., 1st and 2nd Sess. (Washington, D.C.: Government Printing Office, 1949), p. 24.

[4]Federal Trade Commission, *Report on Corporate Mergers and Acquisitions* (Washington, D.C.: Government Printing Office, 1955), p. 168.

[5]United States, *House Report No. 1191*, 81st Cong., 1st Sess. (Washington, D.C.: Government Printing Office, 1949), p. 11.

[6]353 U.S. 586 (1957).

cent stock interest in General Motors violated the original version of Sec. 7 of the Clayton Act. Du Pont, as a major supplier to General Motors, was found to have lessened competition in automobile paint finishes and automobile fabrics. The Court noted that General Motors was the "colossus of the giant automobile industry" and that "du Pont's commanding position was promoted by its stock interest and was not gained solely on competitive merit." The dissent disagreed that the original version of the Clayton Act was applicable to vertical acquisitions and noted: "Thus, over 40 years after the enactment of the Clayton Act, it now becomes apparent for the first time that §7 has been a sleeping giant all along."

Change in Geographic Market Language

The 1950 amendment also changed the relevant market nomenclature from "such commerce in any section or community," in the original version of Sec. 7, to read as follows: "in any line of commerce in any section of the country." Senator Kefauver urged the deletion of the word "community" on the ground that it might suggest, for example, that a merger between two small gasoline stations in part of a city was forbidden.[7] A Senate Report also expressed fear that a literal interpretation of the word "community" might result in the prohibition of all but *de minimus* mergers.[8]

The pertinent provisions of Sec. 7 of the Clayton Act, after its amendment by the Celler-Kefauver Antimerger Act Amendment of 1950, read as follows:

No corporation engaged in commerce shall acquire, directly or indirectly, the whole or any part of the stock or other share capital and no corporation subject to the jurisdiction of the Federal Trade Commission shall acquire the whole or any part of the assets of another corporation engaged also in commerce, where in any line of commerce in any section of the country, the effect of such acquisition may be substantially to lessen competition, or tend to create a monopoly.

General Objectives of the Antimerger Act

The Supreme Court in its landmark decision, *Brown Shoe Co.* v. *United States*,[9] analyzed in detail the legislative history of the amended Sec. 7 of the Clayton Act. The Court noted the congressional concern with what

[7]United States, *Hearings Before the House Committee on the Judiciary on House Report 515*, 80th Cong., 1st Sess. (Washington, D.C.: Government Printing Office, 1947), p. 260.

[8]United States, Committee on the Judiciary, *Senate Report No. 1775*, 81st Cong., 2nd Sess. (Washington, D.C.: Government Printing Office, 1950), p. 4.

[9]370 U.S. 294 (1962).

was considered to be a "rising tide of economic concentration in the American economy," and the desirability of retaining "local control" over industry and the protection of small business.[10] The amendment to Sec. 7 would not impede, in the opinion of the Court, "a merger between two small companies to enable the combination to compete more effectively with larger corporations dominating the relevant market, nor a merger between a corporation which is financially healthy and a failing one which no longer can be a vital competitive factor in the market." "Taken as a whole," concluded the Supreme Court, "the legislative history illuminates congressional concern with the protection of *competition*, not competitors, and its desire to restrain mergers only to the extent that such combinations may tend to lessen competition."

[10]For the selected views of economists toward antitrust merger policy, see M. A. Adelman, "The Antimerger Act of 1960," *American Economic Review*, Vol. LI (May, 1961), 240; J. M. Blair, "The Conglomerate Merger in Economics and Law," *Georgetown Law Journal*, Vol. XLVI (Summer, 1958), 672; B. Bock, *Mergers and Markets*, 5th ed., "An Economic Analysis of the First Fifteen Years Under the Merger Act of 1950 (New York: National Industrial Conference Board, 1966); J. B. Dirlam, " 'The Celler-Kefauver Act': A Review of Enforcement Policy," in *Administered Prices: A Compendium on Public Policy*, pp. 97–133; J. W. Markham, "Survey of the Evidence and Findings on Mergers," in *Business Concentration and Price Policy*, pp. 141–82, "Merger Policy Under the New Section 7: A Six-Year Appraisal," *Virginia Law Review*, Vol. XL (1957), 489, and "Antitrust Trends and New Constraints," pp. 84–92; D. D. Martin, *Mergers and the Clayton Act* (Berkeley, Calif.: University of California Press, 1959); Nelson, *Merger Movements in American Industry;* G. Stigler, "Mergers and Preventive Antitrust Policy," *University of Pennsylvania Law Review*, Vol. CIV (1955), 176; "The Statistics of Monopoly and Merger," *Journal of Political Economy*, Vol. LXIV (1956), 33–40; and Weston, *The Role of Mergers in the Growth of Large Firms.*

Lists of mergers are published monthly by the National Industrial Conference Board in New York City. Also see Federal Trade Commission, *Report on the Merger Movement: A Summary Report* (Washington, D.C.: Government Printing Office, 1948); United States, House of Representatives Interim Report of the Antitrust Subcommittee of the Committee on the Judiciary, *Corporate and Bank Mergers*, 84th Cong., 1st Sess. (Washington, D.C.: Government Printing Office, 1955); and United States, House of Representatives Staff Report of the Select Committee on Small Business, *Mergers and Superconcentration*, Acquisitions of 500 Largest Industrial and 50 Largest Merchandising Firms, 87th Cong. (Washington, D.C.: Government Printing Office, 1962).

CHAPTER TWENTY-TWO

Determination of the Relevant Market in Merger Cases

The legality of a merger covered by Sec. 7 of the Clayton Act, as amended by the 1950 Celler-Kefauver Antimerger Act, rests in the majority of cases on the following critical language of this Act: "where in any line of commerce in any section of the country, the effect of such acquisition may be substantially to lessen competition, or tend to create a monopoly." The phrase "in any line of commerce" has reference to a particular product market. The phrase "in any section of the country" has reference to a selected geographic area. In order to judge whether or not a merger will "substantially" affect competition adversely, a court must reach a definition of a *relevant market* which takes into account both product and geographic factors.

Defining Product Market Boundaries

The boundaries of a product market are determined by the reasonable interchangeability of use, or the cross-elasticity of demand, between a product and its substitutes. The courts examine such factors as (1) the product's peculiar characteristics and uses, (2) unique production facilities, (3) distinct customers, (4) distinct sellers, and (5) industry or public recognition.

THE BROWN SHOE CASE (1962). In *Brown Shoe Co.* v. *United States*,[1] the Supreme Court found illegal the acquisition by Brown Shoe Company, the

[1] 370 U.S. 294 (1962).

fourth largest shoe manufacturer, of the G. R. Kinney Company, the nation's largest family-style retail shoe chain and twelfth largest shoe manufacturer. The Court held that the relevant lines of commerce encompassed by the acquisition were men's, women's, and children's shoes because (1) the public recognizes these product lines as separate, (2) each line is manufactured in separate plants, (3) each has peculiar characteristics which render it noncompetitive with the others, and (4) each line is directed to a distinct class of customers.

The Court rejected the argument of Brown Shoe that the predominantly medium-priced shoes that it manufactures occupy a product market different from the predominantly lower-priced shoes that Kinney sells. Medium-priced shoes were held to compete with lower-priced shoes. "It would be unrealistic," in the words of the majority of the Supreme Court, "to accept Brown's contention that, for example, men's shoes selling below $8.99 are in a different product market from those selling above $9.00."[2]

Brown Shoe was also unsuccessful in its argument that the product market definition of children's shoes should take account of age and sex differences. For example, Brown argued that "a little boy does not wear a little girl's black patent leather pump." Brown contended that "infants' and babies' " shoes, "misses' and children's" shoes, and "youths' and boys' shoes" should each be considered a separate line of commerce. The Court could find no advantage for Brown Shoe if finer product definitions were employed:

> Brown manufactures significant, comparable quantities of virtually every type of nonrubber men's, women's, and children's shoes, and Kinney sells such quantities of virtually every type of men's, women's, and children's shoes. Thus whether considered separately or together, the picture of this merger is the same.[3]

THE CONTINENTAL CAN (HAZEL-ATLAS) CASE (1964). In *United States* v. *Continental Can Co.*[4] the Supreme Court held illegal a merger between the second largest manufacturer of metal containers (Continental Can) with the third largest manufacturer of glass containers (Hazel-Atlas). The District Court found that glass and metal containers constituted separate lines of commerce, since the containers had different characteristics that could disqualify them from particular uses; the machinery necessary to pack in glass is different from that employed when cans are used; and the users of glass or metal cans do not shift back and forth as relative prices for these containers change. The Supreme Court noted that metal containers and glass containers were separate industries, but held that the inter-industry

[2] *Ibid.*, p. 326.
[3] *Ibid.*, pp. 327–28.
[4] 378 U.S. 441 (1964).

competition between the manufacturers of these two types of containers brought both metal and glass containers under one combined product market for judging the merger. The Court found that both types of containers are used to pack baby food, soft drinks, beer, and other products. Furthermore, metal cans were penetrating, after considerable consumer resistance, a number of traditional glass container markets, such as carbonated soft drinks. Continental Can had been a major factor in promoting the entry of metal cans into the former domain of glass containers in a number of product categories. In the words of the Court,

> Thus, though the interchangeability of use may not be so complete and the cross-elasticity of demand not so immediate as in the case of most intra-industry mergers, there is over the long run the kind of customer response to innovation and other competitive stimuli that brings the competition between these two industries within §7's competition-preserving proscriptions.[5]

A dissenting opinion was written in the *Continental Can* Supreme Court decision by Justice Harlan, and joined in by Justice Stewart. The dissent contended that the majority opinion was a "travesty of economics," since the Court provided "its own definition of a market, unrelated to any market reality whatsoever." Justice Harlan believed that the metal container industry and glass container industry were separate lines of commerce. The grouping of metal and glass containers into one product market, or a combined line of commerce was, in the words of Justice Harlan, "completely fanciful:"

> The bizarre result of the Court's approach is that market percentages of a non-existent market enable the Court to dispense with "elaborate proof of market structure, market behavior and probable anticompetitive effects."[6]

It is interesting to note that the Government did not suggest that "glass and metal containers" constituted a separate line of commerce until submitting their brief to the Supreme Court. Furthermore, the Government deliberately omitted mention of market shares, since "those traditional yardsticks are generally unavailable to measure the full consequences which an inter-industry merger would have on competition."[7] If a market does not exist for "glass and metal containers," *market shares* cannot be meaningfully compiled.

Continental Can argued that the purpose of its merger with Hazel-Atlas was to diversify into the related glass container field. The District Court held that the case involved a "conglomerate merger" between a

---

[5]*Ibid.*, p. 455.

[6]*Ibid.*, pp. 469–70.

[7]Government Brief, p. 22. See 378 U.S. 441, 470.

manufacturer of metal containers and a manufacturer of glass containers. As shown in Table 22-1, Hazel-Atlas accounted for 9.6 per cent of the total shipments of glass containers, and Continental Can accounted for 33.0 per cent of the metal container shipments in the United States.

TABLE 22-1

PERCENTAGE OF METAL AND GLASS CONTAINER SHIPMENTS
ACCOUNTED FOR BY CONTINENTAL CAN AND HAZEL-ATLAS, 1955

	Continental Can	*Hazel-Atlas*	*Continental Can and Hazel-Atlas Combined*
Glass containers	None	9.6	9.6
Metal containers	33.0	None	33.0
Glass and metal containers	21.9	3.1	25.0

The Supreme Court majority opinion held, in effect, that Continental Can had not moved into a separate market by its merger with Hazel-Atlas, but had fortified its position in the combined metal and glass container market. Continental, with 21.9 per cent of the shipments, ranked second in this product market, and Hazel-Atlas, with 3.1 per cent, ranked sixth. In the words of the Court,

> By the acquisition of Hazel-Atlas stock Continental not only increased its own share more than 14% from 21.9% to 25%, but also reduced from five to four the most significant competitors who might threaten its dominant position. The resulting percentage of the combined firms approaches that held presumptively bad in *United States* v. *Philadelphia National Bank*. . . .[8]

Justice Harlan, in his dissenting opinion, objected to the comparison with the *Philadelphia National Bank* case, which involved the merger of the second and third largest banks in the metropolitan Philadelphia area. Both banks were clearly in the same product market, commercial banking, which was a market "sufficiently inclusive to be meaningful in terms of trade realities." In the *Continental Can* case the product market definition was not clear. In such a context, Justice Harlan believed that the presumptively illegal market share approach taken by the majority in *Continental Can* was inappropriate:

> When a merger is attacked on the ground that competition *between* two distinct industries, or lines of commerce, will be affected, the shortcut "market share" approach developed in the *Philadelphia Bank* case . . . has no place.[9]

[8]*Ibid.*, p. 461; and 374 U.S. 321 (1963).
[9]*Ibid.*, p. 475.

THE ALCOA (ROME CABLE) CASE (1964). In the *Alcoa* (Rome Cable) case,[10] decided by the Supreme Court in the same year as Continental Can, the District Court's definition of the relevant product market was also reversed. The District Court held that the acquisition of Rome Cable by Alcoa did not violate Sec. 7 of the Clayton Act. In both *Alcoa* (Rome Cable) and *Continental Can* (Hazel-Atlas), the Supreme Court found the acquisitions to be illegal. In *Alcoa* (Rome Cable) the Supreme Court severed the product market determined by the District Court. In *Continental Can* the Supreme Court joined into one product market the separate lines of commerce found by the District Court.

Both the District Court and Supreme Court in the *Alcoa* (Rome Cable) case agreed that bare aluminum conductor was a product submarket; it had virtually displaced copper in overhead lines used to carry electric power from generating plants to consumers. The courts disagreed on whether bare aluminum conductor and insulated aluminum conductor could be joined into one product market, namely, aluminum conductor.

The District Court found that insulated *aluminum* conductor could not be treated as a separate line of commerce from insulated *copper* conductor, since both are functionally interchangeable by the users; the conductor industry does not differentiate between copper and aluminum insulated products; both may be produced interchangeably on the same fabricating machinery; and neither has distinct customers or specialized vendors.

The Supreme Court found that despite the competition existing between insulated aluminum and insulated copper conductors, insulated aluminum could be treated as a separate line of commerce. The Court noted that the price of most insulated aluminum conductor is 50 to 60 per cent of the price of insulated copper conductor of the same size. Furthermore, the growth of insulated aluminum conductor in the market for insulated overhead lines, from less than 10 per cent in 1950 to over 75 per cent in 1959, reflected advantages for this product.

Having found that insulated aluminum conductor constituted a line of commerce, the Supreme Court went on to hold that aluminum conductor (bare and insulated) constituted the relevant product market. This was, in the words of the majority of the Court, merely "a logical extension of the District Court's findings." The dissent, written by Justice Stewart, and joined in by Justices Harlan and Goldberg, could find little justification for grouping bare and insulated aluminum conductor together. The combination was not recognized by the industry as a separate line of commerce, and different equipment and engineering skills were required for their manufacture and sale. Thus the dissent concluded:

---

[10]*United States* v. *Aluminum Company of America*, 377 U.S. 271 (1964).

But even if insulated aluminum conductor is a proper line of commerce, there is no basis in logic, or in the competitive realities of the conductor industry, for lumping together in one line of commerce bare and insulated aluminum conductors.[11]

Diversification was the avowed purpose of the mergers in both the *Alcoa* (Rome Cable) and *Continental Can* (Hazel-Atlas) cases. Continental Can, a producer of metal containers, merged with Hazel-Atlas in order to enter the field of glass containers. Alcoa, a fully integrated aluminum producer, acquired Rome Cable in order to enter the insulated copper conductor market and broaden its insulated aluminum conductor line.

The District Court in the *Alcoa* (Rome Cable) case found that Alcoa "lacked the 'know-how' to manufacture the more complicated types of insulated wire and cable for which there was a growing demand." Alcoa believed that the time required to obtain such competence from its own organization, and the expense involved, necessitated the acquisition of a company that already had this ability in the insulating field. At the time of the merger, Alcoa was the leading producer of primary aluminum ingot (38.6 per cent) and the leading fabricator of bare aluminum conductor (32.5 per cent). Alcoa produced no copper conductor cable or wire.

Rome was predominantly a copper manufacturing company. In 1958 Rome was one of the ten largest manufacturers of copper conductor in the United States. Its share of the bare aluminum conductor market was insignificant (0.3 per cent). As shown in Table 22-2, the combined Alcoa-Rome share of the combined aluminum and copper conductor, bare and insulated, was 3.2 per cent. Their combined share of the total insulated copper and aluminum market was 1.6 per cent. The District Court found that the market shares of Alcoa and Rome in these broad product markets were insufficient for a finding of a lessening of competition as a result of the merger.

TABLE 22-2

PERCENTAGE OF ALUMINUM AND COPPER CONDUCTOR MARKET
ACCOUNTED FOR BY ALCOA AND ROME CABLE IN 1958

	Alcoa	*Rome*	*Alcoa-Rome Combined*
Aluminum conductor	27.8	1.3	29.1
Bare	32.5	0.3	32.8
Insulated	11.6	4.7	16.3
Total aluminum and copper conductor	1.8	1.4	3.2
Bare	10.3	2.0	12.3
Insulated	0.3	1.3	1.6

[11]*Ibid.*, p. 286.

The Supreme Court, by treating aluminum conductor as the relevant market, was able to achieve more substantial market shares. The Court held that Alcoa by acquiring Rome Cable was able to add 1.3 percentage points to its already leading share (27.8 per cent) of the aluminum conductor field. This increment of 1.3 percentage points was sufficient to make it reasonably likely that the merger would produce a substantial lessening of competition within the meaning of Sec. 7 of the Clayton Act. There was no mention of the finding by the District Court that Alcoa's share of aluminum conductor was steadily declining for the past decade, and continued to decline after the merger. The Alcoa-Rome share of aluminum conductor fell 4.3 percentage points from 29.1 per cent in 1958, the year preceding the merger, to 24.8 per cent in 1961. Thus, in the aluminum conductor market, Alcoa increased its share by 1.3 percentage points in 1959 by the acquisition of Rome Cable, but lost this amount plus an additional 3 percentage points by 1961.

Rome Cable represented, in the opinion of the Supreme Court, "the prototype of the small independent that Congress aimed to preserve by §7."[12]

Defining Geographic Market Boundaries

The geographic market boundaries in which the competitive effects of a merger are judged are normally the area or "section of the country" in which the acquired company and acquiring company can be expected to conduct business. The coverage of a geographic market is not confined to political subdivisions such as states or cities. But the availability of data often requires a particular region, state, or metropolitan area to be selected as an approximation to a more accurate area of effective competition. Trade associations often compile data by political subdivisions and, consequently, the parties must settle for the best available data. In recent years the Federal Trade Commission and Department of Justice have made a few special surveys to obtain market data otherwise unavailable to the parties in litigation.[13] These agencies, empowered with broad subpoena power, are in an advantageous position for gathering data deemed crucial to the defense or prosecution in an antitrust proceeding.

THE BETHLEHEM-YOUNGSTOWN CASE (1958). In *United States* v. *Bethlehem Steel Corp.*[14] the District Court rejected the defendants' argu-

---

[12]*Ibid.*, p. 281.

[13]See *Pillsbury Mills, Inc.*, 50 F.T.C. 1110 (1954). But cf. *Union Bag-Camp Paper Corp.* v. *Federal Trade Commission*, 233 F. Supp. 660 (D. C. N.Y., 1964).

[14]168 F. Supp. 576 (1958).

ment that the geographic market for steel products was not nationwide but consisted of three separate sections covering the United States: eastern, mid-continent and western. Since all of Bethlehem's plants were located in the eastern and western areas, and all of Youngstown's plants were located in the mid-continent area, the defense maintained that the proposed merger of these companies could not substantially lessen competition. The gist of the defense was that the high cost of transporting steel products confined the operations of the two companies to separate markets:

> The substance of the defendants' argument is: that within each of the three areas there are natural or regional markets adjacent to the locations of the steel plants; that steel consumers prefer to purchase from steel plants which are located nearby in order to avoid excess freight charges; that steel producers prefer customers located nearby in order to reduce freight absorption when that is necessary; that the greater the distance between the customer and the steel plant, the less effective is the steel plant in the competition for the customer's business; that the competitive force of a steel plant's shipments decreases as sales are made further away from the so-called natural market. Accordingly the defendants maintain that Bethlehem is an "effective competitor" only in the Eastern and Western Areas where its plants are located and that Youngstown is an "effective competitor" only in the Mid-Continent Area where its plants are located. Conversely they classify themselves as marginal suppliers in those areas where they do not have plants and contend that their competitive positions in their non-plant areas are minor and subordinate to steel producers with plants located there.[15]

The District Court found that Bethlehem was not an effective competitor of Youngstown. In 1955, the year preceding the proposed merger, Bethlehem accounted for 9.1 per cent and Youngstown accounted for 5.7 per cent of the total steel shipments into the states of Michigan and Ohio. In the same year Bethlehem accounted for 5.2 per cent and Youngstown 9.4 per cent of the total industry shipments into the state of Ohio, where over half of Youngstown's ingot capacity was located. Similar overlaps of sales were found in the state of Michigan, a number of multistate regions, and in the United States as a whole. Specifically, the District Court held that the relevant geographic markets included: (a) the United States as a whole, (b) the northeast quadrant of the United States, (c) Michigan, Ohio, Pennsylvania, and New York, (d) Michigan and Ohio, (e) Michigan, and (f) Ohio. Finally, the District Court noted that the "section of the country" must be determined with respect to both buyers and sellers:

> The determination must be made on the basis of not only where the companies have in the past made sales, but also on the basis of where potentially they could make sales and where buyers could reasonably turn to them as alternative substantial sources of supply.[16]

[15] *Ibid.*, p. 597.
[16] *Ibid.*, p. 599.

THE BROWN SHOE CASE (1962). In *United States* v. *Brown Shoe Co.*[17] the Supreme Court found that the relevant geographic market at the *manufacturing* level was the entire Nation. "The relationships of product value, bulk, weight and consumer demand enable manufacturers to distribute their shoes on a nationwide basis, as Brown and Kinney, in fact, do." However, for judging the effect of the acquisition at the *retail* level, the relevant geographic market was held as cities "with a population exceeding 10,000 and its immediate contiguous surrounding territory in which both Brown and Kinney sold shoes at retail through stores they either owned or controlled."

Both the District Court and the Supreme Court rejected the contention by Brown Shoe that the relevant geographic market for retailing should in some cases include only the central business districts of large cities, and in others, should encompass "standard metropolitan areas" within which smaller suburban communities are found. Brown Shoe was, in effect, arguing that the relevant geographic market should in some cases be small enough to separate center-city shoe markets (where Brown Shoe's outlets were primarily located) from the surrounding suburban shoe markets (where Kinney's stores were primarily located).[18] The Supreme Court found that shoe stores in the outskirts of cities compete effectively with stores in the central downtown areas. Therefore, the relevant geographic market was held to include both downtown and suburban areas:

> Such markets are large enough to include the downtown shops and suburban shopping centers in areas contiguous to the city, which are the important competitive factors, and yet are small enough to exclude stores beyond the immediate environs of the city, which are of little competitive significance.[19]

THE PHILADELPHIA BANK CASE (1963). In *United States* v. *Philadelphia National Bank*[20] the Supreme Court held that the proper question to ask in determining the appropriate geographic relevant market is "not where the parties to the merger do business or even where they compete, but where, within the area of competitive overlap, the effect of the merger on competition will be direct and immediate."[21] In applying this test the Court found that the relevant geographic market for judging the economic effects of the proposed acquisition by Philadelphia Bank of Girard Trust was the four-county Philadelphia metropolitan area (Philadelphia, Montgomery, Bucks,

---

[17]370 U.S. 294 (1962).
[18]Bock, *Mergers and Markets*, 5th ed., p. 80.
[19]370 U.S. 294, 339 (1962).
[20]374 U.S. 321 (1963).
[21]*Ibid.*, p. 357.

and Delaware counties) in which the merging banks were permitted under state law to operate branches, and from which the bulk of their business originated.

The Supreme Court rejected the finding of the lower court that the relevant geographic market consisted of the northeastern United States, or at least New York City and the entire Delaware Valley (*i.e.*, Philadelphia, Bucks, Montgomery, Delaware, and Chester counties in Pennsylvania; and in New Jersey, Burlington, Camden, and Gloucester counties). The Supreme Court noted that large borrowers and depositors in the four-county area did considerable business with New York City banks, and were in need of a large bank in the Philadelphia area to avoid going to other cities for major financing. In contrast, the smaller bank customers are influenced by convenience and generally confine their banking activities to local banks. Therefore, the Court observed in a footnote: "the four-county area remains a valid geographic market in which to assess the anticompetitive effect of the proposed merger upon the banking facilities available to the smaller customer — a perfectly good 'line of commerce' . . . "[22] However, the four-county area was also deemed a workable compromise for all customers, both large and small. In the words of the Court,

. . . in banking the relevant geographical market is a function of each separate customer's economic scale means simply that a workable compromise must be found: some fair intermediate delineation which avoids the indefensible extremes of drawing the market either so expansively as to make the effect of the merger upon competition seem insignificant, because only the very largest bank customers are taken into account in defining the market, or so narrowly as to place appellees in different markets, because only the smallest customers are considered. We think that the four-county Philadelphia metropolitan area which state law apparently recognizes as a meaningful banking community in allowing Philadelphia banks to branch within it, and which would seem roughly to delineate the area in which bank customers that are neither very large nor very small find it practical to do their banking business, is a more appropriate "section of the country" in which to appraise the instant merger than any larger or smaller or different area.[23]

The boundaries of a relevant geographic market may extend beyond the area of actual competition and encompass areas of potential competition. In the following two merger decisions, decided in 1964, the Supreme Court rested its principal finding of illegality on the fact that potential competition was actually present, or in view of a rapidly expanding market, could be expected to occur in the near future between the acquired and acquiring companies.

[22]*Ibid.*, p. 360, fn. 37.
[23]*Ibid.*, p. 361.

THE EL PASO CASE (1964). In *United States* v. *El Paso Natural Gas Co.*,[24] the Supreme Court found illegal the acquisition between the sole company licensed by the Federal Power Commission to distribute natural gas from out of state into the state of California (El Paso) and the only other important interstate pipeline company licensed to operate west of the Rockies (Pacific Northwest Pipeline). Pacific Northwest operated a pipeline from the San Juan Basin, New Mexico, to the state of Washington, and was authorized to receive large quantities of Canadian gas.

Prior to the acquisition, Pacific Northwest had attempted unsuccessfully to obtain a license to distribute natural gas into the rapidly expanding California market. Pacific Northwest also entered into negotiations with the Southern California Edison Company for the sale of natural gas which would be delivered at a point on the California-Oregon border. Edison, which was the largest industrial user of natural gas in Southern California, used El Paso gas, which it purchased through a distributor on a low-priority "interruptible" basis, *i.e.*, subject to interruption during periods of peak demand. Upon learning of the negotiations between Pacfic Northwest and Edison, El Paso succeeded in getting one of its distributors to give Edison a contract on a noninterruptible basis. A few months later El Paso acquired control of Pacific Northwest.

The Supreme Court held that Pacific Northwest, though it had no pipeline into California, was a substantial factor in the California market at the time it was acquired by El Paso. "We would have to wear blinders," stated the Court, "not to see that the mere efforts of Pacific Northwest to get into the California market, though unsuccessful, had a powerful influence on El Paso's business attitudes within the state."[25] Pacific Northwest was therefore found to be a potential competitor of El Paso at the time of the acquisition.

The following passage reflects the interest of the Supreme Court in the outlying area of potential competition occupied by Pacific Northwest:

Pacific Northwest had proximity to the California market — 550 miles distant in Wyoming, even nearer in Idaho, only 250 miles away in Oregon. Moreover, it had enormous reserves in the San Juan Basin, the Rocky Mountains, and western Canada. Had Pacific Northwest remained independent, there can be no doubt it would have sought to exploit its formidable geographic position vis-à-vis California. No one knows what success it would have had. We do know, however, that two interstate pipelines in addition to El Paso now serve California — one of the newcomers being Pacific Gas Transmission Co., bringing down Canadian gas. So we know the opportunities would have existed for Pacific Northwest had it remained independent.[26]

[24]376 U.S. 651 (1964). Also see *Cascade Natural Gas Corp.* v. *El Paso Natural Gas Co.*, 386 U.S. 129 (1967).

[25]*Ibid.*, p. 659.

[26]*Ibid.*, p. 661.

THE PENN-OLIN CASE (1964). In *United States* v. *Penn-Olin Chemical Co.*[27] the Supreme Court held that the formation of a joint venture by two chemical companies to produce sodium chlorate in the southeastern quadrant of the United States would be unlawful under Sec. 7 of the Clayton Act if either of the parent companies would have entered this market individually, with the other remaining at the edge of the market as a potential competitor. Prior to the formation of Penn-Olin, one of the parents of the joint venture, Pennsalt Chemicals, produced sodium chlorate at its plant in Portland, Oregon. Under the terms of a sales arrangement, the other parent, Olin Mathieson, sold a third of the plant's output in the southeastern part of the United States. This sales arrangement was entered into on a temporary basis for the purpose of testing the southeastern market with a view toward the formation of a joint venture located at Calvert City, Kentucky.

The District Court found that, at the time of the formation of the joint venture, Pennsalt was not an effective competitor in the southeast because it labored under a freight handicap in shipping from Oregon. Pennsalt's competitors, American Potash and Hooker Chemical, each had a sodium chlorate plant located in Mississippi, and together accounted for over 90 per cent of the sodium chlorate sales in the southeast. After Penn-Olin was formed, Pittsburgh Plate Glass announced that it would build a sodium chlorate plant in Louisiana. The District Court found that Pennsalt and Olin Mathieson each possessed the resources and general capability needed to build its own plant in the southeast. However, this factor was not controlling, in the opinion of the District Court, except as a factor in determining whether *both* companies would have probably entered the market as individual competitors if the Penn-Olin joint venture had not been formed. "Only in this event would potential competition between the two companies have been forclosed by the joint venture."[28]

The Supreme Court held that the District Court had used the wrong test. In the words of the Court,

. . . Certainly the sole test would not be the probability that *both* companies would have entered the market. Nor would the consideration be limited to the probability that one entered alone. There still remained for consideration the fact that Penn-Olin eliminated the potential competition of the corporation that might have remained at the edge of the market, continually threatening to enter. Just as a merger eliminates actual competition, this joint venture may well foreclose any prospect of competition between Olin and Pennsalt in the relevant sodium chlorate market. . . .[29]

The case was remanded to the District Court, which found that the evidence did not show that, but for the joint venture, Pennsalt as a matter

[27]378 U.S. 158 (1964).
[28]217 F. Supp. 110, 130 (1963).
[29]378 U.S. 158, 173 (1964).

of reasonable probability would have individually entered the southeastern sodium chlorate market.[30]

Interrelation of Product and Geographic Market Definitions

The fact that two merging firms compete in only a small fraction of the geographic-product market in which either operates, does not necessarily place the merger outside the scope of the Clayton Act. The Supreme Court has emphasized the word *any* in the following language from Sec. 7 of the amended Clayton Act: "where in any line of commerce in any section of the country, the effect of such acquisition may be substantially to lessen competition, or to tend to create a monopoly."

In the *Philadelphia National Bank* case, the Supreme Court in determining the relevant market, stated that the proper question to be asked is "not where the parties to the merger do business or even where they compete, but where, within the area of competitive overlap, the effect of the merger on competition will be direct and immediate."[31]

In the *Continental Can* (Hazel-Atlas) case the Supreme Court accepted the Government's argument that wherever "meaningful competition" exists, a "line of commerce" is to be found. Thus, the majority stated:

. . . we hold that the inter-industry competition between glass and metal containers is sufficient to warrant treating as a relevant product market the combined glass and metal container industries and all end uses for which they compete.[32]

The purpose of delineating a particular line of commerce and section of the country is to provide a basis or framework for appraising the effects of a given merger. In this posture the relevant market analysis, both as to product market boundaries and geographic market boundaries, becomes an essential part of the jurisprudence of antitrust law. The market facts and commercial attributes are observed in order to select an appropriate arena in which to judge the effects of a merger. The court must consider not only the effects on the competition between the merging parties but also the probable effects or injuries on third parties (competitors, suppliers, or customers).[33]

---

[30]246 F. Supp. 917 (1965); *affirmed per curiam*, 389 U.S. 308 (1967).

[31]374 U.S. 321, 357 (1963).

[32]378 U.S. 441, 457 (1964).

[33]B. Bock, *Mergers and Markets*, 4th ed. (New York: National Industrial Conference Board, 1965), p. 59, and "Relativity of Economic Evidence in Merger Cases — Emerging Issues Force the Issue," *Michigan Law Review*, Vol. LXIII (June, 1965), 1355–72.

CHAPTER TWENTY-THREE

Conglomerate Mergers

As American firms diversify and broaden their lines of commerce, the significant problems in antitrust become less concerned with the monopolization of a given product market. The single product analysis of monopoly and oligopoly theory has become inadequate for explaining the more general economic behavior of firms selling a multitude of different products. Rational business conduct can no longer be identified with the short-run profit maximization of a particular market. The firm that attempts to accommodate customers with a broad product line will often incur losses or low profit margins on some of its items. Consequently, the firm must subsidize some of its operations by profits earned in several of its other product markets. By analyzing the practice of subsidization, one can perceive the firm in terms of an aggregation of product markets. Furthermore, the focus of antitrust can be reoriented from the single product analysis of monopoly to the problems concerning multiple product forms of competition.

The Concept of Conglomerate Power

The legal and economic problems associated with conglomerate mergers are present where the merging companies do not directly compete with each other nor stand in a buyer-seller relationship. A major issue is whether diversified firms, which take the merger route to grow, enjoy unique advantages over smaller single product competitors. The complex of these advantages has been labeled "conglomerate power" by Professor Corwin Edwards:

This aspect of the power of large concerns becomes more conspicuous as the diversity of operations becomes greater, that is, as the likelihood that the large concern has monopoly power in any particular market becomes less. When the large company spreads across many products throughout a wide geographical area and covers a series of stages in production and distribution, its opportunities for multiple contacts with other large concerns are at their greatest, and the advantage to be derived from an effort to get the best of another large company at a particular point is least evident. Similarly, such a company has the maximum chance to discipline or destroy any particular small company by a localized attack without serious inconvenience to itself, and has the minimum vulnerability to attack from a single small company.... Differentials in size rather than in monopoly power are the source of such advantages. The large concern has a special status, even though it may operate in an industry so large that its percentage of the total market is small. The small enterprise lacks these advantages even though it may operate in an industry so small that it has a practical monopoly from which it derives other advantages.[1]

Conglomerate Power as a System of Subsidization

The advantages of "conglomerate power" can also be shown to accrue to any large company which is able to take funds from one geographic or product market, or from one stage of production, and use these funds to subsidize other areas under its operation. When a firm maintains a broad line of goods, some of which are carried at a loss or low profit margin, it is following a business policy which reflects that what is not earned on some items carried in stock will be more than compensated by the additional profits earned on the remaining goods. Subsidization can be shown to encompass not only rational conduct for the multiple-product firm, but even for the single-product firm.

Initially, it should be noted that the market for any single product can be conceived alternatively as a cohesion of submarkets. A manufacturer with several stages of production is actually producing a series of products, starting from a crude raw material or basic structure up to the finished end product. Some of the intermediate products could be sold, conceptually at least, to other fabricating firms. What constitutes an actual stage of pro-

---

[1]"Conglomerate Bigness as a Source of Power," in *Business Concentration and Price Policy*, p. 336. For various views on conglomerate mergers, see M. A. Adelman, "The Antimerger Act, 1950–60," *American Economic Review* (Proceedings, 1961), p. 236; Blair, "The Conglomerate Merger in Economics and Law," pp. 672–700; B. Bock, *Mergers and Markets:* A Guide to Economic Analysis of Case Law, 2nd ed. (New York: National Industrial Conference Board, 1962), Studies in Business Economics No. 77; and D. Turner, "Conglomerate Mergers and Section 7 of the Clayton Act," *Harvard Law Review*, Vol. LXXVIII (May, 1965), 1313–95. Also see M. Gort, *Diversification and Integration in American Industry*, National Bureau of Economic Research (Princeton, N. J.: Princeton University Press, 1962); and J. C. Narver, *Conglomerate Mergers and Market Competition* (Berkeley, Calif.: University of California Press, 1967).

duction can often be a matter of cost accounting rather than the actual ability of a producer to resell a partially finished product. Similarly, geographic markets can be split up into various accounting units and treated as separate markets. It is more the rule than the exception that a firm will operate one of its stages of production, or sell in one of its geographic markets, at a lower profit margin than other stages or markets. The more profitable markets are subsidizing or partially carrying the less profitable ones. Whatever the justification — maintaining an efficient level of production, broadening a sales base for protection against seasonal fluctuations, anticipating future company growth — the practices of every firm reflect instances of subsidization, in one form or another, in almost every facet of its business behavior.

There are many forms of subsidization. In some cases the subsidization appears as an attempt by corporate management to equalize its profits in various markets or stages of production. Other times the firm is covering an actual loss resulting from a product sold below cost. Finally, a firm could be using subsidization for the "price squeezing" of smaller independent nonintegrated firms. It will, therefore, be useful for the later discussion of conglomerate mergers to distinguish these alternative concepts of subsidization.

SUBSIDIZATION AS THE EQUALIZATION OF PROFIT RATES. The first interpretation of subsidization covers every accounting transfer of profit between different products of a firm, or any manipulation of a rate of return between different stages of production. The fact that neither product is sold actually at a loss is not significant. The higher profit earner is treated as carrying more than its share of the total investment of the firm. Thus, if a 2 per cent profit is made on product A, and a 10 per cent profit is made on product B, the second product is considered to be subsidizing the first. Similarly, under this interpretation, the fact that some of the products from different stages of production are not sold by the firm on the open market, and therefore the firm earns no actual profit, is not relevant. The vertical stage of production with the higher rate of return is treated as carrying more than its share of the total investment of the firm; it serves as the source of subsidization for the remaining stages of production.

In *United States* v. *New York Great Atlantic and Pacific Tea Company* the Circuit Court employed this interpretation of subsidization in analyzing the pricing of A & P in various geographic markets:

When the gross profit rate is reduced in Area X, it is an almost irresistible conclusion that A & P had the power to compensate for any possible decline in net profits by raising the gross profit rate and retail prices in Area Y, where it was in a

²67 F. Supp. 626 (E.D. Ill., 1946), *affirmed* 173 F. 2nd 79 (7th Cir., 1949).

competitive position to do so. The record is replete with instances of deliberate reductions of gross profit rates in selected areas. . . . There must inevitably be a compensation somewhere in the system for a loss somewhere else, as the overall policy of the company is to earn $7 per share per annum on its stock.[3]

This type of subsidization, seen as an equalization of profit rates, occurs even though products are not sold at a loss. All that is required is a disproportionate accrual of earnings or rates of return between different geographic markets, or product markets.

SUBSIDIZATION AS A COMPENSATION FOR A LOSS. The second meaning of subsidization requires a company to use profits from its operations in one market to support *actual losses* in a second market. The requirement that one of the products of a company be sold at a loss is often illusory. In vertical integration, for instance, the products from earlier stages of production may not even be sold on the open market. Therefore, under this interpretation of subsidization, seen as a compensation for a loss, one must assume that if, hypothetically, the firm sold its products from a particular vertical stage of production, the firm would sustain a loss on the open market.[4]

Under the second interpretation of subsidization, the answer to the question of whether or not subsidization is present can be expected to depend in some instances upon the accounting method selected. Similarly, as the firm increases in complexity either through vertical integration or diversification, the determination of precisely which departments, stages of production, or products are responsible for the over-all profit level of the firm can be ambiguous as a result of the problem of complementarity. Different products, or stages of production, share in the use of capital equipment, management, and selling expenses. Therefore, profits which are attributable to the complementary interactions of elements within the aggregate structure of a firm are often rather arbitrarily allocated by cost accounting methods to specific stages of production or distribution.

SUBSIDIZATION AND THE "PRICE SQUEEZING" OF NONINTEGRATED INDEPENDENTS. The final interpretation of subsidization is related to the act of "price squeezing" by a vertically integrated firm. Some of the profits derived from market sales of products from one stage of production are used to carry another stage operated at or below cost, with the result that competing nonintegrated, independent firms are either destroyed or in-

[3] *Ibid.*, p. 87.

[4] Reference to the literature on internal transfer pricing can be found in J. A. Menge, "The Backward Art of Interdivisional Transfer Pricing," *Journal of Industrial Economics*, Vol. IX (July, 1961), 215–32.

jured. Accompanying this type of subsidization is usually a restriction of supply, or an overcharging on price, by the vertically integrated firms to its customers. These customers are generally independent processors or fabricators, who depend upon the vertically integrated firm for raw materials, and must also face the vertically integrated firm in the market for the final product. In this context the term subsidization carries opprobrium and is classified as a method of cutthroat competition.

The previous discussion of the *Alcoa* case pointed out that the offense committed by Alcoa was the forward subsidization of the sheet manufacturing operation, which was performed at a near loss, by the "profits" made at the earlier stage of ingot production. The court segregated the various technological levels of the integrated firm and treated each as an independent operation. Alcoa was found guilty of squeezing the competing fabricators that purchased ingot from Alcoa at allegedly enhanced prices, and then had to meet Alcoa's unduly low prices for fabricated sheet. Similarly, it was argued by the Government in the *A & P* case that the "profits" earned by A & P in its earlier vertical stages of manufacturing private brands were used to subsidize its retail operations. Since A & P neither held a monopoly over the supply of goods it manufactured, nor sold any of these items to its competitors, it could not be accused of squeezing rival firms.[5] Furthermore, A & P could not have earned profits at its higher stages of production, which had no sales. The term "rate of return" should have been used to describe these earnings.[6]

A & P was alleged to have followed a business strategy of cutting prices in a particular area in order to increase volume, which in turn would lower expenses, and permit a higher over-all rate of return to be earned at a lower mark-up. A & P would accept a low return or loss in the interim between the time when prices were lowered and the time a larger volume was attained. If A & P was successful in achieving a larger volume in a particular area, it would earn a higher return relative to its initial position; if A & P was unsuccessful in its price reduction campaign, it would sustain a loss or lower return on an unchanged volume.[7]

The problem of subsidization in relation to predatory pricing can be analyzed in terms of Fig. 23-1, which depicts three cases involving rates of

[5] The A & P Court of Appeals Main Brief, at page 194; J. Dirlam and A. Kahn, "Integration and Dissolution of the A & P Company," *Indiana Law Journal*, Vol. XXIX (Fall, 1953), 4.

[6] "No man can make a profit selling to himself." M. A. Adelman, *A & P: A Study in Price-Cost Behavior and Public Policy* (Cambridge, Mass.: Harvard University Press, 1959), p. 245. Also see "Trouble Begins in the 'New' Sherman Act: The Perplexing Story of the A & P Case," *Yale Law Review*, Vol. LVIII (May, 1949), 969–82.

[7] M. A. Adelman, "The A & P Case: A Study in Applied Economics," *Quarterly Journal of Economics*, Vol. XLIII (May, 1949), 238–57.

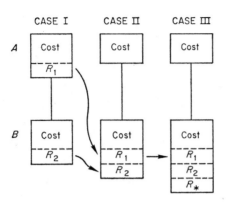

CASE I   CASE II   CASE III

Fig. 23-1. *Subsidization Between Vertical Stages of Production*

return at different vertical stages of production. Case I illustrates vertical integration, where the firm earns the same rate of return or a "normal profit" from both the A and B stages of production. Case II shows a situation where the integrated firm decides to take all its return in the lower B stage by using the higher A stage as a source of subsidy. The firm earns the same rate of return on its investment in the B stage of production $(R_1 + R_2)$ as it formerly earned on a combined basis from the A stage (R_1) and the B stage (R_2). Case III shows a firm earning an additional "monopoly profit" (R_*) as a result of predatory pricing practices.

The issue raised in both the *Alcoa* and *A & P* cases concerns the extent to which subsidization may be carried on before it becomes an unfair predatory practice. Professors Dirlam and Kahn ask,

How "disporportionate" must be the returns from different activities before an illegal "abuse" of integration may be said to have occurred? It is impossible to lay down arithmetical rules. The courts can decide only on the basis of historical pattern of action, the relative size of the protagonists, and the intent deducible therefrom, the practices in the trade, and the economic impact of the "subsidization," whether an unreasonable restraint of trade has been effected.[8]

Furthermore, the cost and ease of entry of new firms must be considered, since predatory competition to eliminate or browbeat competitors and then raise prices can succeed only if there exist barriers to entry. To quote Professor Adelman: "Predatory competition is an expensive pastime, undertaken only if monopoly and its fruits can be obtained and *held*."[9]

[8]Dirlam and Kahn, "Integration and Dissolution of the A & P Company," p. 3. Also see the reply by M. A. Adelman, "Integration and Dissolution of the A & P Company— A Reply," *Indiana Law Journal*, Vol. XXIX (Spring, 1954), 367–70; and Rejoinder by Dirlam and Kahn, *ibid.*, pp. 371–75.

[9]*Ibid.*, p. 369. Also see J. S. McGee, "Predatory Price Cutting: the Standard Oil (N. J.) Case," *Journal of Law and Economics*, Vol. I (October, 1958), 137–69.

SUBSIDIZATION AND THE FALLACY OF PRODUCTION AT COST. A fallacy often found in the discussion of subsidization is that the return on capital for some of the vertically integrated stages of production can be neglected by a firm. When a firm sells a product at cost from any of its various stages of production, and receives no return on the corresponding capital involved in the production process, it is working for nothing. No firm can possibly survive in the long run unless, sooner or later, it begins to make a profit. Therefore, the vertically integrated firm cannot survive by continually obtaining goods at cost from its earlier stages:

> An integrated firm, by definition, demands a larger investment than its non-integrated rival. If it is to secure a return on that additional investment, its profits will be larger. It can obtain raw materials at cost from its vertically integrated source of supply only by the sacrifice of return on its investment in that source. It can distribute its products at "cost" through profitless retail stores only if it is willing to forego interest on the money invested in the retail enterprise.[10]

An example of the production at cost fallacy appears in the *A & P* case with reference to the Atlantic Commission Company, abbreviated as ACCO, which acted as sole buyer for A & P. ACCO also traded as a broker with the rest of the food trade. The court described the "advantages" which A & P derived from ACCO as follows:

> Suppose an item was selling in the market at 100, ACCO could buy for A & P and have its choice of the quality at 95. The balance of the trade could buy at 100 and pay ACCO a 5% brokerage. Thus, the price to A & P was 95 and to A & P's competitors 105.[11]

The court ignored the additional investment made in ACCO by A & P. A & P did not "save" 5 per cent brokerage any more than a company "saves" interest when it uses its own internal funds which could be invested and earn interest elsewhere. The court compounded the fallacy by first stating that the price to A & P was 95 (ignoring A & P's investment in ACCO), and second, by stating that the price to outsiders was 105 (ignoring the savings in capital for those who use ACCO and do not have to organize their own brokerage division).

The above discussion of subsidization and the fallacy of production at cost in no way denies that the temporary consumption of capital may be lucrative in the long run. By selling at or below cost, the firm may be achieving either the outright destruction of competitors or the subjugation of competitors to passive price followers. This type of cutthroat competi-

---

[10]Hale and Hale, *Market Power: Size and Shape Under the Sherman Act*, pp. 224–25.
[11]173 F. 2nd 79, 85 (1949).

tion can handsomely compensate the stronger firm for its temporary expenditure of capital.

The vertically integrated firm is in no different position from the non-integrated firm when it consumes its own capital through the selling of products at or below cost. "If, during the short run, it is willing to forego a normal return upon its investment, it may sell below cost, thus hurting its competitors. But a non-integrated firm may do likewise. Although some type of integration may be helpful for providing a cushion of profit to sustain the price cutter during his foray, local price cutting to drive a competitor out of business is not a phenomenon limited to vertically integrated firms."[12] Therefore, the advantage possessed by the integrated firm for price cutting is the probable existence of larger financial resources that can be drawn upon in the consumption of internal capital.

Legal Interpretations of Conglomerate Power in Merger Cases

The concept of conglomerate power has at its foundation a belief that a diversified firm, by virtue of its multiplicity of geographic and product markets, has a competitive advantage over a single product firm. Alternatively, the emphasis can be changed from different horizontal product markets to vertical stages of production, and the concept would embrace the belief that an integrated firm, by virtue of "profits" or higher rates of return at various stages of production, has a competitive advantage over the nonintegrated firm.

The horizontal aspects of conglomerate power were discussed *In the Matter of Procter & Gamble Company*.[13] In summarizing the reasons for finding illegal the acquisition of the Clorox Chemical Company, a manufacturer of household bleach, by the Procter & Gamble Company, a manufacturer of soap and detergents but not household liquid bleach, the Hearing Examiner stated:

... the deciding factor is the ability of Proctor & Gamble's conglomerate organization to shift financial resources and competitive strength through a broad front of different products and markets and its ability to strategically alter the selected point of greatest impact as time, place and market conditions require. ... The test of conglomerate power is whether a corporation is able to concentrate its competitive efforts at one point by shifting its financial resources and competitive strength from one industry or market to another.[14]

---

[12]G. Hale, "Vertical Integration," *Columbia Law Review*, Vol. XLIX (November, 1949), 940.

[13]Docket No. 6901, Second Initial Decision (February 28, 1962).

[14]*Ibid.*, p. 62 of the mimeographed text.

The Supreme Court also held the acquisition was illegal. The Court viewed the merger as one of "product extension", rather than purely conglomerate, since packaged detergents and household liquid bleach are used complementarily in the washing of fabrics and in general household cleaning.[15] Furthermore, the products of Procter & Gamble and Clorox were sold generally to the same customers, at the same stores, and by the same merchandising methods.

At the time of the acquisition, Clorox was the leading manufacturer of household liquid bleach, with 48.8 per cent of national sales. It had annual sales of approximately $40 million and had an annual advertising and promotion budget over $5 million. Purex, the second leading producer accounted for 15.7 per cent; Roman Cleaner, the third largest, accounted for 5.9 per cent. The remaining thirty per cent of the sales of household liquid bleach was accounted for by approximately 200 small firms.

Although the Commission and the Circuit Court expressly refused to find that a reasonable probability existed that Procter & Gamble would have entered the household liquid bleach market on its own, the Supreme Court nevertheless held that Procter & Gamble was the most likely entrant into this field. "It is clear," stated the Court, "that the existence of Procter at the edge of the industry exerted considerable influence on the market." Furthermore, the number of potential entrants into the household liquid bleach field was "not so large that the elimination of one would be insignificant."

Procter & Gamble, as a multi-product producer, was found by the Court to enjoy substantial advantages in advertising and sales promotions. For example, Procter & Gamble, by obtaining discounts on radio and television commercials, could advertise at a lower unit cost than a firm with only one product. Clorox, in contrast, was unable to obtain substantial advertising discounts and, of course, had less to spend on advertising. The Supreme Court feared that " . . . the substitution of the powerful acquiring firm for the smaller, but already dominant, firm may substantially reduce the competitive structure of the industry by raising entry barriers and by dissuading the smaller firms from aggressively competing." Entry barriers would be raised by the substitution of the larger advertising capabilities of Procter & Gamble for those of Clorox. There were no technological barriers to entry because capital requirements for producing liquid bleach are small. Thus, the likelihood that a new entrant would have greater reluctance to face Procter & Gamble than smaller Clorox constituted, in the opinion of the Supreme Court, a heightening of the barriers to entry in the household liquid bleach field. The Court reasoned that smaller firms would be dissuaded from competing by their fear of retaliation by Procter &

[15]*Federal Trade Commission* v. *The Procter & Gamble Co.*, 386 U.S. 568 (1967).

Gamble. But Justice Harlan, in his concurring opinion, observed that it could equally be assumed that smaller firms would become more aggressive in competing because of their fear that otherwise Procter & Gamble might ultimately absorb their markets.

It should be noted that even before the acquisition Clorox, as an independent company, had greater economic power than its rivals. In terms of market shares of household liquid bleach Clorox accounted for nearly half of the industry sales and was three times larger than the Number 2 firm in its industry and eight times larger than the Number 3 firm. The finances of Clorox, although not comparable with Procter & Gamble's, appeared adequate in view of its relative size and success in its industry. Furthermore, as a result of the popularity of its product, Clorox was also able to obtain ample shelf space in chain stores and supermarkets.

In contrast, the acquired firm in *Reynolds Metals Co.* v. *Federal Trade Commission*[16] did not already possess a relatively greater size than its competitors before the acquisition took place. Reynolds Metals, the largest producer of aluminum foil in the world, with assets in 1957 over $730 million, acquired one of its customers, Arrow Brands, one of "eight or ten" small producers of decorative aluminum florist foil with assets under $1 million. Arrow accounted for approximately 33 per cent of the sales in this industry. From the initial facts one might easily conclude that the antitrust offense was the foreclosure of suppliers by vertical integration. That is, Reynolds by acquiring one of its customers, Arrow Brands, could now foreclose other competing foil suppliers, such as Alcoa, from selling to Arrow Brands. But the Federal Trade Commission expressly stated that even if Reynolds did not supply aluminum foil to Arrow Brands, the acquisition would still be considered illegal. The Circuit Court characterized the acquisition by Reynolds as "the intrusion of 'bigness' into a competitive economic community otherwise populated by commercial 'pygmies'." In holding the acquisition illegal, the Circuit Court stated,

> Arrow's assimilation into Reynolds' enormous capital structure and resources gave Arrow an immediate advantage over its competitors who were contending for a share of the market for florist foil. The power of the "deep pocket" or "rich parent" for one of the florist foil suppliers in a competitive group where previously no company was very large and all were relatively small opened the possibility and power to sell at prices approximating cost or below and thus to undercut and ravage the less affluent competition.[17]

When the subsidization constitutes a potential resort to a "deep pocket," the concept of conglomerate power approaches its furthest degree of devel-

[16]309 F. 2nd 223 (1962).
[17]*Ibid.*, pp. 229–30.

opment. A second product or geographic market, or several stages of production, are no longer required for subsidization. Furthermore, a second company may not even be required for conglomerate power to be exercised. For there is no reason why a single company cannot dip into its cash reserves and consume its capital structure by selling at or below cost, and thereby simulate the same system of subsidization alleged to exist in most conglomerate merger cases.

All investment as well as innovation is basically a form of subsidization. When a firm starts a research and development department, it is financing one department with the profits earned at another stage of production. A new product that a firm is attempting to introduce to the public is almost invariably an initial losing proposition because of low volume, and high advertising and distribution costs. The building of a new plant requires financing from either a bank, internal reserves, a "deep pocket" from another company, a horizontal subsidy from another geographic product market, or another vertical stage of production.

Conflicting desiderata may arise if we attempt to preserve the structure of industries composed of numerous independent units and simultaneously encourage larger companies to enter the research and development of new products and industries. Sometimes the protection of numerous independent competing firms can bring greater economic growth and competition than could be expected from the domination of a field by a few large firms. But there may be other cases in which the growth potential and benefits to the nation are resolved in favor of larger firms.

At the core of the concept of conglomerate power is a belief that a substantial disparity in the size of firms in the same market may be incompatible with the forms of competition which our antitrust laws are expected to preserve. A market structure of a large number of firms, no one of which has significant market power, does meet some of the requirements for the classical definition of "pure" competition. But in a market structure of a limited number of firms, equality in size may not be more desirable than some degree of inequality of size. Inequality of size may be a vital stimulus for the smaller firms to improve their product, to compete more vigorously, and, as an over-all policy, to refuse to settle for a smaller share of the market. There exists no ready answer to the question whether an industry composed of firms approximately the same size can be expected to be more or less competitive than an industry whose firms are different in size.

TABLE OF CASES

General Electric Co. v. Masters Mail Order Co., 244 F. 2d 681 (2d Cir., 1957) *cert. denied* 355 U.S. 824 (1957)/*120*

General Foods Corp., In the Matter of, 52 F.T.C. 798 (1956)/*237*

Gerber Products Co. v. Beech-Nut Life Savers Co., 160 F. Supp. 916 (S.D.N.Y., 1958)/*238*

Goodyear Tire & Rubber Co. v. Federal Trade Commission, 331 F. 2d 394 (7th Cir., 1964), *affirmed* 381 U.S. 357 (1964)/*200*

Griffith; United States v., 344 U.S. 100 (1948)/*49*

Grinnell Corp; United States v., 384 U.S. 563 (1966)/*61–62*

Harley-Davidson Motor Co., In the Matter of, 50 F.T.C. 1047 (1954)/*202*

Heaton Peninsular Button Fastener Co. v. Eureka Specialty Co., 77 F. 288 (6th Cir., 1896)/*189*

Henry v. A.B. Dick, 244 U.S. 1 (1912)/*189*

International Business Machines Corp. v. United States, 298 U.S. 131 (1936)/*188*

International Salt Co. v. United States, 332 U.S. 392 (1947)/*203*

Interstate Circuit, Inc. v. United States, 306 U.S. 208 (1939)/*112-13, 118*

Jerrold Electronics Co.; United States v., 187 F. Supp. 545 (E.D. Pa., 1960), *affirmed per curiam*, 365 U.S. 567 (1961)/*188, 199*

Judson L. Thomson Mfg. Co. v. Federal Trade Commission, 150 F. 2d 952 (1st Cir., 1945), *cert. denied* 326 U.S. 776 (1945)/*203*

Leitch Mfg. Co. v. Barber Co., 302 U.S. 458 (1938)/*201*

Loew's Inc.; United States v., 371 U.S. 38 (1962)/*199-201*

Manufacturers Hanover Trust Co.; United States v., 240 F. Supp. 867 (S.D.N.Y., 1965)/*126-29*

Maryland and Virginia Milk Producers Assn.; United States v., 167 F. Supp. 799 (D.D.C., 1958), 362 U.S. 458 (1960)/*214-15*

Maryland Baking Co. v. Federal Trade Commission, 243 F. 2d 716 (4th Cir., 1957)/*226*

Masonite Corp.; United States v., 316 U.S. 265 (1942)/*113*

Mercoid Corp. v. Mid-Continent Investment Co., 320 U.S. 661 (1944)/*189, 201*

Milk and Ice Cream Can Institute v. Federal Trade Commission, 152 F. 2d 478 (7th Cir., 1946)/*229*

Minneapolis-Honeywell Regulator Co., In the Matter of, 44 F.T.C. 351 (1948), *reversed*, 191 F. 2d 786 (7th Cir., 1951), *cert. dismissed*, 344 U.S. 206 (1952)/*238*

Moore v. Mead's Fine Bread Co., 348 U.S. 115 (1954)/*226*

Morgan Envelope Co. v. Albany Perforated Paper Co., 52 U.S. 425 (1893)/*191*

Morton Salt Co. v. G. S. Suppiger Co., 314 U.S. 488 (1942)/*189–91, 201*

Motion Picture Patents Co. v. Universal Film Mfg. Co., 243 U.S. 502 (1917)/*189, 191–92, 201*

Mueller Company v. Federal Trade Commission, 323 F. 2d 44 (7th Cir., 1963)/*237*

Muller, E. B. & Co. v. Federal Trade Commission, 142 F. 2d 511 (6th Cir., 1944)/*226*

National Lead Co. v. Federal Trade Commission, 49 F.T.C. 791 (1953), *modified* 227 F. 2d 825 (7th Cir., 1955), *reversed*, 352 U.S. 419 (1957)/*113, 229, 232*

New York Atlantic and Pacific Tea Co.; United States v., 67 F. Supp. 626 (E.D. Ill., 1946), *affirmed* 173 F. 2d 79 (7th Cir., 1949)/*261-65*

Northern Pacific Railway Co. v. United States, 356 U.S. 1 (1958)/*196–97, 201, 203*

Ohio Valley Electric Corp. v. General Electric Co., 244 F. Supp. 914 (S.D.N.Y., 1965)/*14–115, 122*

Old Dearborn Distributing Co. v. Seagram Distillers Corp., 299 U.S. 183 (1936)/*119*

Osborn, S. Kriete, v. Sinclair Refining Co., 286 F. 2d 832 (4th Cir., 1960), *cert. denied*, 366 U.S. 963 (1961)/*197, 200*

Paramount Pictures, Inc., United States v., 334 U.S. 131 (1948)/*113*

Parke, Davis and Co.; United States v., 362 U.S. 29 (1960)/*121*

Penn-Olin Chemical Co.; United States v., 217 F. Supp. 110 (1963), 378 U.S. 158 (1964), 246 F. Supp. 917 (1965), *juris. noted*, 386 U.S. 906 (1967)/*257-58*

Pevely Dairy Co. v. United States, 178 F. 2d 363 (8th Cir., 1949), *cert. denied* 339 U.S. 942 (1950)/*113*

Philadelphia, City of v. Westinghouse Electric Corp., 210 F. Supp. 483 (E.D. Penn, 1962)/*114–122*

Philadelphia National Bank; United States v., 374 U.S. 321 (1963)/*127–28, 131, 249, 254–55, 258*

Pick Mfg. Co. v. General Motors Corp., 80 F. 2d 641 (7th Cir., 1935), affirmed per curiam, 299 U.S. 3 (1936)/*188*

Pillsbury Co. v. Federal Trade Commission, 50 F.T.C. 1110 (1954), 354 F. 2d 952 (5th Cir., 1965)/*252*

Procter & Gamble Co. v. Federal Trade Commission, Second Initial Decision (February 28, 1962), 358 F. 2d 74 (1966), 386 U.S, 568 (1967)/*266–68*

Reynolds Metals Co. v. Federal Trade Commission, 309 F. 2d 223 (1962)/*268*

Schwegmann Brothers v. Calvert Distillers Corp. and Seagram Distillers Corp. 341 U.S. 384 (1951)/*119*

Signode Steel Strapping Co. v. Federal Trade Commission, 132 F. 2d 48 (4th Cir., 1942)/*203*

Sinclair Refining Co.; Federal Trade Commission v., 261 U.S. 463 (1923)/*201, 203*

Staley Manufacturing Co., A.E.; Federal Trade Commission v., 324 U.S. 746 (1945)/*229–31*

Standard Motor Products, Inc. v. Federal Trade Commission, 265 F. 2d 674 (2d Cir., 1959), cert. denied 361 U.S. 826 (1959)/*233*

Standard Oil Co. of Calif. v. United States, 337 U.S. 293 (1949)/*200*

Standard Oil of Indiana; Federal Trade Commission v., 355 U.S. 396 (1958) *217–18, 232–33, 238*

Standard Oil of New Jersey v. United States, 221 U.S. 1 (1911)/*27–36, 38, 48*

Sugar Institute, Inc. v. United States, 297 U.S. 553 (1936)/*116–17*

Sun Oil Co. v. Federal Trade Commission, 371 U.S. 505 (1963)/*234–36*

Sunshine Biscuits, Inc. v. Federal Trade Commission, 306 F. 2d 48 (7th Cir., 1962)/*233*

Tag Manufacturers Institute v. Federal Trade Commission, 174 F. 2d 452 (1st Cir., 1949)/*117*

Tampa Electric Co. v. National Coal Co., 365 U.S. 220 (1961)/*200*

Theater Enterprises, Inc. v. Paramount Film Distributing Corp., 346 U.S. 537 (1954)/*111–12*

Times-Picayune Publishing Co. v. United States, 345 U.S. 594 (1953)/*190, 198–99*

Trans-Missouri Freight Assn.; United States v., 166 U.S. 290 (1896)/*29–31, 122*

Trenton Potteries Co.; United States v., 273 U.S. 392 (1927)/*113–14*

Triangle Conduit & Cable Co. v. Federal Trade Commission, 168 F. 2d 157 (1948)/*232*

Union Bag-Camp Paper Corp. v. Federal Trade Commission, 233 F. Supp. 660 (D.C.N.Y., 1964)/*252*

United Shoe Machinery Co. of New Jersey; United States v., 247 U.S. 32 (1918) *51*

United Shoe Machinery Corp. v. United States, 258 U.S. 451 (1922)/*51, 202–4*

United Shoe Machinery Corp.; United States v., 110 F. Supp. 295 (D. Mass., 1953), affirmed per curiam 347 U.S. 521 (1954)/*51–53*

United States v. (See under name of other party).

United States Steel Corp.; United States v., 251 U.S. 417 (1920), 223 F. 55 (1915)/*37–41, 50*

Utah Pie Co., v. Continental Baking Co., 386 U.S. 685 (1967)/*226*

Index

274